Experiencing Poverty
Voices from the Bottom

SECOND EDITION

D. STANLEY EITZEN
Colorado State University

KELLY EITZEN SMITH
University of Arizona

PEARSON

Boston • New York • San Francisco
Mexico City • Montreal • Toronto • London • Madrid • Munich • Paris
Hong Kong • Singapore • Tokyo • Cape Town • Sydney

Executive Editor: *Jeff Lasser*
Series Editorial Assistant: *Lauren Houlihan*
Marketing Manager: *Kelly May*
Production Editor: *Judy Fiske*
Editorial-Production Service: *Omegatype Typography, Inc.*
Composition Buyer: *Linda Cox*
Manufacturing Buyer: *Debbie Rossi*
Electronic Composition: *Omegatype Typography, Inc.*
Cover Administrator: *Linda Knowles*

For related titles and support materials, visit our online catalog at www.ablongman.com.

Between the time website information is gathered and then published, it is not unusual for some sites to have closed. Also, the transcription of URLs can result in typographical errors. The publisher would appreciate notification where these errors occur so that they may be corrected in subsequent editions.

ISBN-13: 978-0-205-54795-1
ISBN-10:   0-205-54795-8

Library of Congress Cataloging-in-Publication Data

Eitzen, D. Stanley.
   Experiencing poverty : voices from the bottom / D. Stanley Eitzen,
Kelly Eitzen Smith.—2nd ed.
       p.   cm.
   Includes bibliographical references and index.
   ISBN-13: 978-0-205-54795-1 (pbk.)
   ISBN-10: 0-205-54795-8 (pbk.)
   1. Poverty—United States.   2. Poor—United States.   3. Economic
history—1945–   4. United States—Economic conditions—1945–   I. Smith,
Kelly Eitzen.   II. Title.
   HV91.E39   2009
   362.50973—dc22

                                                                    2008007192

Printed in the United States of America

10 9 8 7 6 5 4 3 2 1   12 11 10 09 08

If statistics are the language of the "New Economy," the personal story is the language of the "Under Economy."

Beth Kelly, Director of People United for Families (2001)

Many in our country do not know the pain of poverty. But we can listen to those who do.

George W. Bush (inaugural address, 2001)

ABOUT THE EDITORS

D. Stanley Eitzen (Ph.D., University of Kansas, 1968) is professor emeritus in sociology from Colorado State University. He is author or co-author of twenty-four books, many of which are in multiple editions. His other books in this field include *Social Problems*, 11th edition (Allyn and Bacon, forthcoming 2008); *Solutions to Social Problems: Lessons from Other Societies*, 4th edition (Allyn and Bacon, 2007); *Solutions to Social Problems from the Top Down: The Role of Government* (Allyn and Bacon, 2007); *Solutions to Social Problems from the Bottom Up: Successful Social Movements* (Allyn and Bacon, 2007); *Inequality: Social Class and Its Consequences* (Paradigm, 2007); *Paths to Homelessness: Extreme Poverty and the Urban Housing Crisis* (Westview, 1994); and *The Reshaping of America* (Prentice-Hall, 1989). His major research interests are social problems, social inequality (race/class/gender/sexuality), families, power, and sport.

Kelly Eitzen Smith (Ph.D., University of Arizona, 1999) is the associate director of the Center for Applied Sociology and a lecturer at the University of Arizona. Her dissertation, under the direction of David A. Snow, was an ethnography of the lives of homeless women. At the Center for Applied Sociology, she conducted extensive research in the areas of day labor, homelessness, poverty, and housing issues. Her sociological interests include gender, family, sexuality, and social inequality.

CONTENTS

Poverty is one of the most persistent social problems in America. Looking at poverty from the "top down," sociologists, political scientists, and economists have counted and classified the poor by income, race, ethnicity, gender, household and family status, and geographical location. These social scientists have also described how the poor live and theorized as to why they are poor. There are also important studies that look at poverty from the "bottom up" (e.g., Kozol, 1988; Liebow, 1993; MacLeod, 1995; Snow and Anderson, 1993), but many of them have provided disembodied information that ignores what it is like to be poor from the perspective of the poor themselves. Our goal is to add to their insights about poverty by focusing on the voices of the poor, not on the information filtered by social scientists. We seek to know how the poor define their situations; the reasons for their plight; the problems they face; their coping strategies for providing the daily necessities of food, clothing, shelter, transportation, and health care; and their perceptions of government and charity efforts.

If we ignore the voices of the poor, we have dehumanized them, making their humanity invisible. As Eric Alterman argues in an essay for *The Nation* (2000:12), "While we hear that 43 million Americans lack health insurance, rarely do we read or hear about what it's like to raise a sick child without it." Similarly, we know little about how working-poor families manage when they pay more than half of their income for housing; how the shift from a manufacturing economy to one based on knowledge/service has left them behind; how the 1996 welfare legislation has affected former AFDC mothers who now work for minimum wages while paying for child care, transportation, clothing, and other costs of working outside the home; how the poor pay more for goods and services; and how natural and social disasters abruptly push people into poverty. Hidden in their answers to these and other questions is the answer to the core question of whether the reason for poverty is fundamentally one of character or is the result of structural forces outside their control.

Without hearing the voices of the impoverished our understanding of their social life is incomplete. Analyses from the top down miss the insights that only those experiencing poverty can articulate. This omission has important implications for those policymakers interested in solving social problems. In this regard, Alan Wolfe (1991:23) has said:

> *If policymakers are going to respond adequately to the transformations America has been experiencing, they ought first to consult, not quick and shallow public opinion polls nor the well-financed view of those with an immediate stake in whatever policy is being debated, but instead those whose lives constitute and are constituted by the policies they make. It is a long way from the "bottom up" to the "top down"—longer than from the "top down" to the "bottom up"—but like many longer journeys, the rewards at the end of the trip are more lasting. [emphasis added]*

This collection of readings will provide the voice, the presence, and the perspective of the poor who live on the margins and are generally invisible to the middle and upper classes. Our goals are twofold: (1) to bring the realities of the lives of the impoverished as close to the reader as possible, and (2) to get the reader to listen carefully to these voices of the poor in order to enhance their understanding of:

- How the poor became poor.
- How the poor are treated by individuals and organizations in the community.
- What keeps the poor poor.
- How the poor manage day-to-day.
- What theory of causation best explains poverty.
- The consequences of the welfare-to-work federal legislations.
- The best solutions for ending poverty.

We seek answers to these issues by listening to those on the bottom. To accomplish this, we divided the book into six parts. Part I provides an overview of poverty in the United States (from the "top down") and the sociological perspective for understanding this social problem. Part II, using voices of the poor, seeks answers to the question: Why are the poor poor? Part III is a new section to this edition, and focuses on how the poor and the near poor are extremely vulnerable in situations such as war, natural disasters, job loss, family disruption, and health problems. Part IV explores the issue of survival while living on the economic margins. Part V examines the impact that society's prominent institutions have on the lives of poor people. The final section, Part VI, demonstrates efforts by poor people to create viable lives even when they face difficult situations. These efforts include the organization and use of an underground—hidden, irregular, and sometimes illegal—economy; family networks for exchange of goods and services; neighborhood organizations; and collective efforts such as strikes and boycotts to change work conditions, welfare regulations, and school policies.

We have selected a variety of essays that provide the voices of the poor. The voices come from three sources: (1) those who are currently living in poverty; (2) those who were once poor and can look back on their experiences while impoverished; and (3) social scientists who include voices of the poor along with their analyses.

To aid the reader we provide an introductory essay that puts poverty in perspective by providing data on the extent and distribution of poverty in the United States. It concludes with a discussion of the sociological imagination as a way of seeing and understanding poverty through the experiences of those at the bottom of society. The remaining parts and the chapters within them are each preceded by a brief overview that provides the context and alerts the reader to the important issues discussed. Each essay opens with an overview that contextualizes it and provides focus questions that link the articles together. Pertinent web sites, scholarly references, and a glossary are also included.

ACKNOWLEDGMENTS

Several friends and colleagues have helped us by providing ideas and essays that we have included. Our very special thanks in regard to Kathryn D. Talley, Michelle Navarre Cleary, Beth Kelly, and Lauren Davis-Delano. Special thanks to Jeffrey Lasser, our editor, for his support of this project.

BIBLIOGRAPHY

Alterman, Eric (2000). "Still with Us," *The Nation* (April 24):12.

Kozol, Jonathan (1988). *Rachel and Her Children: Homeless Families in America*. New York: Crown.

Liebow, Elliot (1993). *Tell Them Who I Am: The Lives of Homeless Women*. New York: The Free Press.

MacLeod, Jay (1995). *Ain't No Makin' It: Aspirations and Attainment in a Low-Income Neighborhood*. Boulder, CO: Westview Press.

Snow, David A., and Leon Anderson (1993). *Down on Their Luck: A Study of Homeless Street People*. Berkeley: University of California Press.

Wolfe, Alan (1991). "Introduction," pp. 1–13 in *America at Century's End*, Alan Wolfe (Ed.). Berkeley: University of California Press.

PART I

Poverty in the United States and the Sociological Imagination

This introductory essay provides an overview in two ways. First, it provides the official statistics on poverty in the United States in terms of extent and distribution. While necessary and important, these numbing statistics miss what is happening in individual lives, a void that the essays in this book will fill. Second, hearing and understanding these voices requires a way of listening and interpreting sociologically—"sociological imagination"—a perspective that is elaborated in the final section of this essay.

THE EXTENT AND DISTRIBUTION OF POVERTY IN THE UNITED STATES

A common boast by Americans, not without some truth, is that the United States is the richest country on earth. The United States has great natural resources, the most advanced technology, and a very high standard of living. At the same time, when compared with other industrial democracies of the West, the United States has the highest proportion of its population living in poverty. Consider the following international comparisons, where the United States does not fare well:

- According to the United Nations' Human Development Reports, out of seventeen high-income countries, the United States scores the worst on the Human Poverty Index. This index measures early mortality rates, illiteracy rates, poverty, and long-term unemployment. Sweden, Norway, and the Netherlands received the best (i.e., the lowest) scores on the index.

- The probability of living in poverty is more than twice as high for a child born in the United States as for a child born in Belgium, Germany, or the Netherlands (Block et al., 2006).
- The poverty thresholds as defined by the United States are much higher than international standards. If the United States used the most common international measure, which counts people who live on less than half of a country's median income as poor, than almost 55 million people would be counted as poor (rather than 37 million) (Block et al., 2006).

In effect, then, despite its richness, the United States has a serious problem with poverty.

This section provides a brief survey of what is known about poverty in the United States from the "top down." We present how the government defines poverty and what census figures tell us about the distribution of poverty by race, gender, age, and place. Also examined is the extent that people in poverty experience **upward mobility.**

The Poverty Threshold

This official poverty line, the **poverty threshold,** is based on what the Social Security Administration considers the minimal amount of money required for a subsistence level of life. The number is computed by multiplying by 3 the cost of a basic nutritionally adequate diet. This multiplier is based on a 1955 finding that poor people spend one-third of their income on food. Since then the poverty level has been readjusted annually to account for inflation. Using this official standard ($10,160 for one person under age 65, $15,277 for a family of three, and $20,144 for a family of four), 12.6 percent of Americans (37 million) were poor in 2005 (the statistics for this section are taken largely from DeNavas-Walt, Proctor, and Lee, U.S. Bureau of the Census, 2006).

While the government's arbitrary line dividing the rich from the poor is the standard measure, it minimizes the actual extent of poverty in the United States. Critics of this measure argue that it does not keep up with inflation, that housing now takes up a much larger portion of the family budget than food, that there is a wide variation in the cost of living by locality, and that the poverty line ignores differences in medical care needs of individual families. Were a more realistic formula used, the number of poor would more likely be at least 50 percent higher than the current number (i.e., 18.9 percent or 55.5 million impoverished Americans).

The official number of poor people is also minimized because government census takers miss so many poor people. Those most likely overlooked in the census live in high density urban areas where several families may be crowded into one apartment, or in rural areas where some homes are inaccessible. Some workers and their families follow the harvest from place to place and therefore have no permanent home, as well as transients and homeless people who are also likely to be missed by the census. The inescapable conclusion is that the number of the poor in the United States is underestimated because the poor tend to be invisible, even to the government. This undercount by the census and the formula used to determine the poverty line have policy consequences. The official numbers on poverty determine eligibility for federal programs such as Head Start, food stamps, and housing subsidies. When these numbers understate the real extent of poverty, they reduce the size of government programs to aid the impoverished.

Despite these difficulties and the understating of actual poverty by the government's poverty line, the official government data provide useful information about the distribution of poverty in the United States. See Table 1 for a summary of the statistics used in this overview.

Racial Minorities

Income in the United States is maldistributed by race. Using three-year average medians from 2003–2005, the Census Bureau finds that the median household income for Asian American households was $59,877, compared with $50,677 for White households, $33,627 for Native American and Alaskan Native households, $35,467 for Latino households, and $31,140 for African American households. Not surprisingly then, in 2005 8.4 percent of Whites were officially poor, compared with 10.9 percent of Asian Americans, 22 percent of Latinos, 24.7 percent of African Americans, and 25.3 percent for Native American and Alaskan Natives. These summary statistics mask the differences within each racial/ethnic category.

TABLE 1:   People and Families in Poverty by Selected Characteristics: 2005

Characteristic	Number Below Poverty	Percent
Total People	36,950,000	12.6
Under 18	12,896,000	17.6
65 Years +	3,603,000	10.1
Native-born	31,080,000	12.1
Foreign-born	5,870,000	16.5
Naturalized Citizens	1,441,000	10.4
Not Citizens	4,429,000	20.4
White, non-Hispanic	16,227,000	8.3
Black	9,168,000	24.9
Asian and Pacific Islander	1,402,000	11.1
Latino	9,368,000	21.8
Inside Metropolitan Areas	30,098,000	12.2
Inside Central Cities	15,966,000	17.0
Outside Metropolitan Areas	6,852,000	14.5
Married-couple Family	2,944,000	5.1
Female Household, No Husband Present	4,044,000	28.7

Source: U.S. Bureau of the Census, 2006, "Income, Poverty, and Health Insurance Coverage in the United States: 2005," Current Population Reports, pp. 60–231.

For example, Americans of Cuban descent, many of whom were middle-class professionals in Cuba, have relatively low poverty rates, whereas Puerto Ricans, Mexicans, and Central Americans have disproportionately high poverty rates. Similarly, Japanese Americans are much less likely to be poor than those Asians from Cambodia, Laos, and Vietnam.

Nativity

In 2005, 5.9 million of the foreign-born individuals in the United States (16.5 percent) were poor. Of the poor foreign-born, 39 percent were naturalized citizens and the remaining were noncitizens, for poverty rates of 10.4 percent and 20.4 percent, respectively. These official statistics do not include the 12 million undocumented immigrants who enter the United States illegally to work at menial jobs.

Age

The nation's poverty rate for children under age 18 was 17.6 percent (1 out of every 6 American children) in 2005. For those children under age 6, the rate was 20 percent. Related children under age 6 living in families with a female head of household, no husband present, had a poverty rate of 52.9 percent, a rate more than 5 times that for their counterparts in married-couple families (9.9 percent). Although there are more White children in poverty, children of color are disproportionately poor. In 2005 the rate for White children under age 18 was 14.4 percent, compared to 34.5 percent of African American children, and 28.3 percent of Latino children.

Contrary to popular belief, the elderly (those 65 and older) have a lower poverty rate (10.1 percent) than the general population (12.6 percent). The poverty rate of the elderly varies greatly by state, from a high of 24 percent in Mississippi to a low of 7 percent in Utah and Vermont. Women are especially vulnerable to poverty as they age due to a lifetime of lower earnings and fewer retirement benefits.

Children have a higher poverty rate than the elderly because government policy provides programs such as Social Security and Medicare for the aged and these programs are typically indexed for inflation. On the other hand, welfare programs targeted for poor children (e.g., Aid to Families with Dependent Children) have been eliminated or reduced, especially since 1980.

Gender

Women are more likely to be poor than men (24.1 percent compared to 17.9 percent) because of prevailing sexism in society. The United States has a dual labor market, with women found disproportionately in lower paying jobs. This dual market is reflected in the female-to-male earnings ratio (or sex pay gap). In 2005 the female-to-male earnings ratio was 0.77 (i.e., women earned 77 cents for every dollar earned by men). The relatively high frequency of divorce and the large number of never-married women with children, coupled with the cost of child care, housing, and medical care, have resulted in the high numbers of single-female headed families, with no husband present, being poor (28.7 percent of single-headed families in poverty, compared to 5.1 percent for married-couple families). In fact, of the female-headed families with children under age 18 and no husband present, 42.8 percent lived in poverty in 2005. This trend has been called the **feminization of poverty,** a term which implies that the large proportion of poor women is a relatively new phenomenon in the United States. However, this term obscures the fact that women have always been more economically vulnerable than men, especially older women and women of color.

Place

Poverty is not randomly distributed geographically; it tends to cluster in certain places. Regionally, the area with the highest concentration of poverty in 2005 was the South (14 percent), compared to 12.6 percent in the West, 11.3 percent in the Northeast, and 11.4 percent in the Midwest. The South and West have the highest poverty rates because they have the largest concentrations of African Americans, Latinos, and a relatively large number of recent immigrants. The three places with the highest average poverty rates in 2004 were the District of Columbia (18.3 percent), Louisiana (19.2 percent), and Mississippi (19.3 percent). The states with the lowest poverty rates were New Hampshire, Minnesota, and New Jersey.

In metropolitan areas, the poverty rate in 2005 was higher in the central cities (17.5 percent) than in suburban areas (9.1 percent). For those living outside of metropolitan areas, the poverty rate was 14.2 percent. One especially relevant trend regarding poverty in the central cities is that it is becoming more and more geographically concentrated. This spatial concentration of poverty means that the poor have poor neighbors, and the area has a low tax base to finance public schools and a shrinking number of businesses because businesses tend to move to areas where the local residents have more discretionary income. These factors mean a reduction in services and the elimination of local jobs.

Although poverty generally is more concentrated in cities, the highest concentration of U.S. poverty exists in four nonmetropolitan regional pockets where the economic engine has broken down: the Appalachian mountain region, where the poor are predominantly White; the old Southern cotton belt from the Carolinas to the Louisiana delta, where the poor are mostly African American; the Rio Grande Valley/Texas Gulf Coast, where the poor are largely Latino; and the Native American reservations of the Southwest.

Poverty is greatest among those who do not have an established residence. People in this category are typically the homeless and migrant farm workers. The homeless, estimated at about 1 million, are those in extreme poverty. Migrant workers—adults and children who are seasonal farm laborers working for low wages and no benefits—are believed to constitute about 3 million. Latinos are overrepresented in this occupation.

The Working Poor

Having a job is not necessarily a path out of poverty. United States census data show that over 2.8 million full-time workers were below the poverty line in 2005, plus another 6.4 million workers who worked at least part time. Despite working, these people remain poor because they hold menial, dead-end jobs that have no benefits and pay the minimum wage or below. In 2003, 2.1 million workers were paid the minimum wage or less, yet this wage does not support a family. The federal minimum wage of $5.15 an hour adds up to only $10,712 for full-time work (falling over $5,000 short of the poverty line for a family of three, and almost $10,000 short for a family of four). Just above the minimum wage are more than two million Americans working in nursing homes: they earn, on average, between $7 and $8 an hour. The median wage of the estimated 2.3 million child care workers is $6.00 to $7.00 an hour, usually without benefits. Workers in other occupations—such as janitors, health care aides, hospital orderlies, funeral attendants, and retail sales clerks—typically make similarly low wages (Reich, 2000).

The lot of the working poor is similar to that of the nonworking poor on some dimensions, and worse on others. They do society's dirty work for low pay and few, if any, benefits. They live in substandard housing, and their children go to underfinanced public schools. They are poor, but unlike the nonworking poor, they are not eligible for many government supports such as subsidized housing, medical care, and food stamps. Compounding the economic woes of the poor is a lack of health insurance coverage. In 2005, 46.6 million people were without health insurance.

The Near-Poor

The **near-poor** are people with family incomes at or above their poverty threshold but below 125 percent of their threshold (i. e., with the official poverty line at $15,277 for a family of three, 125 percent of that number is $19,096.) In 2005, 16.8 percent of the population was near poor, a significant portion of those being under the age of 18.

The Severely Poor

Use of the official poverty line designates all people below it as poor whether they are a few dollars short of the threshold or far below it. In reality, most impoverished individuals and families have incomes considerably below the poverty threshold. In 2005, for example, the average dollar amount needed to raise a poor family out of poverty was $8,125 (i.e., the average family needed $8,125 *additional* income to reach the poverty threshold). For poor individuals not in families, the average income deficit was $5,361, and for poor women in female-headed households the average income deficit was $8,610.

In 2005, 15.9 million Americans were **severely poor** (those people living *at or below half of the poverty line*). Some facts about these people who are among the poorest of the poor are the following (Pugh, 2007):

- Approximately 1 in 3 are children under age 17.
- Nearly 2 out of 3 are female.
- In this category, 4.3 million are African Americans and 3.7 million are Latinos. Severely poor Blacks are more than three times as likely as Whites to be in deep poverty, while extremely poor Latinos are more than twice as likely.
- Typically, the severely poor must use at least 50 percent of their meager income for housing.

The Dynamics of Poverty: The Likelihood of Moving Out of Poverty

Crucial to our understanding of poverty is to know whether poverty is a transient phenomenon for individuals and families or whether it is a permanent condition. Research has shown that most poor people move above the poverty line in less than two years, whereas about 20 percent of those in poverty at any point in time have been poor for seven or more years (summarized by Rodgers, 2000). It is significant that most of those who escape poverty remain economically marginal and vulnerable. "Living on the margins means that if they encounter any economic adversity (e.g., sickness or injury, job loss, divorce), many of the former poor are in jeopardy of falling back into poverty" (Rodgers, 2000:66). Thus many people on the economic margins move in and out of poverty throughout much of their lives.

THE SOCIOLOGICAL IMAGINATION

This book is a collection of essays by people who have experienced poverty. Our goal in presenting them is to help the reader develop a better understanding of this social problem as described by those who are or who once were at the bottom of society's social and economic hierarchies. However, the fact that the essays are by poor people and their unique circumstances does not mean that we want the reader to understand poverty as a personal problem of people who have made choices that have led them to impoverishment. Rather we want the reader to view these essays with a "sociological imagination." C. Wright Mills (1916–1962) in his classic *The Sociological Imagination* (1959) wrote that the task of sociology is to realize that individual troubles are inextricably linked to social forces. Thus, by examining life circumstances, we can see how they are tied to the structure of society. The sociological imagination involves several related components:

- The sociological imagination is stimulated by a willingness to view the social world from the perspective of others.
- It involves moving away from thinking in terms of the individual and his or her problem, focusing rather on the social, economic, and historical circumstances that produce the problem. Put another way, the sociological imagination is the ability to see the societal patterns that influence individuals, families, groups, and organizations.
- Possessing a sociological imagination, one can shift from the examination of a single family to national budgets, from a poor person to national welfare

policies, from an unemployed person to the societal shift from manufacturing to a service/knowledge economy, from a single mother with a sick child to the high cost of health care for the uninsured, and from a homeless family to the lack of affordable housing.

• Developing a sociological imagination requires a detachment from the taken-for-granted assumptions about social life and establishing a critical distance (Andersen and Taylor, 2000:10–11). In other words, one must be willing to question the structural arrangements that shape social behavior.

> The sociological assumption that provides the basis for this critical stance is that the social world is human-made and therefore not sacred. Belief systems, the economic system, the law, the way power is distributed—all are created and sustained by people. They can, therefore, be changed by people. (Eitzen and Baca Zinn, 2007:7).

• When we have this imagination we begin to see the solutions to social problems not in terms of changing problem people, but in terms of changing the structure of society.

NOTES AND SUGGESTIONS FOR FURTHER READING

Andersen, Margaret L., and Howard F. Taylor (2000). *Sociology: Understanding a Diverse Society*. Belmont, CA: Wadsworth.

Armour, Stephanie (2001). "Tough Times for Laid-Off, Low-Income Workers." *USA Today* (October 30):1A–2A.

Barrington, Linda (2000). *Does a Rising Tide Lift All Boats?* New York: The Conference Board, Research Report 1271-00-RR.

Belluck, Pam (2001). "New Wave of the Homeless Floods Cities' Shelters." *New York Times* (December 18). Retrieved from www.nytimes.com/2001/12/18/national/18HOME .html

Block, Fred, Anna Korteweg, Kerry Woodward, Zach Schiller, and Imrul Mazid (2006). "The Compassion Gap in American Poverty Policy." *Contexts* 5(2):14–20.

Children's Defense Fund (2001). *The State of America's Children: 2001*. Washington, D. C.

DeNavas-Walt, Carmen, Bernadette D. Proctor, and Cheryl Hill Lee, U.S. Census Bureau, Current Population Reports, P60-231 (2006). "Income, Poverty, and Health Insurance Coverage in the United States: 2005." Washington, D.C.: U.S. Government Printing Office.

Economic Policy Institute (2000). "The Myth of Economic Mobility." Retrieved from www .epinet.org/books/swa2000/graph.htm

Ehrenreich, Barbara (2001). *Nickel and Dimed: On (Not) Getting By in America*. New York: Metropolitan Books.

Eitzen, D. Stanley, and Maxine Baca Zinn (2007). *In Conflict and Order: Understanding Society*, 11th ed. Boston: Allyn and Bacon.

Glasmeier, Amy K. (2006). *An Atlas of Poverty in America: One Nation, Pulling Apart, 1960–2003*. New York: Routledge.

Katz, Michael B. (1989). *The Undeserving Poor*. New York: Pantheon Books.

Kushnick, Louis, and James Jennings (Eds.) (1999). *A New Introduction to Poverty: The Role of Race, Power, and Politics*. New York: New York University Press.

Maggi, Laura (2000). "The Poor Count." *The American Prospect* (February 14):14–15.

Michael, Marie (2001). "What Is the Poverty Line?" *Dollars and Sense*, No. 233 (January/February):43.

Miller, Juanita E. (2000). "The Working Poor." Ohio State University Extension Fact Sheet. Retrieved from www.ag.ohio-state.edu/ohioline/hyg-fact/5000/5703.html

Mills, C. Wright (1959). *The Sociological Imagination.* New York: Oxford University Press.

Miringoff, Marc, and Marque-Luisa Miringoff (1999). *The Social Health of the Nation: How America is Really Doing.* New York: Oxford University Press.

Mishel, Lawrence, Jared Bernstein, and John Schmitt (2000). *The State of Working America:2000/2001.* Ithaca, NY: Cornell University Press.

Pollitt, Katha (2001). "Childcare Scare." *The Nation* (May 14):10.

Pugh, Tony (2007). "U.S. Economy Leaving Record Numbers in Severe Poverty." *McClatchy Newspapers.* Retrieved from www.realcities.com/mld/krwashington/16760690.htm?template=contentModules/prin

Reich, Robert B. (2000). "The Great Divide." *The American Prospect* (May 8):56.

Rodgers, Harrell R., Jr. (2000). *American Poverty in a New Era of Reform.* Armonk, NY: M. E. Sharpe.

Sanders, Bernard (2000). "The 'Booming' Economy." *Sanders Scoop* (Spring):3.

Schwarz, John E., and Thomas J. Volgy (1992). *The Forgotten Americans.* New York: W. W. Norton.

Sen, Amartya (1995). *Inequality Reexamined.* Cambridge, MA: Harvard University Press.

Smeeding, Timothy M., and Peter Gottschalk (1998). "Cross-National Income Inequality: How Great Is It and What Can We Learn From It?" *Focus* (University of Wisconsin-Madison Institute for Research on Poverty), Volume 19 (Summer/Fall): 15–19.

Solow, Robert M. (2000). "Welfare: The Cheapest Country." *New York Review of Books* (March 23):20–24.

Wilson, William Julius (1996). *When Work Disappears: The World of the New Urban Poor.* New York: Alfred A. Knopf.

Winfield, Nicole (2000). "U.S. Scores an 'F' on Efforts to Cut Poverty Among U.S. Women." *Associated Press* (June 8).

PART II

Theories of Poverty: Why Are the Poor Poor?

"By design, we live in a society that is very competitive. After adding individual differences to handicaps/advantages of race, class, and sex, it turns out that some people run faster than others. Those who run very fast are highly rewarded. Those who run at an average pace do pretty well most of the time. For a variety of reasons, seldom if ever any fault of their own, some poor people and some homeless people . . . can't run fast at all."

Elliott Liebow (1993)

"Dealing with poverty is not a viable political issue in America. It jars with a cultural sense that the poor bring things upon themselves and that every American is born with the same chances in life."

Paul Harris (2006)

"I had three kids. I was paying $275 every two weeks. . . . I was only getting $247 by that time. One day I came home, there was a padlock on the door. So I took my kids to a friend's, but it was too crowded, then I moved to another friend's, then another. . . . I tried to get into the shelters, but the shelter system turned me away. . . . [I realized] it's got to be something not just wrong with me. It's got to be something wrong in the world, in the system."

Kensington Welfare Rights Union member (cited in Baptist and Bricker-Jenkins, 2002)

Theories of Poverty: Who or What Is to Blame for Poverty?

How are we to explain the paradox of poverty amidst plenty—why are there so many people poor in affluent America? There are two very different answers to this question. One answer is that the poor themselves are the cause because of their biological inferiority, their self-defeating culture, or their bad personal choices. The opposite answer places the blame on the structure of society. That is, some people are poor because society has failed to provide equality of educational opportunity, because institutions discriminate against women and minorities, because private industry has failed to provide enough good paying jobs, or because businesses have relocated to where labor is cheaper. In this view, society works in such a way as to trap some people and their offspring in a condition of poverty.

INDIVIDUAL THEORIES/CULTURAL EXPLANATIONS

Innate Inferiority

Social Darwinism is the notion that social life is competitive, with the best and the brightest rising to the top of the social hierarchy and the slow and the weak found at the bottom. An early proponent of this idea, sociologist Herbert Spencer said in 1882: "[Poverty was nature's way of] excreting . . . unhealthy, imbecile, slow, vacillating, faithless members of society in order to make room for the 'fit,' who were duly entitled to the rewards of wealth" (quoted in *The Progressive*, 1980:8). The contemporary articulation of the "innate inferiority" argument is best illustrated by Richard Herrnstein and Charles Murray. They argue in their book *The Bell Curve* (1994) that the economic and social hierarchies found in society reflect a single dimension–cognitive ability, as measured by IQ tests. In effect society is a **meritocracy** (social classification by ability) developed by a sorting process. This reasoning assumes that people who are close in mental ability are likely to marry and reproduce, thereby ensuring social classes by level of intelligence.[1]

Cultural Inferiority

Most Americans intuitively accept the explanation for poverty known as "**the culture of poverty.**" First articulated by anthropologist Oscar Lewis (1959), this

---

[1]For critiques of the innate ability theories, see especially Ryan (1976); Gould (1994); Reed (1994); *Contemporary Sociology* (1995); and Fischer et al. (1996).

13

theoretical position argues that many poor people develop a way of life that keeps them poor in adapting to their deprived condition. Individuals in this culture of poverty share feelings of marginality, helplessness, dependence, and inferiority. The poor have weak ego structures, a lack of impulse control, and a strong present-time orientation with relatively little ability to defer gratification and plan for the future. They are more permissive in raising their children, less verbal, more fatalistic, and less interested in formal education than the more affluent. Most significant, these different values and lifestyles that comprise the culture of poverty explain continued poverty because they are transmitted from generation to generation. Moreover, these character traits are so ingrained that they will survive even if poor people suddenly left poverty. Eventually, their values and behaviors would very likely put them back into poverty because they would be impulsive and not oriented toward the future.

A variant of the culture of poverty explanation is the notion of **underclass** as presented by, among others, Auletta (1999), Lemann (1986), and Kaus (1992). The underclass is a relatively small group, perhaps 10 to 20 percent of the poverty population. The underclass are conceptualized as mired in poverty, living in the inner city, and, typically, non-White. This group adopts its own values and behaviors which differ from mainstream society. The behavioral characteristics include a strong propensity for crime and other antisocial behaviors, welfare dependency, and out-of-wedlock births. A major facilitator of these deviant cultural values and behaviors is the welfare system, because it breaks down the work ethic by paying benefits as a matter of entitlement rather than as a consequence of work.

The most serious criticism of this notion that poverty results from the pathology of the weak is that it undercuts claims for collective obligation to design a better society (Robinson, 2001).[2] For example, by blaming the poor for their condition, adherents to this position see unequal schooling as justified. Why should school boards provide equal sums of money for similar programs in middle-class schools and lower-class schools, and why should teachers expect the same performance from poor children as from children of the more well-to-do? The result of such beliefs is, of course, a self-fulfilling prophecy. Low expectations beget low achievement (Eitzen and Baca Zinn, 2007:202).

Critics of the culture-of-poverty hypothesis argue that the poor are an integral part of society; they do not abandon the dominant values of society but, rather, retain them while simultaneously holding an alternative set of values. This alternative set is a result of adaptation to the conditions of poverty. Elliot Liebow, in his classic study of lower-class African American men, took this view. For him, street corner men strive to live by society's values but are continually frustrated by externally imposed failure.

> From this perspective, the street corner man does not appear as a carrier of an independent cultural tradition. His behavior appears not so much as a way of realizing the distinctive goals and values of his own subculture, or of conforming to its models, but rather as his way of trying to achieve many of the goals and values of the larger society, of failing to do this, and of concealing his failure from others and from himself as best he can. (Liebow, 1967:222)

[2]For critiques of the culture of poverty and underclass theories see especially Liebow (1967); Ryan (1970); and Reed (1980).

Most Americans believe that poverty is a combination of biological and cultural factors. Judith Chafel reviewed a number of studies on the beliefs of Americans and found that they "view economic privation as a self-inflicted condition, emanating more from personal factors (e.g., effort, ability) than external-structural ones (e.g., an unfavorable market, racism). Poverty is seen as inevitable, necessary, and just. . . ." (Chafel, 1997:434).

STRUCTURAL EXPLANATIONS

Michael Harrington, whose book *The Other America* was instrumental in sparking President Lyndon Johnson's war on poverty, said this in that classic: "The real explanation of why the poor are where they are is that they made the mistake of being born to the wrong parents, in the wrong section of the country, in the wrong industry, or in the wrong racial or ethnic group" (Harrington, 1963:21). In other words, the structural conditions of society are to blame for poverty, not the intellectual and cultural deficits of the poor.

Consider the way the U.S. economy works. The basic tenet of capitalism— that who gets what is determined by private profit rather than collective need— explains the persistence of why some people are impoverished. Because of the primacy of profits, employers continually act to keep wages and benefits as low as possible. The business community lobbies Congress opposing the raising of the minimum wage, resisting efforts to allow maternity leave for workers, and arguing against "equal pay for equal work" provisions for women. Typically, employers have tried to keep unions out of the work place because unions organize to increase wages and benefits for workers. Business owners also make investment decisions to reduce costs by the use of new technologies, such as robots to replace workers. Similarly, owners may shut down a plant and shift their operations to a foreign country where wages are significantly lower. In short, the capitalist system is an economic system that perpetuates inequality.

Most good jobs require a college degree, but the poor cannot afford to send their children to college. Scholarships go to the best-performing students, but children of the poor most often do not perform as well as the children of the privileged. This underformance by poor children results from the lack of enriched preschool programs for them, low expectations for them by teachers and administrators, and by systems of tracking by ability as measured on class-biased examinations. Problems in learning and test-taking may also arise because English is their second language. Because poverty is often concentrated geographically and schools are funded primarily by the wealth of their district, children of the poor usually attend inadequately financed schools. All these acts result in a self-fulfilling prophecy—the poor are not expected to do well in school, and they do not. They fall behind the children of privilege in developing the skills for college and marketable skills that lead to success in jobs. Because they are failures as measured by objective indicators (such as the disproportionately high number of dropouts, discipline problems, and the low number of those who desire to go to college), the school feels justified in its discrimination toward the children of the poor.

The traditional organization of jobs and schools in U.S. society deprive racial minorities of equal opportunities for education, jobs, and income. As a result, African Americans, for example, are half as likely to be wealthy and twice as likely to be poor as Whites. They are also twice as likely as Whites to be unemployed. Structuralists would argue that these differences are not the result of the flaws in African Americans but result rather from historical and current discrimination in communities, schools, banks, and the work world. Similarly, women typically work at less prestigious jobs than do men, and, when working at equal-status jobs, receive less pay and have fewer chances for advancement. These differences are not the result of gender differences but because of personal, social, and societal barriers to equality based on gender.

The structural explanation for poverty, then, rests on the assumption that the way society is organized perpetuates poverty, not the characteristics of poor people.[3] In the words of Claude Fischer and his colleagues:

Inequality is not fated by nature, nor even by the "invisible hand" of the market; it is a social construction, a result of our historical acts. Americans have created the extent and type of inequality we have, and Americans maintain it. (Fischer et al., 1996:7)

Theories of natural inequality cannot tell us why countries with such similar genetic stocks (and economic markets) as the United States, Canada, England, and Sweden can vary so much in the degree of economic inequality their citizens experience. The answer lies in deliberate policies. (Fischer et al., 1996:9)

Some examples of how the powerful and the privileged make policies that widen the economic gap between them and the poor include (Robinson, 2001):

- Over the last 20 years the New Deal assumption that housing is a fundamental right has withered with declining budgets for subsidized housing while gentrifying neighborhoods have been subsidized through government grants and redevelopment zones.
- President Bush's proposed massive tax cut gives 43 percent of the money to the wealthiest 1 percent of Americans while reducing social investments for health care, schools, and housing.
- Local governments provide subsidies to wealthy owners of professional sports teams to build luxurious stadiums. In Denver politicians put the corporate welfare stadium tax to a public vote, and lobbied for its passage, but do not let the voters decide whether to extend that tax to help low-income renters and homeowners.
- Also in Denver, the city council approved a $65 million public subsidy for a luxury Hyatt hotel. At the same time these officials refused to honor requests to tie this subsidy to an agreement by the Hyatt to allow union organizing at the hotel.

As Tony Robinson states: "In such ways, the privileged make political choices that exacerbate the crisis of the vulnerable, justifying these choices with theories of the pathology of the poor. But politics can be transformed with the understanding

[3]For critiques of the structuralist theories of poverty, see Murray (1984) and Mead (1992).

that the problems of poverty are a human creation, amenable to human solution" (2001:G1).

NOTES AND SUGGESTIONS FOR FURTHER READING_____

Auletta, Ken (1999). *The Underclass,* updated and revised edition. New York: Random House.

Baptist, Willie, and Mary Bricker-Jenkins (2002). "A View from the Bottom: Poor People and Their Allies Respond to Welfare Reform," pp. 195–210 in *Lost Ground: Welfare Reform, Poverty and Beyond,* Randy Albelda and Ann Withorn (Eds.). Cambridge, MA: South End Press.

Chafel, Judith A. (1997). "Societal Images of Poverty." *Youth and Society* 28 (June):432–463.

Contemporary Sociology (1995). "Symposium: The Bell Curve." Volume 24 (March):149–161.

Eitzen, D. Stanley, and Maxine Baca Zinn (2007). *In Conflict and Order: Understanding Society.* Boston: Allyn and Bacon.

Fischer, Claude S., Michael Hout, Martin Sanchez Jankowski, Samuel R. Lucas, Ann Swidler, and Kim Voss (1996). *Inequality by Design: Cracking the Bell Curve Myth.* Princeton, NJ: Princeton University Press.

Gould, Stephen J. (1994). "Curveball." *The New Yorker* (November 28):139–149.

Herrnstein, Richard J., and Charles Murray (1994). *The Bell Curve: Intelligence and Class Structure in American Life.* New York: The Free Press.

Kaus, Mickey (1992). *The End of Equality.* New York: HarperCollins.

Kushnick, Louis, and James Jennings (Eds.), (1999). *A New Introduction to Poverty: The Role of Race, Power, and Politics.* New York: New York University Press.

Lemann, Nicholas (1986). "The Origins of the Underclass." *The Atlantic,* Part I (June):31–55; Part II (July):54–68.

Lewis, Oscar (1959). *Five Families: Mexican Case Studies in the Culture of Poverty.* New York: Random House.

Liebow, Elliot (1967). *Talley's Corner.* Boston: Little, Brown.

Marks, Carole (1991). "The Urban Underclass." *Annual Review of Sociology* 17:445–466.

Mead, L. M. (1992). *The New Politics of Poverty: The Nonworking Poor in America.* New York: Basic Books.

Murray, Charles (1984). *Losing Ground.* New York: Basic Books.

O'Connor, Alice (2001). *Poverty Knowledge: Social Science, Social Policy, and the Poor in the Twentieth-Century U.S. History.* Princeton, NJ: Princeton University Press.

The Progressive (1980). "Out of the Bottle." Volume 44 (August):8.

Reed, Adolph, Jr. (1990). "The Underclass as Myth and Symbol: The Poverty of Discourse about Poverty." *Radical America* 24 (January/March):24–40.

Reed, Adolph, Jr. (1994). "Looking Backward." *The Nation* (November 28):654–662.

Robinson, Tony (2001). "Poor, Poorer, Poorest: the Politics of Poverty." *The Denver Post* (March 4):G1.

Ryan, William (1970). "Is Banfield Serious?" *Social Policy* 1 (November/December):74–76.

Ryan, William (1976). *Blaming the Victim,* rev. ed. New York: Random House (Vintage).

Sidel, Ruth (1996). *Keeping Women and Children Last: America's War on the Poor.* New York: Penguin Books.

Poverty or At Home in a Car

JACKIE SPINKS

*According to the Department of Housing and Urban Development, in
2005 there were 754,000 homeless people across the country, approximately 300,000 more people than available beds in shelters. While these
numbers are staggering, what is it really like to be one of the severely poor,
without a home? This essay was written by a 40 year old White male at the
"bottom of America's class system." Living in his car, eating at the local
mission, he ruminates about being poor. As you read his essay, consider
the following questions: Does the author reveal how he became poor? How
has he adapted to his situation? Which theories of poverty (cultural/indi-
vidual/structural) are reflected in this reading, and why? What role should
society play, if any, in helping people like this author?*

For seven months, my home has been my 1973 Dodge van. Life in a car is similar
to life in a garbage can: trash filled, cramped, and with a smell to die from. Before
that, I lived in a shed. I live here because I was kicked out of the shed.

Guys, suited in black worsted, the authority clothes of caliphs-in-waiting, circle around me; avoiding eye contact.

Sometimes I wonder what's going through their minds when they see me? Do
they ever wonder what's going through mine? Or do they give a damn? Or maybe
they assume I don't have a mind? Or are they thinking, "Bum! Loser! What's the
matter with you? There's work out there. It isn't a recession. You corks think you're
too good to work. So okay, be a stiff, but why do I have to support you, and why do
you dirty up nice streets? Where's your pride? Where's your work ethic?"

Yeah, I pretty much know them. But they don't know me from marmalade. So
here's to making my acquaintance.

I'm one of those seedy guys at the bottom of America's class system, who
knows that he's going to stay there. I'm not taken in by that "rags to riches" hooey
our teachers, parents, media; in fact, the whole culture, fed us. I am 40-years-old,

SOURCE: Jackie Spinks, "Poverty or At Home in A Car," *Z Magazine* 9 (February 1996), pp. 57–60.
Reprinted by permission of the publisher.

and have not earned more than $20,000 in my entire life, which means I've lived on less than $100 a month, for the past 20 years. So I know, after all this time, I'm not going anywhere.

Before I go on I'd better forewarn you: I'm not a curator of America's art of scrimping, a chronicler of poverty's abasements, or a bemoaner of its inequality. I'm just a down-and-outer trying to puzzle out my life, figure out how guys like me get where they are, especially when they don't have the excuse of alcohol or dope for their downward spiral.

I sold my Yamaha for $100 and bought this beater I'm living in for $75 dollars. Pretty lucky break. I got it for $75 because the interior was gutted, the windows broken, the roof rusted through. It was ready for the compactor, so nobody bid on it at the city auction. Thus, I have a home—my first in a long time.

I tinkered with it and got it moving. The reverse gear needs money to fix, so I can only go forward. The back brakes are bad (more money) and I worry driving, because of the brakes. So I don't drive it far. Besides, I have to hang onto my space, where my car's parked. But every once in a while I take a spin around the block just to keep my beater alive, as who knows when the local Praetorians will hustle me off. They'll give me a ticket for something, probably driving without registration. The constabulary knows and hates me. Not only am I an outcast, but being only five and a half feet tall, I'm an easy nab.

Mostly I stay where I am. What's important is keeping my corner. Three other guys have found my spot and are now parked near me. If I move my car, they'll grab it, as it is the best space, so I protect my claim. It's particularly valuable to me, as it's the only place where I can move forward and don't need to go into reverse.

It's a challenge, living in a crouched position in my van: minus toilet, water, telephone, electricity, and privacy. But the toughest part is the temperature: 95 degrees in the summer and freezing in winter.

I eat at the mission. Before I forced myself to check out the place (I was afraid of it), I lived on stuff like vanilla wafers, nachos, half-eaten pizzas, or sandwiches I found lying around.

Why the mission spooked me was, first, it was strange; and second, a lot of beefy guys with nothing to lose hung around the entrance. I had no weapon, no back-up, and there's always some guy hankering to beat up a little guy. On the one hand, poverty makes brutes, but on the other hand, people are poor because they're basically passive. Telling myself they all just want to be somebody and have you recognize it, I stiffened my mettle.

Nevertheless, just to avoid trouble, I smiled. I'm the kind of guy who smiles a lot, tells jokes, shows he's a regular guy. But I confess the adrenaline was pumping, and a rigid smile was shellacked on my face when I ambled cool, but not cocky, into the mission. It smelled like fat frying, a good smell, and the eating space was big—a high-ceilinged room with about 80 guys and 2 women sitting at long tables.

A lot of the guys were Mexican farmworkers, all talking in Spanish. They had serious faces. A couple years back, I climbed on a field bus and for about two weeks, picked strawberries. Those people were fast, about four times as fast as me. A little girl about 10 picked faster than I ever could—if I lived to be 100. I watched her to figure out her method. She'd kind of hold the bush and pull three or four berries at one reach. And did it with miniature fingers, that didn't crush the berries—such ingenuity wasted on a berry bush. She said she wanted a house and three kids when she grew up.

The food at the mission will never disturb McDonald's, but it fills me up and that's what counts. For instance, on my first day, they gave us two choices: bean soup or venison soup. We have a lot of deer hunters in this part of the country and most of them dislike venison, so the mission gets a lot of venison.

Most of the guys chose venison soup, but I chose bean soup. I'm a vegetarian, more by necessity than by conviction, but I think going without meat is a good idea. Besides, I have a soft spot for deer.

The mission, also, gets a lot of good pastries, the kind you buy at a bakery, usually about a week old. I eat a lot of doughnuts. You can take them with you when you leave. Sometimes we have ripe bananas. Sometimes we even have salad.

Often the food at the mission is spoiled, but nobody reports it, as it's better to be sick than risk closure. The bathroom, which is next to the kitchen, has been without toilet paper or paper towels for months. Four of the six toilets don't flush and nobody mops or uses cleanser, so you can figure it's a shopping mall of microbes, but nobody expects Trump Towers. Often I puke. Once, I did it for two days, but as one guy said, "How do you know it was the food at the mission. It could have been the flu."

Illness is for the rich. The poor that try to join that club, get two minutes and a swift heave-ho. It's been 20 years since I've been to a doctor. A few weeks back, I drove a guy with a severed finger to emergency, and sat with some mothers, who said they'd been waiting three hours. The mothers held their sick kids and scolded the others.

Many of the guys at the mission are here illegally. Nervous. Worried about trouble, too. Like me. And they're dirty. Like me. I can't speak Spanish, maybe a few words like "por favor, como esta, adios, and gracias." Wish I knew more. A big regret—flunking Spanish in high school. Their English is better than my Spanish, but still hard to understand. So mostly we just smile at one another.

My little forays into conversation with mission Saxons usually consist of mutual brag-a-thons. You'd think we'd all just dumped our portfolios with our brokers and decided to do a little slumming. And, if not that, we all have ships that will be tooting in, around the bend, any minute.

According to all of us displaced whites (I gas along with the best), we just need a little capital to get started. Some of the guys have pretty good ideas. One guy, a wood carver, thought he'd make Sasquash dolls and sell them at local fairs and bazaars. Another guy built a toilet for car dwellers, but fearing theft of his idea, was cagey in explaining how it operated. I listened up on that one. Then his paranoia took over, and he clammed up. Another had an idea for paper blankets.

It's all just talk. Nobody will ever do anything. To build up our self-esteem, we peg ourselves as 20th century pariahs, like frontier sheep farmers. We perceive ourselves as urban pioneers staking out claims, front runners of things to come.

We carve out places, on the street, protect our turf, think of ourselves as prototypes of those guys who straggled over the Cascades without a penny to their names: sometimes desperate, often lonely, frequently surviving by their wits. They were giants. Stoics. Squatters like us. Our heroes. Deep in all of us, we mourn not having been born in the 18th century. Because we believe (probably incorrectly), that then poverty was a clean and honorable estate, not just wacko actions and fantasizing, like it is today.

How does a homeless, jobless, middle-aged man occupy his day? Well, first off I sleep. Besides sleeping I post myself in the library. I arrive at opening time, ten in the morning, and stay most of the day. It's cool in there. Air conditioned. But temperature is only a minor reason I like the library. The main reason is the people. The people are quiet. No one bothers me or tells me to move on.

I read everything: religion, carpentry, mechanics, electrical, police training, political, biographies, nutrition, baseball novels, and a lot of gun, boat, news, and alternate press magazines. Sometimes I walk along the docks, examine the boats, imagine stowing away on a Russian cargo ship.

I scrutinize, with the eye of a tourist: buildings, factories, guys working—and I especially like to study bees. When I've exhausted looking, I sit in my car and read.

How do I live? Well, I use a can for my bowels and dump my loo near some pole beans and tomatoes in a garden nearby. I expected big beans and red, ripe tomatoes in that spot, but to my surprise they're limping along. One of my fellow car-dwelling aficionados said, "Living on the streets, you probably got toxic crap." I do my "miss congeniality" smile, but don't think it's funny. I don't think he meant it to be funny. I use recycled newspaper for toilet paper.

I mosey up to the college about once a month and sneak a shower in the college gym. I'm careful to use it when it's empty, shower as quickly as possible, just in case I get caught.

Probably the biggest problem for guys like me is water. I'm always looking for water. Every chance I get, I fill up a jug I carry everywhere in my backpack and haul it back to my Dodge. And that's strictly for drinking—not to wash hands, face, dishes, or clothes.

Apart from begging, the thing about poor people that riles rich people the most is our grime. Cleanliness is identified with goodness in America. It's next to Godliness. Dirt is evil. I think we're supposed to clean up and pretend we're real. I don't oppose cleanliness. It's that cleanliness for someone living in a car is a labyrinthine ordeal.

First, to wash and dry two loads of clothes—it costs about $5.00 total. Plus, you need a way to get to the laundry; plus, you need soap; plus, you need something to wear while you're washing the clothes.

But now and then a car-dwelling paisano does spiff up. Once cleaned up, he isn't too bad. I wonder why I've been going on ad nauseam about cleanliness and appearance? I must have some insecurity there. But then, so when aren't we insecure?

As for work, in my 20s when hope bloomed, I choo-chooed along, the little engine that could—but not anymore. Now, it's "tote that barge, lift that bail, wish to hell I could land in jail." I've worked for bosses that were drill sergeants with little concern about their oxen's safety who expected it to plow away at minimum pay. I got chemical burns on my hands that ate away chunks of the flesh, burns that still eat my fingers ten years later. I have no hope for anything better than a grinding $4.60 an hour.

A guy at the mission said, "I'd rather be poor than work. Why should I help make the rich richer?"

I'm anxious all the time. Until I found the mission, I worried constantly about where my next meal was coming from; I was anxious about my future; anxious about people. But mostly I was anxious that if—by some remote possibility I landed a decent job—that after so many years of non-work, with its absence of punctuality, drive, and concentration, I would fail again.

Hey, I sound like the mother of all belly-achers, bitching about contaminated food, cleanliness, jobs, pisspots, anxiety. I forget the other class has troubles, too; that they whip themselves, unmercifully, if some friend gains on them. That if their cash flow falls from ten million to two million, they worry they're finished and stumble home, get swacked, and feel like they'll never be a real player.

I heard some social worker-type talk about homelessness being a new deviant career. Sure am glad I have a career at last. Deviant or otherwise. Is homelessness better than being male, white, 40, and working at McDonalds? Yeah, I guess so, but then, Hell, McDonalds wouldn't hire a bum like me—even if he did have nice teeth.

The inner awareness I live with, and fight every day is that I'm nothing. To get rid of this feeling, I'd like to try Prozac. But two bucks for a pill, without a buzz. Then again, maybe I'm lucky. At some later date, they'd probably discover Prozac caused some kink, like edema of the brain, or elephantiasis, or more likely, an old stand-by like high blood pressure or cancer. They always find some pea to stick in our comfort zone. So I sleep Prozacless.

Because I sleep a lot, the books I've read label me depressed. I question that, as I've never contemplated suicide; but maybe I am depressed and don't know it. Or maybe I sleep because I'm bored. About the only truism about poverty in America in the 1990s is that it's one giant yawn.

Maybe that's what depression is—nothing to do. Rutsville. And doing the rut alone, at ebb tide, and feeling its all your fault. That everything's your fault. Feeling something's wrong with you because you would rather be poor than be under the foot of a master. So who wants to think. Better to sleep.

About our depression, whenever you channel onto a poor person's wave, male or female, what you discover is that—underneath the defenses, they're thinking, "There's something haywire with me. I'm worse than second-rate, I'm rotten. I can't do anything right. Nobody will ever hire a creep like me for any job that has a future. I'll never do anything that's even slightly smart."

To illustrate, a guy at the mission, came out from lunch and found the side of his Kawasaki dented. A few minutes before he'd been chair of the brag-a-thon. Now, you'd expect the guy to say, "I'll, gonna kill the bastard who did this." But no, all this poor jerk could do was stare and mutter, "It's all my fault. I can't do anything right."

We all walked away, but it hit close. We understood.

In contrast to Americans, who place so much emphasis on individualism, people from other countries don't blame themselves. A Hindu cab driver, so black that he felt forced to reiterate three times, to our uninquiring minds, that he was Caucasian, told us about an experience he had here. He was sitting in a park and noticed several Americans going over to a marble protrusion, bending over it, and when water gushed out, drinking. Being thirsty, he went over to the protrusion, bent over it, but no water came out. He bent over it several times, still no water. Finally, he walked away, telling himself even the water over here in America is prejudiced.

Now that's what we considered an intelligent response, the kind we wish we could make.

It's like the world has a negative image of us, so we absorb that image, make it ours, and agree with the world, that, yes, because we aren't successes, we're slime.

Yeah, we're lazy. The dictionary definition of lazy is slow moving, resistant to exertion, slothful. And gadzooks, the perfect definition of depression.

Those active, employed people, who run around doing this and that, who talk briskly, walk with that high-stepping gait, who complain about have too much on their calendar, who, after a quick handshake, dash of to another appointment, are as strange to us as a bidet. We watch, wonder, and shuffle off, when we're around them. I guess they don't understand us either; the passive, the depressed, the underclass. Yet, we all share the same boat and it's gaining water. And maybe we know it better than they do.

Whatever. So, I sleep about 11 or 12 hours a day. Wish it were the sleep of the frazzled or anesthetized, but it's a half awake sleep. When awake I contemplate ways to make our world better. On good days, I dream of a revolution in concept. On bad days I decide, "Blow 'er up. Start over."

As I lie here, watching the rain drip alongside the car window, I forage around for something positive to say about poverty. What I come up with is freedom. Yeah, I have freedom—no worry about stocks or kids or lovers. I click around the idea of freedom for a while and finally decide, next to a high IQ, freedom is the most over-rated quality any sociologist ever extolled.

The Armstrongs: An Oral History of a Homeless American Family

STEVEN VANDERSTAAY

Steven VanderStaay introduces this selection in the following way: "The Armstrongs lived in Bellevue, a young, largely affluent city east of Seattle, until a medical emergency and the sudden loss of Mark's job forced the family to seek emergency housing. Since Bellevue has little emergency housing, the Armstrongs were advised to seek shelter in nearby Seattle. Eventually, the family was moved to a large public housing project in the city's Central District. Each morning they awake at 5:00 for the long bus ride back to Bellevue for work and school. Mark and Linda both work, as do their teenage children. Speaking to them, I am struck that they are the quintessential American family: hard-working, supportive, patriotic, loving. And now homeless. The Armstrongs' difficulties—underemployment, housing, grocery bills, health costs, insurance problems—mirror those of other homeless families driven from affluent communities. They are African Americans in their early thirties." As you read the following selection, what issues are raised by Mark's words about the minimum wage? The minimum wage has since been raised; is this enough to raise the Armstrong family out of poverty? How would individuals from the different theoretical perspectives analyze this family's situation?

MARK: I designed and built conveyor belts, and was good at it. I was making over $15 an hour. And I can go back there right now and get you a letter of recommendation from the company and let you read what they wrote about me. That in itself tells you what kind of worker I am.

The company went out of business. Bang! Didn't even know it was coming. I was between jobs three or four months. I could have found work right away if I wanted to make minimum wage, but I got pretty high standards for myself I don't even want to make what I'm making now. We could barely afford rent then, how

SOURCE: Steven VanderStaay, *Street Lives: An Oral History of Homeless Americans* (Philadelphia, PA: New Society Publishers, 1992), pp. 172–176. Reprinted with permission of the author.

can we now? But when you got kids to feed and bills to pay, you have to do the best you can.

But minimum wage—that's insulting. I don't knock it for high school students. They're getting training, learning about working, making their pocket money. That's fine. But you take a person . . . I got six kids. $3.35, $4 an hour, I spend more than that wage in a day's time on a grocery bill. I mean you can accept some setbacks, but you can't tell a person, "I don't care if you've been making $15 something an hour, the minimum is what you've got to make now." If I hand you this letter, give you my resume, my military record, show you the kind of worker I am, talk about my family, how can you degrade me by offering me the minimum wage?

Then we had trouble with the house we were renting. And, well, the biggest part of it was hospital bills. My son had to have emergency surgery. Since the company was going out of business it let the insurance lapse, so I got stuck with the bill. Spent every penny we had saved and there's still fourteen hundred dollars on it. You would think by being medical that it wouldn't affect the credit, but it does.

Now I'm working with Safeway's warehouse. I work in the milk plant. Swing shift. Sometimes I'm off at 12:30, 1:00 at night, and then turn right around and go back at 8:30 the next morning. Yeah, it's hard sometimes. I'm not making half of what I used to. I'm a helper—I used to have people working for me. I'd worked my way up through the ranks. But like I was saying, you adjust, you do what you have to do. I'm the kind of person, I get with a company I want to stay, be a part of it. I like to get along with people and work, get my hands dirty. See something accomplished. I'm low man on the totem pole but I'll stay and work my way up.

The warehouse, it's refrigerated on one end and kind of hot on the other. They make their own milk cartons out of plastic so you have to deal with heat and cold. You have to know how to dress 'cause you're dealing with both extremes.

LINDA: I've been a custodian, nurse's aide; now I work at K-Mart. I still have to bus back to the East side [Bellevue] every day. It's okay but I'm looking for something else. You know, it's $4 an hour, and there's no benefits, no discounts at the store, nothing like that.

And I'm in school now, too. I'm going for business training, probably computers or administration. When school starts I'll either bring the little ones there with me or have one of the older ones bring them home.

Working full-time and going to school. Six kids, seventeen on down to twelve. Three in high school, three in grade school. Two of them work at Jack in the Box. They've been working the same shift but my oldest, he's on the football team, so he might be working at a different time than my daughter. And then there's the church, and those football games. Yes we're busy! Just an all-American family. One that's hit a string of bad luck, that's all.

The hardest thing is getting up early enough to bus back over there. As soon as school gets started that's really going to be a problem. It might be a couple of hours, both ways. And if they find out our kids are living here they'll want them in school in Seattle. But they like the schools there and I like them. They're better. And that's where we've lived, that's where we work.

But we get by. The kids, they cook, they clean, they wash and iron their own clothes. And the older ones, they all work. We're so proud of them. Oh, we have the same problems everybody else has, with teenagers and so forth. But we get through 'em. Just thank God they're not on drugs. That's the biggest problem here.

MARK: When we had to move and lost the house, when I lost my job, we told the kids the truth, the flat out truth. With no misconception; none whatsoever. Kids are not dumb. If you lie to kids, why should they be honest with you? They know exactly what we're going through and they know why.

Same thing when we moved here—six kids, three rooms, writing all over the walls, the drugs and crime. We tried to avoid the move but we didn't have any choice. They knew exactly where we were moving to, as best I could explain it. We told them we didn't want to come, but if it came down to it we were coming. And we did.

Now my worst fear . . . there's so much drugs in this area. And people think every apartment in the projects is a drug house. They knock on the doors, knock on the windows—they stop me out there and ask where it is. It's here, so close to us all the time. And all the shooting and fighting . . . You can look out the window any given night and see the police stopping people and searching everyone.

If I can't look out my door and see my kids, I send for 'em. And I'm afraid when I can't see 'em. 'Cause when they get to shootin' and fightin' and carryin'-on, a bullet don't got no names on it. Sometimes when I come in from work, three, four o'clock in the morning, I wonder just when they're going to get me. But my worst fear, my worst fear is the kids.

LINDA: Over in Bellevue they think if you can't afford it then you shouldn't be there. You know, who cares if you work there.

The first house that we had, we were the first blacks in the neighborhood. When I moved over there I said, "Where the black people?" [laughs, then moves her head from side to side as if searching] . . . no black people? Then the neighbors, they got to looking, came out, they were surprised, too. "Oooh, we got black people over here now" [laughs]. The kids were the only black kids around.

MARK: People don't want to rent to a family. And you know the kind of rent they're asking over there in Bellevue, that's not easy to come up with. And you need first, last month's rent, security. . . . And then people automatically assess, they stereotype you. Maybe sometimes it's 'cause we're black—I'm not saying this is true, I'm saying that sometimes I *felt* that the reason we didn't get a place was because we were black. But most of the time it's the family. People would rather you have pets than kids these days.

One guy, he had six bedrooms in this house. But he didn't want a family. Why would you have six bedrooms if you didn't want to rent to a family? May not be legal, but they do that all the time.

Now there is some validity in what they say about children tearing up things. But the child is only as bad as you let him be. You're the parent, he's going to do exactly what you let him do and get away with. If my kids tear something up, I'll pay for it. But me, I tell my kids that if I have to replace something they've destroyed, then one of their sisters or brothers isn't going to get something they need. And when they do something they answer to me.

I'm not bitter . . . I mean I'm somewhat so. I'm not angry bitter. It's just that I don't like dragging my kids from one place to the next, and I don't think we've been treated right. We had to take places sight-unseen, just to get 'em. We paid $950 a month, and during the wintertime $300, $400 a month for electric and gas bills. Then bought food, kept my kids in clothes. How you supposed to save to get ahead with all that?

And the house, when we moved in the landlords said they'd do this and that, fix this and that. Said we would have an option to buy it. We said "Okay, and we'll do these things." We had an agreement.

We never got that chance to buy, and they never fixed those things. But we kept paying that $950 a month. They had a barrel over us: we needed some place to go. And they made a small fortune those years. A month after we moved out we went by: all those things they wouldn't do were done.

Before that the guy decided to sell his house, just like that, and we had to move. It was December, wintertime. For a while we were staying with her mother in a two-bedroom. Nine people. We had to be somewhere so we took that second place before we had even seen it.

Everybody has to have a place to live. And people will do what they have to do to survive. A lot of things that you see going on around here are for survival [he sweeps his hand, indicating the housing projects]. I'm not taking up for them, there's a lot of things happening here that I oppose. But where there's a will there's a way, you know.

Feeling Trapped

NIKKIE THOMPSON

The United States has the highest rate of teenage pregnancy and birth in the Western industrialized world. According to the National Campaign to Prevent Teen Pregnancy, approximately 750,000 teenage girls get pregnant each year, and 80 percent of them will end up on welfare. In addition to an increased risk of poverty, there is an increased risk for health problems to both the child and teenage mother. Going beyond the statistics, what is it like being a teen parent in poverty? Thinking sociologically, analyze this essay by a single, former teenage mother. What is her experience with the welfare system? What faults of the system does she point to? Which theories are best reflected in her essay and why?

Have you ever felt trapped? Not physically, but emotionally and financially. I have been a single parent for almost a decade and I have never been without stress. Being a parent is not easy, not to mention if you are a teenager. I could've done away with my responsibility, but I chose to take it on and become a woman.

Over the years I have been through homelessness, violence, and abandonment. Sometimes life should not offer so much strain. My first child clearly was not planned and my second was planned in the dream that daddy would always be there. Being on welfare with two kids has been no day at the beach.

My children are the most important thing to me. Can you believe that people ridiculed me and talked bad about me because I didn't have a job and lots of money? When I was growing up, my mom, grandma, and great grandma never had money. They managed some how to raise the people who raised me. They washed, scrubbed, wiped, bathed, and hard labored their asses off for pennies.

The rich people used the backs of the slaves to build the cities we live in now. I feel that times really have not changed. Let's start with the County Human Service Departments. Denver alone has around a $55,000,000 surplus. A family needing assistance for the TANF program (in some cases) has to complete a mandatory

SOURCE: Nikkie Thompson, "Feeling Trapped," People United For Families (PUFF) Poverty to Prosperity Newsletter (November 2000). Reprinted by permission of the publisher.

amount of work hours before they can receive any assistance. Or come to our job skill classes and receive no job skills at all.

Most of these programs teach you how to dress for an interview and how to get better self-esteem. And they encourage you into believing that you will be self-sufficient with a good job.

When you leave you will wonder what did I learn in these classes. And why do I have a low income, dead end ass job. Most people that leave these programs end up with a job in the $5.15–$8.50 range. That is not enough when considering housing, food, child-care, transportation, healthcare, clothing, phone, utilities, and taxes.

In my experience the government has a plan to keep the low-income and poverty level individuals just that. The system is set already to have us be dependent on it and not ourselves. They say "Give them welfare and make it hard to afford life." Then they'll say, "Take the welfare back and sell a false dream that they'll be self-sufficient from welfare to work programs."

We are these people just like my elders washing, picking, scrubbing, and cleaning up the city's filth. In today's society it takes money to make money. How can we as poor people get and keep anything with the GREED DOG on our back trying to take everything we get.

I am a 24-year-old working mom of two kids, making a little over minimum wage. I am stressed. I don't eat, sleep, or have time for my kids anymore. Just because I thought that I would be self-sufficient. I went to these programs made to "help." I ended up with a low paying job with hope of making more in the future. My money can never be saved because I don't make enough to save. Bills consume my whole check. Just from the little money I make, I am no longer eligible for any kind of assistance.

GREED is what this system is all about. How can we as the working poor ever afford the necessities of life? The minute we get some money it is gone. That sounds like TRAPPED to me!

No 40 Acres and a Mule: An Interview with a Displaced Black Farmer

ROBERT D. BULLARD

The following selection is an interview with Gary Grant, an African American, North Carolina farmer. The selection points out the importance of land ownership to African Americans since the time of slavery. As you read this selection, think about the issue of institutional racism, which occurs when social arrangements and accepted ways of doing things in society create a disadvantage for a racial group. How does Grant's story illustrate institutional racism? What components are evident from the structural perspective of poverty?

The federal government created the Freedmen's Bureau to provide assistance to former slaves. It also promised the former slaves parcels of land and the loan of a federal government mule to work the land. The federal government never lived up to its promise of "forty acres and a mule." Nevertheless, some African American farmers were able to buy or lease parcels of land under these programs. However, during Reconstruction under President Andrew Johnson, many of the powers and activities of the Freedmen's Bureau were dismantled and much of the land that had been leased to black farmers was taken away and returned to Confederate loyalists.

Despite open hostility, racial discrimination, and institutional racism practiced inside and outside of government, African American farmers were able to amass an impressive amount of farmland holdings. By 1910, they owned over 16 million acres of farmland. By 1920, there were 925,000 African American farmers. In 1999, African American farmers number dwindled to less than 17,000 and less than 3 million acres of land.

Racial discrimination practiced against African American farmers was never eradicated. In 1997, African American farmers brought a lawsuit against the USDA charging it with discrimination in denying them access to loans and subsidies. The

SOURCE: Robert D. Bullard, "No 40 Acres and a Mule: An Interview with a Displaced Black Farmer," Environmental Justice Research Center (June 25, 1999). Reprinted by permission of the author.

lawsuit was filed in August, 1997 on behalf of 4,000 of the nation's 17,000 black farmers and former farmers. A Consent Decree was signed in January, 1999. The estimated cost of the settlement ranges from $400 trillion to more than $2 billion. To view the full court opinion click www.dcd. uscourts.gov/district-court.html

This interview was conducted with Gary Grant, a Tillery, North Carolina resident and a plaintiff in the Black farmers' lawsuit. Grant is president of the Black Farmers and Agriculturalists Association or BFAA. His family was forced out of farming in 1991. The interview was conducted by Robert D. Bullard, director of the Environmental Justice Resource Center, in June 1999.

QUESTION: What is your feeling about the black farmers settlement offered by a federal judge?

GRANT: It is a bittersweet victory. Sweet in the fact that we did succeed in the courts, having the USDA admit to discrimination and being certified as a class. Bitter in the fact that I still believe that this consent decree will ensure the demise of black farmers in two to five years. First of all, there is nothing in the document that returns land to us. In addition, there is nothing in the document that will pay off debt that has been incurred because of racist actions of USDA officers. Many of the farmers no longer owe USDA but owe private lenders. If their property is freed up, then the private lender will be able to come after it with less reserve.

QUESTION: What reservations do you have about how the settlement will be carried out?

GRANT: The settlement follows basically a two-track process. Track A is the track that will allow a farmer to go after $50,000 and have his debt written off and that's all. Track B is where a farmer provides records of bias from 1983–97, the period covered in the settlement. Black farmers have to prove with a "preponderance of the evidence" their case of discrimination. That will allow them to collect money from damages as well as to have debt written off to collect money for what they lost in not being able to farm. Track B would add up to more than $50,000. Getting into track B is just entirely too cumbersome for farmers to prove the discrimination in the atmosphere where racism ruled the day and people reacted based on their knowledge and understanding of how you act where racism is prevalent.

QUESTION: Which track do you feel the farmers will take?

GRANT: I really think that most of the farmers will be accepting the $50,000. It is virtually impossible to describe what people have been through and what most folk are saying. Most of them just want the USDA out of their lives. And when you hear the horror stories that people have to tell, you can understand why. Also, most of them have already been driven out of farming. They have lost their livelihood and a way of life. Once again, the government is asking the "victims" to prove discrimination. The burden of proof is on black farmers instead of the lawbreakers. That is not fair. That is not just. But, that's the American way. The government records are filled with examples where black farmers were systematically treated different from white farmers. Black farmers were routinely given less money for the same land than white farmers. They were also denied access to programs that aided white farmers. These were common practices. Fifty thousand dollars is not a lot of money. We are talking about a small business stolen, people's jobs, credit rating, and livelihoods ruined, life savings and investments taken, and spirits broken. No amount of money can repay the pain and suffering inflicted on black farmers. I wonder how much money the government would have offered us if we were white.

QUESTION: What guarantees do African American farmers have that the USDA will not allow the same thing to happen again?

GRANT: We have no guarantees. The government refused to put into the settlement document a clause that said it would enforce its civil rights policies. This means that they won't have a watchdog over them. Many of the farmers are displeased and frustrated. The farm advocate groups are most disturbed that for the long term there is nothing in the document that really helps us out. There is nothing in this document that guarantees that this kind of racism will not occur again within the USDA. To my knowledge, none of the USDA agents who perpetrated this injustice have been terminated. As a matter of fact, nobody was fired that I know of and some of them are getting promotions.

QUESTION: How has your family been hurt by the actions of the federal government?

GRANT: My community, Tillery, is a New Deal Resettlement community established in the 1940s. The federal government bought 18,000 acres of former plantation land and divided it up into forty to eighty-acre tracts and made it possible for black people to purchase that land. The black landowners have been the thorn in the side of the political power in Halifax County, North Carolina ever since, because we have not been dependent on them for our survival. Through our struggle, we've managed to save most of the land. Now the population of Halifax is about 52% African American and the community of Tillery is 99% African American. We still probably own 90% of the land, however white farmers are farming 98% of it.

Tillery had over 300 black farmers in the 1950s. Today, it has none. My family has been in foreclosure for 23 years and we continue to raise that issue. I am part of the class action because the USDA denied me the opportunity to assume my father's debt and to continue to operate our farm. My nieces and nephews have grown up in that 23 year time with a very bitter taste in their mouths and hearts about farming because they have seen the toll taken on my father and mother and my brother and his wife. We are not sure that any of them will enter farming. We are not even encouraging them that strongly, but it has brought us together much closer to the understanding of the power of the land.

QUESTION: How important is African American land ownership?

GRANT: Land ownership has to be a major theme that takes the African American community into the 21st century. As a people, we must understand the value and the power of land ownership. One generation removed from slavery, black folks were able to acquire more than 16 million acres of farmland. We have nearly lost it all. This land has been in my family for 52 years and another tract that was in jeopardy has been in my family for about 100 years. The only power that there really is in this country is land ownership, which produces economics, which is green stuff. Even for you to have money you have to own land first, so that the money has somewhere to be produced from. The constitution and the founding fathers believed that if you were not a member, if you were not a land owner you could not run for office, if you were not a land owner you could not vote. The lessons of the land have been there ever since the beginning. African Americans just seem to have problems with understanding and connecting to it. Also, as we lose this land no one is asking what happens to it and that is where we can also bring in the issue of environmental racism and environmental injustice. On much of this land is where the siting of polluting industries are being set.

QUESTION: How have you been treated by the federal courts?

GRANT: We were successful in keeping our case in court only because of the strong evidence pointing to racism practiced and condoned by USDA. It was time for America to come to grips with the ugly face of racism. America needs to know that a group of people was wronged. We were not satisfied with the January 1999 proposed settlement. On March 2, 1999, U.S. District Judge Paul Friedman held a fairness hearing to amend the lawsuit settlement. We brought close to 500 black farmers to Washington DC. We overflowed two federal court rooms. At that time, we had an opportunity to present to the judge our differences with the consent decree that had been filed. After that hearing, Judge Friedman made 14 recommendations based on what he heard in the courtroom that day. Our attorneys and the government attorneys only accepted four of those with a great modification and those four would not impact the actual actions of the consent decree.

QUESTION: What lessons can African Americans learn from the plight of black farmers?

GRANT: I think that the first lesson is the continuing fact that institutional racism is alive and well in this country. Black people still have to fight like hell to enjoy the rights that whites take for granted. I think the real lesson lies in what we can do as a people if we really will come together. Our case proved that we do have some political power. We got the statute of limitations set aside. We learned quickly that the media is largely controlled and our images manipulated in the headlines to suit the stereotypes of white people. Finally, it became clear that the African American community does not understand the real value and power of black landowners and black farmers. This is true for many of our black churches, civil rights organizations, political groups, colleges and universities, and professional associations. For the most part, we did not have a whole lot of mass support from the 40 million African Americans.

QUESTION: Why do you feel the black farmers' issues did not become a rallying point for many African Americans?

GRANT: Black farmers have produced more professional people than any other area of our society. We still are not getting widespread support from the black community. When you say black farmer and ask someone what image comes to mind, many will see a dirty, ignorant, barefoot, uneducated person. Many blacks see the stereotype. They don't understand that the black farmer has been a mathematician, a scientist, a meteorologist, a doctor, a veterinarian, and even a lawyer. Until we are able to destroy that stereotype, black farmers will always be misunderstood and unappreciated by our professional people.

QUESTION: What would you like to see black organizations, black institutions, and ordinary black citizens do to assist you in this struggle?

GRANT: First, I would like black institutions and black people to believe that the black farmers know what is needed. Second, I would also like them to contribute financially, morally, physically, and spiritually. Third, we need to begin a massive education program with our children on the importance of owning land. The historically black colleges and universities or HBCUs, and especially the Land Grant schools, need to get on board. The black farmers' struggle was a wake up call, and some of our institutions are still asleep. Our struggle challenged the plantation system. Many of our brothers and sisters do not want to stand up anymore and take a stand. Our land grant universities need to design outreach and research that encourage their students to work with black farmers and the black community.

QUESTION: What legacy would you like to see your struggle leave for generations?

GRANT: This country has not had to listen to black farmers because the black community has not said we are worth saving. I don't believe any of us will survive and progress unless we can come together around the central issue of the survival of black farmers. It is imperative that we maintain land ownership so we can make sure our food supply is not poisoned. Land ownership is economic power, political power, and is the only avenue that we really have to ensure our children a legacy.

Notes of a Racial Caste Baby

BRYAN K. FAIR

This selection is by Bryan K. Fair, an African American man from Colum-
bus Ohio, who is now a lawyer, a professor of constitutional law, a uni-
versity administrator, and an author. This is his personal narrative of
growing up as one of 10 children to a single mother in a Black ghetto.
Which theory of poverty do you think the author advocates? How does the
author appear to feel about the welfare system? What lessons can society
learn from his experiences?

RACIAL POVERTY

In Columbus, race is largely a proxy for economic status. Some blacks in the city belong to the middle class and have gone to college and perhaps graduate or professional school. A handful of black doctors and lawyers have practices, and some blacks operate small businesses, on Mount Vernon, Long, Main, or Livingston. Others include teachers and ministers. But most blacks live in one of the ghettos. It is hard to separate race and poverty in black Columbus; they have blended into racial poverty. By contrast, many whites belong to the middle or upper class, living in essentially all-white communities like Bexley, Upper Arlington, Berwick, or Westerville. Thus, if you are black, you aren't expected to be there, especially after dark, and the local police see to it that suspicious (that is, black) people are questioned.

For most of my childhood, my family required Aid for Families with Dependent Children (AFDC), or welfare. But it was not nearly enough for food, housing, and clothing. Part of the welfare money was spent immediately on food stamps. Under the food stamp program, a welfare recipient can buy an allotment of food stamp coupons for less than their face value. For example, one can buy $200 in food stamps for about $125. That may sound like a windfall, but anyone who has lived on AFDC and food stamps, especially in a large family like mine, knows that the stamps and food always run out well before the end of the month.

For the first two weeks of each month we had milk and cereal, peanut butter and jelly, and plenty of bread. For dinner we ate spaghetti, chili, or Hamburger

SOURCE: Bryan K. Fair, *Notes of a Racial Caste Baby: Color Blindness and the End of Affirmative Action* (New York: New York University Press, 1997), pp. 14–26. Reprinted by permission of the publisher.

Helper. Occasionally, we had pot roast or stew. As the month passed, we ate lots of liver and onions over rice, neck bones, or navy beans and corn bread. We also ate luncheon meat, hot dogs, and beans. Except for watermelon on the Fourth of July and oranges at Christmas, we didn't eat fruit. We rarely had balanced meals.

Balanced or not, all too soon the food ran out. Sometimes with ten or more days remaining in the month, we had no more food stamps. The menu then consisted of mayonnaise, sugar, and syrup sandwiches. Among the eleven of us, we could almost always scrape together enough change for bread. We flavored it with whatever we found. Occasionally, we drank sugar water to fill our stomachs. Once, while foraging through the cabinets, I found what I thought was a chocolate candy bar, which I hastily gulped down. But it turned out to be ExLax, a laxative, with predictable, counterproductive results.

If our school had free breakfast or lunch programs, we had at school what was, on some days, our only meals. At other times, I ate at the homes of schoolmates. But sometimes I was too ashamed to accept their parents' offer, even though my stomach ached from hunger. Ironically, few people talk about the stigma or shame of poverty. Instead, they talk about the supposed stigma or harm of remedial affirmative action that can eliminate poverty. Without AFDC, some free meals at school, and generous friends and their parents, I would have gone hungry more often and would have been even more malnourished. That was true for my siblings as well, but we rarely talked about it. Beyond anger, frustration, and hunger, an empty stomach provides little incentive for conversation.

All across the United States every day, millions of people wake up and go to bed hungry; such is life in "the richest nation in the world." Many days and nights, I sat up hoping that Dee would bring home something, anything, to eat. The voices of teachers talking about the importance of abstract educational skills were often hard to hear over the distracting growling of my stomach.

Even with welfare, there was not enough money for basic clothing or adequate shelter for my family. Dee never had money for clothing or shoes. We didn't have hand-me-downs either. I will never forget the humiliation of either having to wear my sister's shoes to school or not go. Local charities occasionally gave clothing and shoes to needy families. Charity Newsies was one of the largest aid groups in Columbus, and every couple of years, Dee took some of us to a local warehouse where Charity Newsies stocked its clothing: shirts, pants, coats, and shoes. We could pick out three outfits, a coat, and shoes. Usually the selection was limited to two or three styles, colors, and patterns. We reluctantly wore these clothes to school, knowing that some of the kids would recognize where they came from. Nevertheless, we wore those clothes until they were tattered. Even though I was always embarrassed when we went to the warehouse, I was grateful for the charity's help. As I grew older and began working, I proudly bought my own clothes.

After buying food stamps, most of the rest of the welfare check went to pay part of the rent. Rent in the ghetto is artificially inflated because so many blacks are competing for the same slum tenements and because few can afford to live elsewhere. Rich people rarely allow low-income housing in their communities, using zoning restrictions to keep out undesirable housing and people, a practice that also artificially inflates the value of their property. Zoning is another way in which the law upholds white privilege.

My family lived almost exclusively on the east side of Columbus, in older housing. We almost always lived in houses because apartments were simply too small. Occasionally, we lived in houses owned by the local housing authority. We had to move often in search of cheaper housing, in some cases when we couldn't get any more extensions from the landlord. In my twelve years of school in Columbus, we moved seven times, all within the same ghetto.

Each house that we lived in was at least fifty years old, really just a shell providing only minimal protection from the elements. Some had leaking roofs, others holes that welcomed rats and field mice. None was large enough to accommodate eleven people. We always shared rooms and sometimes beds, depending on the number living at home. I shared a room with my two younger brothers until I moved in with my oldest brother and his wife during my final year of high school.

Our large number was a test for any house, but much greater for one that was small, poorly insulated, and infested with roaches and rats. We had no money for repair, maintenance, or exterminator services. If the landlord didn't pay for them, we did without them. At night, after most of the lights were off, the roaches took over. When we switched on the lights, they scattered for cover. Sometimes, a rat or mouse scurried past in the shadows cast by the blue light of the rented television. When we saw a rat, we would bring home traps and place them strategically around the kitchen, some more conspicuous than others. Eventually, while checking the traps, one of us would discover a rat still struggling to escape, or after a few days, the stench confirmed a kill.

Dee never had enough money to pay our high utility bills. She regularly did mental gymnastics to determine which bill was the most urgent, nearest the disconnection stage. Telephone service was a luxury we could only occasionally afford, and our service was often restricted to local calls. After it was disconnected, the telephone company required a deposit and reconnection fee. To avoid these costs, Dee arranged for someone to give her a gift telephone package that had no additional fees. Eventually the phone company recognized the scheme, and we went without a telephone.

Money was sometimes so short that we had no gas heat or hot water during frigid Ohio winters. At those times, racial poverty became surreal. How could there be no heat when the temperature was below zero? The only way to stay warm then was to wear layers of clothing, even in bed. I dreaded the mornings. Each time I stepped into the icy shower, I was sure I would break any neck from jumping around. In the summer a cold shower is bracing but refreshing; in the winter it leaves you trembling, almost numb. I often brooded over how little we had.

Racial poverty was the constant feature in my life in black Columbus. At an early age I was an expert on racial poverty. When I should have been learning to read, write, and play with other kids, I was hungry, cold, and learning about being black. When I should have been developing cognitive skills, I was learning that if a person is hungry enough, he or she will steal for food. Before I could read, I learned how to case a store, locate its clerk, grab something to eat, and walk out without paying. Jequeta's, M&R's, Demler's, Lawson's, Big Bear, Kroger's, and other stores along Livingston or Main were my training ground. Occasionally, when I slipped up, clerks chased me through streets and alleys. I'm lucky no one ever shot at me. I never wanted to steal; it was not a game. But sometimes I was so hungry that I didn't know what else to do.

At times, we look to others to blame for our difficult circumstances, and I did, too. I was ashamed of my racial poverty. But I didn't blame the "white man," and since I didn't know my father, I blamed Dee. For years my relationship with my mother was strained because I blamed her for not telling me who my father was and for all that we didn't have. But Dee was not responsible for my father, and she wasn't lazy or idle. She had graduated from high school and had gone to work. But not every occupation was open to her. I didn't understand then that in Columbus and elsewhere black women could work in only certain jobs.

Undoubtedly, some readers will ask why Dee had ten children. I don't know why she did. But I do know that some states have restricted access to contraceptives and have criminalized abortion. And I do know that Dee's family did not have access to general health care. I assume she couldn't afford or didn't want to have an illegal, back-alley abortion. I also suspect she didn't realize she would have sole responsibility for all of us. As her eighth child, I'm glad, of course, that she didn't stop at seven. Yet even if I believed that having ten children was a bad decision—a point that I'm not willing to concede—it was a decision aggravated by her educational and employment limitations: Dee did women's work for women's wages, and any number of jobs for which she might have qualified were simply closed to her. Dee was not to blame for those constraints. The costs of gender tracking and the devaluation of women's labor are enormous for families headed by single women, forcing most of them into a standard of living below the poverty line. For minority women, race and gender discrimination intersect, pushing even more families into poverty.

Those of us living in the ghetto were not destined for poverty because of inferior genetics or poor values. Rather, we were poor because we had limited opportunities as blacks and because of our circumstances. When I left the ghetto in the seventh grade, my life took a new direction. Escaping black Columbus also taught me that whites are not superior to blacks in regard to genetics or values. If you locked whites in ghetto conditions and denied them rewarding opportunities, most of them would be poor, too. Indeed, in pockets of the United States, some of the poorest citizens are white. It is the self-serving racial rhetoric of the white elites in America that has kept blacks and poor whites, including many white women, divided, largely by pitting them against each other and convincing poor whites that by virtue of the color of their skin, they too are superior to blacks.

Critics often charge that welfare itself creates dependency, a peculiar claim because AFDC was started in the 1930s for the opposite reason: to ease the dependency of poor children. To qualify for it, one already had to be dependent. How, then, can welfare create dependency? Some of welfare's critics believe that the current guidelines increase the number of households headed by single women by threatening to terminate benefits if a father or adult male lives in the home. If this is the case, why not change just that part of the policy? Do these critics believe that welfare payments are so large that rational people would rather receive welfare than work? If so, then why don't more Americans choose welfare's "easy street?" Do the critics think that welfare recipients have the luxury of choosing either to work for poverty wages in dead-end jobs with no medical benefits or to receive public assistance with limited benefits? Or do they think welfare is a legitimate option because some Americans don't earn a living wage?

AFDC did not make Dee idle or dependent; she needed it for her dependent children, not herself. Dee did what so many others have done in similar circumstances: she turned to a government that claims not to permit dependent children to go without food, clothing, or shelter. Unfortunately, most of the time we were on welfare, we did not have sufficient food, clothing, and shelter.

Welfare programs currently provide only marginal subsistence for the millions of children they are supposed to aid. The first priority of welfare reform, therefore, must be to ensure that the money spent adequately feeds these children and puts clothes on their backs. In 1990, the federal government spent $14 billion on the Food Stamp Program while spending $10 billion on criminal justice. In 1996, fourteen million people (two-thirds of them children) received AFDC, for which the federal and state governments spend nearly $2.3 billion a year. The money we invest in our children's health and educational development now is far less than what, without the investment, we would spend for additional law enforcement and prisons.

Despite the prevailing assumptions, federal spending on AFDC amounts to less than 1 percent of the national budget; yet some politicians and the media lead us to believe that once we "fix" welfare, the huge federal deficit will disappear. Unfortunately, many of the people talking about welfare seem to know very little about it and seem not to care about our most vulnerable citizens: poor children. If they really do want to reform welfare, they should talk to the real "experts": those kids going without food at the end of the month.

I now regret feeling ashamed and embarrassed about my family's racial poverty and especially rue blaming my mother for it. Only now do I understand how hard it was for her to see us live as we did. Unfortunately, we are not born with knowledge and skills to negotiate such feelings, nor are there enough accessible institutions to help poor people cope with such feelings or provide them with guidance to move out of racial poverty. Plans for welfare reform must increase the funding and accessibility of such agencies—such an agency could have helped nay family a great deal. Under our extraordinary circumstances, Dee was the best mother we could have had. Although she was smart and talented, she had accumulated few material possessions to show for it. Nonetheless, she fashioned an existence for us out of almost nothing, and she never seemed consumed by despair, hers or ours. As a result, I never lost hope. She never talked about hating whites or the men who had abandoned her and her children. Although we had very little, Dee taught us to take care of what we did have, and she made it clear that she expected each of us to help the family whenever we could. I was my siblings' keeper. We all helped out, and Dee stayed and struggled with us. I don't know why she didn't leave, but it never once occurred to me that she might.

REFLECTION QUESTIONS

FOR PART II

The readings in this section contain elements of the different theoretical perspectives and are in no particular order. Analyze each article carefully and group them by individual/cultural and structural theories of poverty. Provide a rationale as to why you think one theory or another is best reflected in each reading.

1. How do the individuals "adapt" to their poverty?
2. Compare/contrast the readings in this section. Do you see any common themes?
3. Using your sociological imagination and the various readings as examples, explain how poverty is structured by race, class, gender, age, and location.
4. The theory you believe is more plausible affects what you think the solutions are. What are the solutions to the different situations? How do the readings compare in terms of solutions? What role should society play in helping the poor?
5. Select one particular essay and analyze it first *without* using a sociological imagination, and then again *with* a sociological imagination.

PART III

Poverty and Vulnerability

"Economic risk is a lot like a hurricane. Hurricanes strike powerfully and suddenly. They rip apart what they touch: property, landscape, and lives. They are common enough to affect many, yet rare enough still to shock. And although they can be prepared for, they cannot be prevented. Some people will inevitably suffer and require help; others will be spared. Recovery is inevitably traumatic and slow. And so it is with families whose lives have been touched by economic risk. What happens in an instant may change a life forever."

Jacob S. Hacker (2006)

While the intention of this book is to examine poverty from the perspective of those experiencing poverty, the reality is that very few individuals in this society are completely secure from the threat of poverty. The readings and the statistics from Part III demonstrate that many of us are just one divorce, one natural disaster, one health problem, or one job loss away from falling under the safety net.

CHAPTER 2

One Step Away

The poor are, by definition, on the economic margins where adequate food, shelter, and medical care are often elusive. Since the Great Depression the government has softened the hardships somewhat with the adoption of Social Security, Medicare, Medicaid, food stamps, the GI bill, subsidized school lunches, welfare for single mothers, and other programs. This safety net, still meager by European standards, has been unraveling since the Reagan administration, causing more and more Americans to feel the sting of poverty. From 2000 to 2005, for example, the number of food stamp participants rose from 17 million to 26 million; the number of people experiencing hunger or the risk of hunger increased from 32 million to 38 million (State of the States, 2006); the number below the government's poverty line increased by 5 million; and the number of Americans without health insurance rose by 4 million to 47 million (Sered and Fernandopulle, 2005).

In natural disasters such as hurricanes, tornados, floods, earthquakes, heat waves or prolonged cold, the poor are the most vulnerable. They live in the flood plain where housing is cheapest, in mobile homes which do not provide adequate protection from strong winds, and in situations where they do not have sufficient means to cool or heat their living quarters adequately. For example, when Chicago experienced a prolonged heat wave in 1995, there were 485 heat-related deaths in one week. Those most likely to die were the elderly, the poor, and the isolated (Klinenberg, 2002). Hurricane Katrina, perhaps the worst natural disaster in modern American history, also took down to poverty many who had not previously experienced that condition.

Middle-class and working-class individuals and families in the United States are increasingly vulnerable to rapid declines in their economic security because of family disruptions, catastrophic illness, corporate downsizing and outsourcing, natural disaster, or war. The downward social mobility may result in bankruptcy, loss of a home, and poverty, situations previously not thought possible by the affected.

Middle-class Americans are increasing economically insecure because economic risks have shifted from government and business to individuals and families. The government has reduced its safety net and businesses which once promised a job, health insurance, and a pension, have reneged on these obligations (the following is from Hacker, 2006). Corporations downsize and move their operations to low-wage economies, putting millions of Americans out of work. Corporate threats to downsize also keep wages low and make the unions relatively powerless to help the plight of workers. Worker benefits have eroded and families are left to fend for themselves. Meanwhile, the price of housing and college education have risen, requiring two earners to maintain a middle-class standard of living. Sudden job loss, divorce, or a catastrophic illness can cause economic turmoil among many of these once stable family units. Consequently, personal bankruptcies are up from 290,000 in 1980 to more than 2 million in 2005. People are losing their homes at record rates. In May 2007, for example, mortgage foreclosures and bank repossession of homes was 90 percent higher than a year earlier (Haviv, 2007). The baby boomers nearing retirement are faced with inadequate pensions because businesses have shifted from a predetermined monthly benefit for the remainder of a worker's life to 401(k) plans in which the worker invests a portion of wages. This shift of the risk to the worker makes them vulnerable to stock market downturns and companies such as Enron, which leave investors (including many of their workers) without a pension when they go bankrupt. The result of all of this: "The incomes of middle-class families aren't much higher today than they were in the 1970s—and they are much more at risk" (Hacker, 2006:15). The *Los Angeles Times* conducted a study of families dealing with economic stresses. They found that there were seven common but potentially destabilizing events:

- divorce or separation
- a decline in a spouse's work hours
- death of a spouse
- birth of a child
- retirement or disability of the main breadwinner
- unemployment
- serious illness

"The *Times* then assessed what fraction of the families touched by any of these episodes suffered a 50 percent or greater decline in their annual income. For every type of setback, the size of the group that took such a huge financial hit climbed substantially between the 1970s and 2000. This occurred even though the odds of at least one of these events befalling a family over the course of a decade remained fairly constant, at about 1 in 5" (Gosselin, 2004:2–3).

NOTES AND SUGGESTIONS FOR FURTHER READING

Food Research and Action Center (2006). *State of the States, 2006: A Profile of Food and Nutrition Programs Across the Nation*. Washington, D.C.

Gosselin, Peter G. (2004). "How Just a Handful of Setbacks Sent the Ryans Tumbling Out of Prosperity." *Los Angeles Times* (December 30): Online: www.latimes.com/business/la-fi/newdeal30dec30,0,769369,print

Hacker, Jacob S. (2006). *The Great Risk Shift*. New York: Oxford University Press.

Haviv, Julie (2007). "U.S. Home Foreclosures up 19 Percent from April." Reuters. Online: www.boston.com/business/articles/2007/06/12/us_home_foreclosures_up_19_percent

Klinenberg, Eric (2002). *Heat Wave: A Social Autopsy of Disaster in Chicago.* Chicago: University of Chicago Press.

Naison, Mark D. (2005). "Black Poverty's Human Face." *Business Week* (September 19):148.

Sered, Susan Starr, and Rushika Fernandopulle (2005). *Uninsured in America: Life & Death in the Land of Opportunity.* Berkeley: University of California Press.

Wickham, DeWayne (2005). "Blacks Suffering Over Race or Class? Some of Both." *USA Today* (September 13):13A.

A Veteran Speaks of the Forgotten Wounded of Iraq

RON KOVIC

The trauma of war haunts many soldiers when they return home. About one-fourth of returning service personnel report some form of mental illness. The most common is post-traumatic stress disorder with symptoms of flashbacks, nightmares, feelings of detachment, irritability, trouble concentrating, and sleeplessness. Many thousands return with physical injuries. Often overlooked in the injuries of war are the consequences of long separations and psychological trauma on the intimate lives of soldiers and their spouses, resulting in a higher than normal divorce rate. Some cannot hold a job and end up in poverty and even homelessness. The Veterans Administration estimates that 500,000 veterans of various wars were homeless some time during 2004 (cited in Alexandra Marks, "Back from Iraq—and Suddenly Out on the Streets," Christian Science Monitor (February 8, 2005).

In the following essay a veteran of the Vietnam War recounts how his life was changed because of that war, and he worries about the fate of soldiers returning from the battles in Iraq and Afghanistan. As you read this selection, think about the similarities between the Vietnam War and the war in Iraq. What can the government do to make sure that the returning soldiers do not suffer the same fate as those from Vietnam?

Thirty-eight years ago, on Jan. 20, 1968, I was shot and paralyzed from my mid-chest down during my second tour of duty in Vietnam. It is a date that I can never forget, a day that was to change my life forever. Each year as the anniversary of my wounding in the war approached I would become extremely restless, experiencing terrible bouts of insomnia, depression, anxiety attacks and horrifying nightmares. I dreaded that day and what it represented, always fearing that the terrible trauma of my wounding might repeat itself all over again. It was a difficult day for me for

SOURCE: Ron Kovic, printed May 29, 2007 Alternet.org. Independent Media Institute. View online at: www.alternet.org/story/52434. This essay was originally published on Truthdig (www.truthdig.com).

decades and it remained that way until the anxieties and nightmares finally began to subside.

As I now contemplate another January 20th I cannot help but think of the young men and women who have been wounded in the war in Iraq. They have been coming home now for almost three years, flooding Walter Reed, Bethesda, Brooke Army Medical Center and veterans hospitals all across the country. Paraplegics, amputees, burn victims, the blinded and maimed, shocked and stunned, brain-damaged and psychologically stressed, over 16,000 of them, a whole new generation of severely maimed is returning from Iraq, young men and women who were not even born when I came home wounded to the Bronx veterans hospital in 1968.

I, like most other Americans, have occasionally seen them on TV or at the local veterans hospital, but for the most part they remain hidden, like the flag-draped caskets of our dead, returned to Dover Air Force Base in the darkness of night as this administration continues to pursue a policy of censorship, tightly controlling the images coming out of that war and rarely ever allowing the human cost of its policy to be seen.

Mosul, Fallouja, Basra, Baghdad, a roadside bomb, an RPG, an ambush, the bullets cracking all around them, the reality that they are in a war, that they have suddenly been hit. No more John Wayne-Audie Murphy movie fantasies. No more false bravado, stirring words of patriotism, romantic notions of war or what it might really mean to be in combat, to sacrifice for one's country. All that means nothing now. The reality has struck, the awful, shocking and frightening truth of what it really means to be hit by a bullet, an RPG, an improvised explosive device, shrapnel, a booby trap, friendly fire. They are now in a life-and-death situation and they have suddenly come face to face with the foreign policy of their own nation. The initial shock is wearing off, the painful reality is beginning to sink in, clearly something terrible has happened, something awful and inexplicable.

All the conditioning, all the discipline, shouting, screaming, bullying and threatening verbal abuse of their boot camp drill instructors have now disappeared in this one instant, in this one damaging blow. All they want to do now is stay alive, keep breathing, somehow get out of this place any way they can. People are dying all around them, someone has been shot and killed right next to them and behind them but all they can really think of at this moment is staying alive.

You don't think of God, or praying, or even your mother or your father. There is no time for that. Your heart is pounding. Blood is seeping out. You will always go back to that day, that moment you got hit, the day you nearly died yet somehow survived. It will be a day you will never forget—when you were trapped in that open area and could not move, when bullets were cracking all around you, when the first Marine tried to save you and was shot dead at your feet and the second, a black Marine—whom you would never see again and who would be killed later that afternoon—would carry you back under heavy fire.

You are now with other wounded all around you heading to a place where there will be help. There are people in pain and great distress, shocked and stunned, frightened beyond anything you can imagine. You are afraid to close your eyes.

To close your eyes now means that you may die and never wake up. You toss and turn, your heart pounding, racked with insomnia . . . and for many this will go on for months, years after they return home.

They are being put on a helicopter, with the wounded all around them. They try to stay calm. Some are amazed that they are still alive. You just have to keep trying to stay awake, make it to the next stage, keep moving toward the rear, toward another aid station, a corpsman, a doctor a nurse someone who can help you, someone who will operate and keep you alive so you can make it home, home to your backyard and your neighbors and your mother and father. To where it all began, to where it was once peaceful and safe. They just try to keep breathing because they have got to get back.

They are in the intensive-care ward now, the place where they will be operated on, and where in Vietnam a Catholic priest gave me the Last Rites. Someone is putting a mask over their faces just as they put one over mine in Da Nang in 1968. There is the swirl of darkness and soon they awaken to screams all around them. The dead and dying are everywhere. There are things here you can never forget, images and sounds and smells that you will never see on TV or read about in the newspapers. The black pilot dying next to me as the corpsman and nurse tried furiously to save him, pounding on his chest with their fists as they laughed and joked trying to keep from going insane. The Green Beret who died of spinal meningitis, the tiny Vietnamese nun handing out apples and rosary beads to the wounded, the dead being carted in and out like clockwork, 19- and 20-year-olds.

There is the long flight home packed with the wounded all around you, every conceivable and horrifying wound you could imagine. Even the unconscious and brain-dead whose minds have been blown apart by bullets and shrapnel make that ride with you, because we are all going home now, back to our country. And this is only the beginning.

The frustrations, anger and rage, insomnia, nightmares, anxiety attacks, terrible restlessness and desperate need to keep moving will come later, but for now we are so thankful to have just made it out of that place, so grateful to be alive even with these grievous wounds.

I cannot help but wonder what it will be like for the young men and women wounded in Iraq. What will their homecoming be like? I feel close to them. Though many years separate us we are brothers and sisters. We have all been to the same place. For us in 1968 it was the Bronx veterans hospital paraplegic ward, overcrowded, understaffed, rats on the ward, a flood of memories and images, I can never forget; urine bags overflowing onto the floor. It seemed more like a slum than a hospital. Paralyzed men lying in their own excrement, pushing call buttons for aides who never came, wondering how our government could spend so much money (billions of dollars) on the most lethal, technologically advanced weaponry to kill and maim human beings but not be able to take care of its own wounded when they came home.

Will it be the same for them? Will they have to return to these same unspeakable conditions? Has any of it changed? I have heard that our government has already attempted to cut back millions in much needed funds for veterans hospitals—and this when thousands of wounded soldiers are returning from Iraq. Will they too be left abandoned and forgotten by a president and administration whose patriotic rhetoric does not match the needs of our wounded troops now returning?

Do the American people, the president, the politicians, senators and congressmen who sent us to this war have any idea what it really means to lose an arm or a leg, to be paralyzed, to begin to cope with the psychological wounds of that war? Do they have any concept of the long-term effects of these injuries, how the struggles of the wounded are only now just beginning? How many will die young and never live out their lives because of all the stress and myriad of problems that come with sending young men and women into combat?

It is so difficult at first. You return home and both physically and emotionally don't know how you are going to live with this wound, but you just keep trying, just keep waking up to this frightening reality every morning. "My God, what has happened to me?" But you somehow get up, you somehow go on and find a way to move through each day. Even though it is impossible, you go on. Maybe there will be a day years from now, if you are lucky to live that long, when it will get better and you will not feel so overwhelmed. You must have something to hope for, some way to believe it will not always be this way. This is exactly what many of them are going through right now.

They are alone in their rooms all over this country, right now. Just as I was alone in my room in Massapequa. I know they're there—just as I was. This is the part you never see. The part that is never reported in the news. The part that the president and vice president never mention. This is the agonizing part, the lonely part, when you have to awake to the wound each morning and suddenly realize what you've lost, what is gone forever. They're out there and they have mothers and fathers, sisters and brothers, husbands and wives and children. And they're not saying much right now. Just like me they're just trying to get through each day. Trying to be brave and not cry. They still are extremely grateful to be alive, but slowly, agonizingly they are beginning to think about what has really happened to them.

What will it be like for them when one morning they suddenly find themselves naked sitting before that mirror in their room and must come face to face with their injury? I want to reach out to them. I want them to know that I've been there too. I want to just sit with them in their room and tell them that they must not give up.

They must try to be patient, try to just get through each day, each morning, each afternoon any way they can. That no matter how impossible and frustrating it may seem, how painful, regardless of the anxiety attacks and nightmares and thoughts of suicide, they must not quit. Somewhere out there will be a turning point, somewhere through this all they will find a reason to keep on living.

In the months and years that are to follow, others will be less fortunate. Young men and women who survived the battlefield, the intensive-care ward, veterans hospitals and initial homecoming will be unable to make the difficult and often agonizing adjustment.

Is this what is awaiting all of them? Is this the nightmare no one ever told them about, the part no one now wants to talk about or has the time to deal with? The car accidents, and drinking and drug overdoses, the depression, anger and rage, spousal abuse, bedsores and breakdowns, prison, homelessness, sleeping under the piers and bridges.

The ones who never leave the hospital, the ones who can't hold a job, can't keep a relationship together, can't love or feel any emotions anymore, the brutal insomnia that leaves you exhausted and practically unable to function, the frightening anxiety attacks that come upon you when you least expect them, and always the dread that each day may be your last.

Marty, Billy Bobby, Max, Tom, Washington, Pat, Joe? I knew them all. It's a long list. It's amazing that you're still alive when so many others you knew are dead, and at such a young age. Isn't all this dying supposed to happen when you're much older?

Not now, not while we're so young. How come the recruiters never mentioned these things? This was never in the slick pamphlets they showed us! This should be a time of innocence, a time of joy and happiness, no cares and youthful dreams—not all these friends dying so young, all this grief and numbness, emptiness and feelings of being so lost.

The physical and psychological battles from the war in Iraq will rage on for decades, deeply impacting the lives of citizens in both our countries.

As this the 38th anniversary of my wounding in Vietnam approaches, in many ways I feel my injury in that war has been a blessing in disguise. I have been given the opportunity to move through that dark night of the soul to a new shore, to gain an understanding, a knowledge, an entirely different vision. I now believe that I have suffered for a reason and in many ways I have found that reason in my commitment to peace and nonviolence.

We who have witnessed the obscenity of war and experienced its horror and terrible consequences have an obligation to rise above our pain and suffering and turn the tragedy of our lives into a triumph. I have come to believe that there is nothing in the lives of human beings more terrifying than war and nothing more important than for those of us who have experienced it to share its awful truth.

We must break this cycle of violence and begin to move in a different direction; war is not the answer, violence is not the solution. A more peaceful world is possible.

I am the living death
The memorial day on wheels
I am your yankee doodle dandy
Your John Wayne come home
Your Fourth of July firecracker
Exploding in the grave.

On the Margins: The Lack of Resources and the Lack of Health Care

JANIS JOHNSON

Adequate health care is something that many Americans take for granted, but health care can be a nightmare for those living in poverty. Janis Johnston is a divorced single mother who recently received her Ph.D. in sociology from Colorado State University. In this essay, she reflects on what it was like when she was poor and had to deal with a problematic health care system. What are some of the problems that she encountered? Can you think of possible alternatives to this system?.

Some days were harder than others. After 13 years of marriage I was in the middle of a divorce, had two kids—Lindsay who was 12 and James who was 6—and I was on unpaid disability leave from the job I'd had for ten years. My kids and I took our clothes and a box of dishes and moved forty-five miles to a town of about 25,000 so I could attend the university there. Because I couldn't work I thought I'd try school, but it was difficult because our only income was from the child support check we received every month.

We didn't have a car so we walked to most of the places that we needed to go and took the bus to school. Because we got only $300 a month, I supplemented our food by finding treasures that the nearest grocery store had thrown into the garbage: old bread, dented cans, and occasionally even frozen meat. It wasn't fun, but I had heard so many horror stories about welfare that I was afraid to go on it, afraid of how people—including members of my own family—would react. That lasted until the night the police came and got me out of a school concert because Lindsay was in the emergency room. While she was riding her bike home from the neighborhood convenience store, a car traveling about 30 miles an hour ran through a crosswalk and hit her, sending her skidding down the pavement. She was unconscious when the ambulance arrived but woke up as they worked on her. She immediately began to protest, saying we didn't have enough money for her

SOURCE: Janis Johnson, "On the Margins: The Lack of Resources and the Lack of Health Care," unpublished essay. Reprinted with the permission of the author.

to go in an ambulance and we surely couldn't afford any hospital. Because of her age they took her anyway.

I was devastated. My daughter was hurt and in pain, and rather than scream-ing for help she was trying to run away from it because we couldn't afford it. As much as that hurt, the reality was that she was right. We couldn't afford it. Her three-block ride to the hospital alone cost more than we lived on for a month. The cost of the emergency room, the doctor, and the x-rays would cost more than we received in a year. To add insult to injury, because she was riding a bike, it was determined that the accident was her fault although she was in a crosswalk and three lanes of traffic had stopped to allow her to cross; the bills were ours alone. The driver of the car called to say his insurance wouldn't pay our bills because it wasn't his fault, and he wondered what I intended to do about the damage to his car. I applied for welfare the next day.

On my walk to the social services center where the local welfare office was located, I kept telling myself over and over that it was OK—that applying for wel-fare didn't mean all those things that I'd heard people say it meant. Applying for welfare didn't mean I was lazy; that I wanted a handout for doing nothing; that I deserved what was happening, and worse, so did my kids. Welfare wasn't who I was at all and I wasn't going to let it define me. After all, I'd been working since I was 14, and for most of my married life I'd held two or three jobs at a time. I wasn't looking for a freebie, but I couldn't make it on my own until I could go back to work. If I could just get a little help—just a little—we could make it. By the time I got to the office, I thought I had myself fairly convinced. I went into the office, filled out the required paperwork, and made an appointment with a caseworker. I stepped out of the building and thought, "There, that wasn't so bad." And then I cried like I would never stop.

We were lucky. My application for welfare was dated the last day of October, which meant that if it were approved, the medical care portion, Title XIX, would cover any medical costs that occurred that month. Lindsay's accident was on Octo-ber eleventh, so if we met the criteria, all of those hospital bills would be paid, follow-up care would be available, and we would get food stamps to help with the cost of food. All I had to do now was get over the idea that being on welfare exposed some inherent flaw in my character. I might actually have been able to do just that if so many people hadn't been telling me welfare really *was* me.

My visit with my caseworker was my introduction to the way people feel about welfare moms. We went over my application to make sure I understood and answered all the questions. Some of the questions seemed ludicrous. One section asked if "anyone in the house owned or was buying any of the following" and then listed 29 possible assets including: "Antiques/Collectibles; Airplane; Busi-ness Inventory; and Burial Policy." Airplane?! It was all I could do not to ask the caseworker whether my Lear jet would disqualify me from receiving the $360 a month stipend the state paid for families of three; it wasn't a plane after all. Luck-ily I didn't mention it because this was a woman who found no joy in her job. Although she never said it directly, it was clear that she didn't understand why I was there. During the interview she mumbled that *she* had two kids and *she* had put herself through college and *she* never needed assistance from the government. I didn't need her to finish her thought; what she'd said was enough to let me know what she thought I deserved. Her treatment of me was a taste of what I would find when I went out into the "real world."

Life on welfare was tough for my kids. I mean we do things as a society to make sure it's obvious who *those people* are, who I am, who Lindsay and James are. It was common for the teacher to say, "Raise your hand if you have a free lunch ticket" to separate the kids who paid for their lunches from those who didn't. In supermarkets people with food stamps had to tell the clerk it was a food stamp order before they rang it up. Announcements such as "Food stamp change to checkstand three." were made on the loud speaker. Whether by design or by accident, all these actions keep welfare recipients in the public eye. For me this meant people could watch what I did, comment on what I bought, and question the way I dressed.

I was grocery shopping one day and a stranger noticed the food stamps in my hand as we waited at the register. I became aware that he was reviewing everything in my cart as well as noting what I was wearing. After a few minutes, he looked right at me and said, "I suppose you think my tax dollars are supposed to buy ice cream and chocolate syrup. And those sandals you have on look pretty expensive. I suppose I bought those for you too." He then backed his cart out of the line and went to the next closest one where he continued to stare at me until my transaction was complete and I walked out the door. Lesson number one. People on welfare have two choices. First, learn how to dress to shop with food stamps—not too nice, not too shabby—and buy only food that's good for you. Second, grow a thick skin to insulate yourself from the stares and comments. I did a little of both.

One of the things about being on welfare that I never counted on was what to do about medical care. Despite the fact that I was on disability from my job, my eligibility for the short-term disability insurance was only good for six months so it was gone. I wasn't eligible for medical care through the university because I wasn't a full-time student, and that meant that if I needed to see a doctor, or if my kids needed to see a doctor, we would have to go as Title XIX patients. Honestly, the pediatricians who took care of the kids were great. It was kind of a pain, because every time we went to see one of them we had to take a coupon, and if we didn't have one—if it hadn't arrived yet or was lost—the kids couldn't be seen. But it was a whole different story when it came to dentists, eye doctors, and doctors for me—worse if we were out of town.

A couple months after we went on welfare, I decided that we needed to get out of town for a break. We still didn't have a car, but a friend let me borrow hers so I could take my kids to see their dad. James had had a cold that I thought was getting better, but on the 45-mile ride to see my ex-husband, it was obvious to me that he was still coughing an awful lot and his fever was back. When we arrived in town, it was a little after 7:00 P.M., so all the doctors' offices were closed. I took him to a "doc-in-a-box," one of those emergency clinics you can go to without an appointment and asked how much it would cost for him to be seen by a doctor. The going rate for a kid with a bad cold was $30.00, plus medicine of course.

According to the receptionist, the clinic didn't take Title XIX and they didn't take charity cases so we left to pool our pennies.

My ex-husband wasn't home—we hadn't called because we didn't have a phone—so the kids couldn't see him. Even worse, I couldn't get any money from him to take James to the doctor. I drove to the place where I'd worked until that August. My former co-workers scratched together $27 so I put that with $2.27 that I had and went back to the clinic. I was sure that $29.27 was close enough, especially when you could see how really sick this poor little boy was, but when we went in the office staff sent us away. They rationalized that the office visit was $30.00, not $29.27, and even if the doctor did see us it wouldn't matter because then we wouldn't have anything left to pay for medicine.

I was furious and at the same time worried and incredibly depressed. Here was a little boy who was getting sicker by the minute—I was starting to think it might be pneumonia—and there wasn't a damn thing I could do about it. We left in spite of my overwhelming desire to throw a big enough fit that they would have to call the cops. I mean at some level I thought if the cops were involved they would see the injustice and make them treat my son, but I didn't have the energy to take the chance and, after all, the cops would probably see things the way the people at the doctor's office did. I always felt that way—like I didn't deserve the same level of respect "normal" people got. But I hated the fact that my kids were being treated that way when there wasn't a fucking thing they could do about it! I was the one who was not working! I was the one who was on welfare! There was nothing about this situation that was their fault and nothing about the way people treated us that they deserved. We drove on.

There was another doc-in-a-box just a few miles from the first one, and we went there hoping that we had enough money for them. This time we had an entirely different experience. The office staff took one look at my son and took us into the inner office immediately. The doctor diagnosed him with an ear infection, bronchitis, and he was dangerously close to pneumonia. They gave us samples of cough medicine and children's Tylenol, enough to last for a couple weeks, and arranged for him to get the antibiotics. Then they refused our $29.27. I was overwhelmed. All the emotions, all the rage and fear and pain that I had carried from the first office seemed to melt and I was suddenly exhausted. I tried to thank them but they insisted it was nothing, headed us toward the car, and recommended that we get James home to bed. Just when I'd given up, there were people in the world who cared, and it wasn't based on how much money we had. I really needed to know that right then.

We weren't quite that lucky when it came to dentists. I tried to find a new dentist when we moved, and the receptionist at the first office I called asked what kind of insurance we had. When I told her we were on Title XIX she explained that the office already had all of *those* people they were required to take and that we would have to look elsewhere. So did the receptionist at the next office, and the next office, and in fact, so did the receptionists at the next seven offices. At the eighth office I was told that they didn't have any more room for people on Title XIX but that if it was an emergency I could go to the emergency room. Going to the emergency room to see if we had any cavities had never crossed my mind, so I asked if they had dentists there. The woman responded that "No, emergency rooms do not have dentists but if it is an emergency situation they can call a dentist who will then come and remove the offending tooth." "But none of these teeth are offensive," I responded. "We're just trying to keep them from getting that way." "Oh," she said, sounding almost disappointed, "I see. Well I don't know anyone who's taking Title XIX right now. You can call back in six months." I quit calling anywhere after that.

Eye appointments were about as easy to get as dental appointments. Lindsay started wearing glasses in the second grade. I wore glasses too, and I was getting headaches and things were blurry, so I thought I'd see if there was any hope that we could see an eye doctor. The short answer was no; Title XIX doesn't cover eyes. Then I got tricky and called to see if I could make an appointment and arrange a way to make payments. They asked if I had insurance and I said no. So did they. This was when family came in handy. For birthday presents my family would take us to the eye doctor and pay for the exam and even glasses if we needed them. I don't know what people on welfare do for dental or eye care if they aren't lucky enough to have access to other resources. I do know what happens to adults, how-ever, when they need to go to a doctor and they're on welfare.

As I mentioned, I was on medical disability. Sometimes that meant that I was in a lot of pain, and sometimes it meant I had a hard time walking, but it was also episodic; I'd be OK for a while and then hit a bad period that might last a couple weeks. In the past, there were times when the doctors treated the injury with medi-cine alone, and sometimes it was a combination of medicine and therapy, but for the most part it was never an emergency. I knew that I needed to find a doctor who would help when it started to get bad and began looking for someone shortly after we moved. Time and time again I was told that the various offices were either not accepting new patients or that there was a significant wait to get in, which was OK as long as I was feeling pretty good. Then I hit a bad period. The doctors who didn't have room for me before had no room for me now so, as was the case with the dentist's office, it was suggested I seek help at the emergency room. This time I took them up on it.

I went into the hospital and asked to see a physician, filled out the paperwork, and waited. When the doctor came to see what my complaint was, I explained it and told him the kind of treatment I usually received—often a combination of painkillers, muscle relaxants, and anti-inflammatory medicines. He looked at me for a second, obviously thinking about something, and then asked why I had come to the emergency room because this was obviously not an emergency. I explained that I was having trouble getting in to see a "regular" doctor because many of them were not accepting new patients, and to get in to see those who were would take several months to a year. So while my case wasn't a real emergency, I couldn't wait that long to be seen either. He was clearly upset because there were real emer-gencies in the hospital and I was taking time away from them. And although he didn't say anything to me and was probably angry at the overall situation, I felt as if it was my fault. It was my fault that there were people who needed treatment that was being delayed because someone who could easily wait was taking up valuable space and time. The situation was awkward because although I needed help, I didn't need it from them, but I couldn't get it anywhere else. They treated me between the real cases and several hours later I went home.

I suppose it wouldn't have been a bad experience if it had happened only once, but the truth is, I began to treat the ER like a doctor's office. They didn't give me excuses as to why they didn't have to take any more welfare cases or why they weren't taking new patients. They didn't ask me to wait for months before I saw a doctor. But I could see the levels of frustration increase. I overheard two of the ER workers talking about people who used their services when it was obviously not an emergency. One of them mentioned a patient who had been in several times in just a couple weeks, and they couldn't get through to him that he needed to find a doctor and quit wasting valuable time and resources in the emergency room. And while I knew they weren't talking about me, they might as well have been. I struggled to find other options but it always came down to the same thing: Go to the emergency room or live with the debilitating pain and risk further damage.

See, that's what most people don't think about with living in poverty. Simple things. Routine exams. Getting your teeth cleaned. Finding a cavity and doing something about it before it means a root canal. Back when I had a real job, I had had a root canal on a back molar and then a crown. Years later when I was on welfare, I lost the crown and was told Title XIX wouldn't cover a replacement. Eventually it got to the point where something had to be done about the tooth and I returned to the dentist who had done the original work. I had known this man for years and even considered a friend. He saw the problem and was immediately angry with me. "How could you let this happen? You should have been in for another crown as soon as you lost the first one. This has never happened to *me* before. I've never had to pull a tooth that I saved." He pulled the tooth and left the room. His nurse finished the work and said she was surprised; she'd never known him to get mad like that, but he was really upset. I never went back.

That one trip to the dentist summed up my time on welfare as well as anything. My "friend" was upset at what I hadn't done because of how it affected *him*, how it made *him* look. And it is one way I will pay for being on welfare for the rest of my life. I have dental problems that I never would have had if I'd had access to preventative care—but I didn't. And I will live with that forever. Some people that I've known for years couldn't deal with my poverty so they are out of my life altogether now, and that too, will be forever. But we were lucky. It could have been worse. My kids and I might have had to exist that way for our lifetimes. For us, it only felt that long.

Personal Voices: An Unnatural Disaster

EMMA DIXON

In 2005 Hurricane Katrina destroyed homes, stores, businesses, roads and bridges along an 80 mile swath of Louisiana, Mississippi, and Alabama coastline. Before Katrina this was an area with a disproportionate number of poor people, primarily African Americans. The per capital income of Blacks in New Orleans in 2000 was $11,332, compared with $31,971 for Whites; 34 percent of Blacks lived below the government's poverty line, in sharp contrast to only 11 percent for the Whites in that city (Naison, 2005). Their plight, already horrible from deprivation and marginalization, became even worse with the loss of life and their meager material possessions by the destructive winds and floods of Katrina. In New Orleans, for example, most Blacks lived in the city's lower-lying areas, and 36 percent of African American households in New Orleans did not own a car so they were the hardest hit by flooding and were less likely than Whites to have an automobile to escape (Wickham, 2005).

As you read this selection, think about the concept of institutional racism. How did institutional racism affect the outcomes of Hurricane Katrina, and what should be done about it?

When Hurricane Katrina tore up the roof of my house, it didn't care that I'm black. My white neighbors, like my black neighbors, saw trees fall on their homes and saw their refrigerators rot and mold. They, like I, lived without electricity or phone for over a week after that color-blind natural disaster.

But an unnatural disaster hit us as well, the institutionalized racism that began centuries ago. The flooded areas of New Orleans were three-quarters black, while in dry areas, African Americans were a minority. Over the years, many well-off white people have left the city for gated suburban communities. The remaining whites tend to live on higher ground.

The unnatural disaster of racism swept away the savings accounts and credit cards with which poor black people could have bought their escape. A century of

SOURCE: Emma Dixon, AlterNet. Posted 11/19/05, printed 6/15/07. Independent Media Institute. View story online at: www.alternet.org/story/28431. Reprinted with permission of alternet.org.

Jim Crow laws barred black families in the South from certain schools and jobs. Social Security benefits were not available at first to domestic and agricultural workers, the occupations of most African Americans at that time. Due to discrimination, most black WWII veterans were unable to use the GI Bill, which gave most white veterans the homeownership and college educations that have made their children and grandchildren so prosperous.

The unnatural disaster of racism swept away the cars with which poor black people could have escaped Katrina. Almost a third of residents of the flooded neighborhoods did not own the cars on which the evacuation plan relied. If the promise to the freed slaves of 40 acres and a mule had been kept, then six generations later, their descendents would own more assets, and the mule would now be a Buick.

Nor has this unnatural disaster abated today, as I learned from my own experience. Almost immediately after Katrina hit my town, I saw spray-painted signs warning that looters would be shot and killed. I was warned by a white neighbor not to move around too much lest I be mistaken as a looter.

When my daughter came to get me from my damaged house and drove me to her home in Indiana, we were turned away by a white motel clerk in Illinois on the pretext that there were no vacancies. A later phone call confirmed what their sign said, that rooms were available. I also experienced first-hand racial discrimination in gas lines, and in food and water distribution lines by a police officer.

The world noticed that the evacuees stuck in the SuperDome and those turned back at gunpoint at the Gretna bridge were mostly black. But who noticed that the first no-bid federal contracts went to white businessmen, cronies of white politicians?

It's hard for me to believe, but this persistent racism is invisible to many white people. A Time Magazine poll taken in September found that while three quarters of blacks believe race and income level played a role in the government response to Hurricane Katrina, only 29 percent of whites felt the same.

The color of money is green, but the color of poverty has a darker hue. Families in the flooded black neighborhoods of New Orleans had a 2004 median income of only $25,759 a year, barely more than half the national average. Why? Louisiana is a low-wage, anti-union state. Many workers have pay so low that they receive public housing and food stamps. New Orleans voters made history by approving a citywide living wage in 2002, but a court blocked it, allowing poverty wages to continue.

Last week I drove home to Louisiana. In my neighborhood I hear the constant buzzing of chain saws removing uprooted trees, and the sounds of hammering as roofers repair endless numbers of damaged roofs. The fragrances of Pine Sol and bleach tinge the air as residents attempt to save refrigerators and rain-soaked carpets. I thank God that my family and I survived the storm, and that the recovery has begun.

Yet I ask myself when the other recovery will begin.

Katrina revealed the racial wealth divide in New Orleans and the unnatural disaster that caused it. When will we rebuild our society so that everyone, regardless of race, has the means to escape the next disaster?

The Domino Effect

SHARON HAYS

As noted previously, there are seven events a person can experience that increase the potential for poverty: divorce or separation, a decline in a spouse's work hours, death of a spouse, birth of a child, retirement or disability of the main breadwinner, unemployment, and serious illness. What happens when a person experiences more than one of these events? In the following selection, the author demonstrates how such events can spiral out of control. How would the different theorists (individual, cultural, and structural) analyze what happened to Sheila?

THE DOMINO EFFECT

It's a downward spiral. And once you hit bottom, you hit hard.

The spiral for Sheila began just after she finished high school. Sheila is white and was 29 years old at the time I met her in the old and notoriously dangerous housing project where she lived, not far from the Sunbelt City welfare office. From a working-class background, she was raised in a small town "with small town values." She was engaged to be married to her high school sweetheart. The summer after they graduated he was killed in an auto accident.

> *I wish that then and there I had just said, "Okay, forward," instead of sitting and mourning and moping and weeping and thinking about what could have and should have and would have been. I should have just gone on ahead to college like I had intended. And I didn't do it. But you know what they say, hindsight is 20–20.*

She moved to Sunbelt City with her parents and took a part-time job. Less than a year later her father left her mother.

> *It was in February. He left a note on the kitchen table. It said, "I'm leaving you for good." And he left the keys to the car that was not paid for. He left one month owing in rent. My mom at the time was not working, and I was still mourning my boyfriend.*
>
> *Shortly after that me and my mom found jobs at a dry cleaners. We opened it in the morning, and we worked for 15 hours a day. We'd come home, go to sleep, get up, and go right back*

SOURCE: Sharon Hays, *Flat Broke with Children: Women in the Age of Welfare Reform* (New York: Oxford University Press, 2003), pp. 141–145. Reprinted with permission of Oxford University Press, Inc.

there. Six days a week. And we were doing good. We had paid up the back rent, and the car was being paid for.

And then my mother got blood clots. She almost lost her leg. And the doctor said she shouldn't work any more. This meant we lost $1,500 a month in income and we were trying to make it on my little $1,200. With the medical bills and the car payments, I got a month behind on rent, and they evicted us.

We were homeless. In all the hoopla and everything, I lost my job. It just kind of dominoed. We were actually homeless, living with friends and things like that. And I mean we went hungry—we ate the throwaways from McDonald's.

A lot of people don't realize how close they live to being homeless. I mean, you're just one or two paychecks away from the street. And once you hit bottom, you're gonna hit and you're gonna hit hard. But you have to remember that once you hit bottom you're as low as you can go. There's only one way to go, and that's up.

Unfortunately for Sheila, the downward spiral had not yet reached its lowest point. It was while she and her mother were homeless that she met the man who was to become the father of her daughter. He was, at that moment, her savior, but only a temporary one:

I met Sam, and I thought he was a very nice gentleman. Sam was living with a friend, and they took the two of us in. I found another job. We were hopeful; even though my mom still couldn't work, we were beginning to get back on our feet.

Sam had told me he was divorced. I was still young; I was 21 at the time. And, like I said, I come from a small community. Well, after we'd been together for almost a year, I got a phone call one morning—and it was his wife! So I used the money I had to put him on a bus back to his wife in Florida. And that's the last I heard of him.

A month later I found out I was pregnant. Sam still doesn't know he's got a daughter. The child support people haven't found him yet.

Putting Sam on that bus meant that pregnant Sheila and her disabled mom were homeless again. And then Sheila was raped:

For a while I wasn't sure if Sam was the father. There was the small issue of the fact that three weeks almost to the day after he left I was raped. That's a part of living on the street; that's a danger for women who live on the street.

And that's how I came to find out I was pregnant—I went to the clinic to check a few weeks after the rape. So there were two possible identities to the father. I had a hard time knowing what to do. But as soon as she was born I saw what she looked like and I knew who she was; I knew who she belonged to. She looks too much like her dad.

Sheila was just 22 years old when she gave birth to her daughter. If things had gone as she had originally planned, she would have been starting her last year of college at that time.

Sheila first went to the welfare office in the last months of her pregnancy, hoping to get medical coverage for the birth.

I was a high-risk pregnancy all the way through my pregnancy. I went down to the welfare office and applied for medical assistance. My mother and I were still homeless. I worked a part-time job until things [with the pregnancy] got too bad. My mother had gotten a job [against her doctor's advice] and we managed, with my first welfare check, to finally get our very own small studio apartment. Just two weeks later my daughter was born.

Sheila's daughter (who was busy with her homework during most of my visit), was seven years old when I met her.

From the time she gave birth to the time of our interview, Sheila had a string of jobs. She went back to work when her daughter was just three months old. That job she described as a "really good one," where she worked her way up to a management position in a fast-food restaurant. The rest of the jobs were temporary or low-paying jobs, mainly entry-level fast foods and unskilled clerical work. She left every one. She quit the good one after more than two years, and she's still sorry about it, even though she remembers well all the time she spent agonizing over that decision. She left because the hours and the bus rides were so long that she was spending over 12 hours a day away from home, and she never had a chance to see her daughter. "My daughter was nearly three years old and she was calling my mother 'mom' and calling me 'Sheila.' It was just too hard. I just wanted to get to know her, to do her ABCs and her 1-2-3s. I wanted to be there."

She went back on welfare and spent almost a year getting to know her daughter before again seeking work. She spoke nostalgically of that time with her three-year-old, but she also emphasized that leaving that job was her "third big mistake," alongside mourning rather than continuing on to college, and getting involved with a married man.

Sheila left subsequent jobs because she hurt her back, loading boxes ("the doctors say I'm not allowed to lift over 15 pounds now"), because the pay was too poor, because the jobs were only temporary (through a "temp" agency), and most recently, because her mother was diagnosed as terminally ill and needed to be cared for. Her mother suffered respiratory failure first, then a massive heart attack and, by the time I met her, Sheila was afraid to leave her alone most of the time. "That's my greatest fear, that I'll go to work, and I'll be at work, and something will happen to my mom. I don't know what to do."

Sheila's combined time on welfare, including the time when her child was born, between jobs, and since her mother's illness, added up to about three and a half years, including the last year and a half since welfare reform. She'd been using the resources offered by the welfare office to train herself on computers and in accounting skills. She told me about the contacts she'd made with state agencies that might hire her, and she was feeling somewhat optimistic, though still quite worried about her mom. Her primary goal was to find an employer flexible enough to allow her to care for both her daughter and her mother.

The sheer number of tragedies in Sheila's young life—her fiancé's death, her father leaving, her homelessness, her affair with a married man, her rape, her high-risk pregnancy, and now her mother's terminal illness—testify to the unique circumstances that led her to go on welfare. But every mother I talked to had a story of hardship to tell. And every mother I met had experienced some version of the domino effect: one problem leading to another and compounding it, until too many dominoes fall and the situation becomes impossible to manage. In this, Sheila's story represents the most prominent pattern in the road to welfare.

REFLECTION QUESTIONS

FOR PART III

The readings in this section demonstrate that many of us are just a health crisis, a job loss, a divorce, or a natural disaster away from falling through the safety net into poverty.

1. Compare and contrast the readings in this section. Are the different individuals and families living on the economic margins affected in the same way?
2. Analyze each article carefully and group them by individual/cultural and structural theories of poverty. What theory is best reflected in each reading? Explain.
3. Using your sociological imagination and the various readings as examples, explain how poverty is structured by race, class, gender, age, and location.
4. What role should the government play in providing a safety net for its citizens? How do we protect people from natural disasters and health crises?

PART IV

Living on the Economic Margins

"In the years since the media's discovery of race and poverty in America's inner cities, much has been written about. . . low-income housing projects. . . . [They] have become must-stops for anyone writing about the nation's so-called 'underclass.' Yet for all the ink and air time devoted to them, it is amazing how little we still know about the people who live there. . . . [R]arely do we get to know the people of the projects as anything other than sociological types, . . . one-dimensional portraits of third- or fourth-generation welfare mothers, violence-prone, drug-dealing gang members or street smart man-children living by their wits. Seldom do writers dare to look beyond the sociology and statistics . . . to see people as individuals rather than as examples of predrawn stereotypes."

Sylvester Monroe (1991)

While this book is devoted to understanding poverty as articulated by the poor themselves, we need to place their comments in the context of what is known about the consequences of living in poverty. This section examines these consequences regarding survival, discrimination, and difficulties in parenting.

CHAPTER 3

Survival and Finances

As we have seen, 37 million people were below the poverty line in 2005, which is considered about $5,000 below the minimum subsistence budget for a hypothetical family of four. This means that the living conditions of the impoverished are, typically, substantially substandard. The poor must forgo medical and dental visits except for emergencies, put up with inadequate heat in the winter, and live in crowded apartments located in hazardous neighborhoods (i.e., neighborhoods with relatively high crime rates and a likelihood of environmental pollution levels significantly higher than found in affluent neighborhoods).

Most significant, the impoverished have inadequate diets. According to the U.S. Department of Agriculture, 11 percent of people in the United States live in households that experience hunger or the risk of hunger (USDA, 2006). The elderly, especially older single women, are especially at risk for hunger. The National Policy and Resource Center on Nutrition and Aging estimates that 60 percent of those 65 and older are at high to moderate nutritional risk (Weaver, 2000).

Inadequate resources often means seeking the cheapest foods, not necessarily the most nutritious ones. As a result, the diet of the poor, typically, is too high in saturated fat (leading to heart problems), salt (a principal culprit in hypertension), and carbohydrates (leading to obesity and diabetes). Children in families below poverty are much less likely than higher income families to have a diet rated as good.

The minimum wage established by Congress has not kept up with inflation. In 2007 Congress agreed (after leaving the minimum at $5.15 for ten years) to raise the minimum in stages to $7.25 an hour in 2009, a wage that is still about $2.00 an hour less than a living wage. Those who work at the bottom of the job and pay hierarchy rarely receive benefits such as health insurance and a pension.

Along with earning lower wages, having few work-related benefits, and paying a large proportion of their income for housing, the poor pay more than the nonpoor for many goods and services. The urban poor concentrated in the inner cities find that food and other commodities cost more since supermarkets, discount stores, outlet malls, and warehouse clubs have bypassed inner-city neighborhoods. Since many inner-city residents do not have transportation to get to the stores where prices are lower, they must buy from nearby stores, giving those businesses monopoly powers.

There are several forms of predatory lending that take advantage of the poor. Banks and savings and loans are rarely located in areas with high poverty concentration. As a result about 10 million poor families do not have bank accounts. This "unbanked" population is forced, then, to rely on a shadow banking industry composed of pawn shops, paycheck cashing businesses, and title brokers that loan money or cash checks to customers with poor credit at enormous costs. Title Brokers in Atlanta, for example, makes small loans to borrowers who use the title of their car for collateral at a high interest rate. A loan of $600 will be repaid at $750 in a month and $1,172 in 90 days (Foust, 2000). Ralph Nader says that the effective interest rate of an auto title pawn is sometimes over 900 percent (Nader, 2000). There are more than 9,000 payday lenders, who typically provide two-week loans for a 15 percent fee. Cash checking firms charge a fee equal to 2 percent to 5 percent of the checks with a $2 minimum. Home loans are only possible for the poor if they are willing to pay a higher interest rate (the "subprime" rate) than those with good credit ratings. There is considerable evidence, as noted in the articles in this section, that some mortgage lenders have used unfair practices in getting low-income homeowners into refinancing existing mortgages with new loans that carry such high rates, high fees, and hidden balloon payments. As a result as many as 2 million subprime borrowers, many of them low-income and minority, will have lost their homes to foreclosure in 2007 (Knox, 2007). And there are rent-to-own businesses that sell appliances and furniture to customers who cannot pay cash. Because of the outrageous interest rates, these consumers often pay two to three times the cash price for their purchases. That the poor pay these high rates is not the result of their stupidity, but more often out of necessity. When you do not have the cash or the credit, sometimes you have no choice but to pay more for what you need.

The poor also pay relatively more in sales taxes for their purchases than the nonpoor. That is, the sales tax is a set tax, costing the same, theoretically, to every purchaser. Yet, charging the same rate means that the lower one's resources, the greater the proportion will be paid in tax, making it a **regressive tax** (an income tax where the rates increase with income is a **progressive tax**). Thus, efforts to move federal programs to the states will cost the poor more, since state and local taxes tend to be regressive.

The facts, then, are clear: the poor have difficulty, sometimes incredible difficulty in meeting their survival needs. The essays included here highlight these difficulties.

NOTES AND SUGGESTIONS FOR FURTHER READING

Edin, Kathryn, and Laura Lein (1997). *Making Ends Meet: How Single Mothers Survive Welfare and Low-Wage Work*. New York: Russell Sage Foundation.

Fine, Michelle, and Lois Weis (1998). *The Unknown City: Lives of Poor and Working-Class Young Adults*. Boston: Beacon Press.

Knox, Noelle (2007). " 'Subprime' Borrowers Help Set Foreclosure Record." *USA Today* (June 15):2B.

Kotlowitz, Alex (1991). *There Are No Children Here: The Story of Two Boys Growing Up in the Other America*. New York: Doubleday Anchor Books.

Nader, Ralph (2000). "The Poor Still Pay More." *The Progressive Populist* (April 1):15.

Snow, David A., and Leon Anderson (1993). *Down on Their Luck: A Study of Homeless Street People.* Berkeley: University of California Press.

U.S. Department of Agriculture (2006). *Household Food Security in the United States, 2005.* USDA Economic Research Service (November).

Weaver, Peter (2000). "Going Hungry: It Still Happens." *AARP Bulletin* 41 (June):9–11.

Ain't No Middle Class

SUSAN SHEEHAN

Originally published in The New Yorker, *this account is the true story of a working-class couple, struggling on the margins. The Mertens live in Des Moines, Iowa, with their two children. She is a nursing home aide, and he is a blue collar worker. Married for 22 years, their story reflects changing economic times, rising inflation, and growing debt. They are a prime example of a family with no safety net—one illness, injury, or job loss away from severe poverty. As you read this selection, think about their finances. What do you see for their future/old age? Is there a solution that will make their situation better? How would different theorists analyze their situation?*

At 10 o'clock on a Tuesday night in September, Bonita Merten gets home from her job as a nursing-home aide on the evening shift at the Luther Park Health Center, in Des Moines, Iowa. Home is a two-story, three-bedroom house in the predominantly working-class East Side section of the city. The house, drab on the outside, was built in 1905 for factory and railroad workers. It has aluminum siding painted an off-shade of green, with white and dark-brown trim. Usually, Bonita's sons—Christopher, who is 16 and David, who is 20 and still in high school (a slow learner, he was found to be suffering from autism when he was eight)—are awake when she comes home, but tonight they are asleep. Bonita's husband, Kenny, who has picked her up at the nursing home—"Driving makes Mama nervous," Kenny often says—loses no time in going to bed himself. Bonita is wearing her nursing-home uniform, which consists of a short-sleeved navy-blue polyester top with "Luther Park" inscribed in white, matching navy slacks, and white shoes. She takes off her work shoes, which she describes as "any kind I can pick up for 10 or 12 dollars," puts on a pair of black boots and a pair of gloves, and goes out to the garage to get a pitchfork.

In the spring, Bonita planted a garden. She and David, who loves plants and flowers, have been picking strawberries, raspberries, tomatoes, and zucchini since

June. Bonita's mother, who lives in Washington, Iowa, a small town about a hundred miles from Des Moines, has always had a large garden—this summer, she gave the Mertens dozens of tomatoes from her 32 tomato plants—but her row of potato plants, which had been bountiful in the past, didn't yield a single potato. This is the first year that Bonita has put potato plants in her own garden. A frost has been predicted, and she is afraid her potatoes (if there are any) will die, so instead of plunking herself down in front of the television set, as she customarily does after work, she goes out to tend her small potato strip alongside the house.

The night is cool and moonless. The only light in the back yard, which is a block from the round-the-clock thrum of Interstate 235, is provided by a tall mercury-arc lamp next to the garage. Traffic is steady on the freeway, but Bonita is used to the noise of cars and trucks and doesn't hear a thing as she digs contentedly in the yellowy darkness. Bonita takes pleasure in the little things in life, and she excavates for potatoes with cheerful curiosity—"like I was digging for gold." Her pitchfork stabs and dents a large potato. Then, as she turns over the loosened dirt, she finds a second baking-size potato, and says "Uh-huh!" to herself, and comes up with three smaller ones before calling it quits for the night.

"Twenty-two years ago, when Kenny and me got married, I agreed to marry him for richer or poorer," Bonita, who is 49, says. "I don't have no regrets, but I didn't have no idea for how much poorer. Nineteen-ninety-five has been a hard year in a pretty hard life. We had our water shut off in July *and* in August, and we ain't never had it turned off even once before, so I look on those five potatoes as a sign of hope. Maybe our luck will change."

When Bonita told Kenny she was going out to dig up her potatoes, he remembers thinking, Let her have fun. If she got the ambition, great. I'm kinda out of hope and I'm tired.

Kenny Merten is almost always tired when he gets home, after 5 P.M., from his job at Bonnie's Barricades—a small company, started 10 years ago by a woman named Bonnie Kuggless, that puts up barriers, sandbags, and signs to protect construction crews at road sites. Some days, he drives a truck a hundred and fifty miles to rural counties across the state to set up roadblocks. Other days, he does a lot of heavy lifting. "The heaviest sandbags weigh between 35 and 40 pounds dry," he says. "Wet, they weigh 50 or 60 pounds, depending on how soaked they are. Sand holds a lot of water." Hauling the sandbags is not easy for Kenny, who contracted polio when he was 18 months old and wore a brace on his left leg until he was almost 20. He is now 51, walks with a pronounced limp, and twists his left ankle easily. "Bonnie's got a big heart and hires people who are down on their luck," he says.

Kenny went to work at Bonnie's Barricades two years ago, and after two raises he earns seven dollars and thirty cents an hour. "It's a small living—too small for me, on account of all the debts I got," he says. "I'd like to quit working when I'm 65, but Bonnie doesn't offer a retirement plan, so there's no way I can quit then, with 28 years left to pay on the house mortgage, plus a car loan and etceteras. So I'm looking around for something easier—maybe driving a forklift in a warehouse. Something with better raises and fringe benefits."

On a summer afternoon after work, Kenny sits down in a rose-colored La-Z-Boy recliner in the Mertens' living room/dining room, turns on the TV—a 19-inch Sylvania color set he bought secondhand nine years ago for a hundred dollars—and watches local and national news until six-thirty, occasionally dozing off. After the newscasts, he gets out of his work uniform—navy-blue pants and a short-sleeved orange shirt with the word "Ken" over one shirt pocket and "Bonnie's Barricades" over the other—and takes a bath. The house has one bathroom, with a tub but no shower. Last Christmas, Bonita's mother and her three younger brothers gave the Mertens a shower for their basement, but it has yet to be hooked up—by Kenny, who, with the help of a friend, can do the work for much less than a licensed plumber.

Kenny's philosophy is: Never do today what can be put off until tomorrow—unless he really wants to do it. Not that he is physically lazy. If the Mertens' lawn needs mowing, he'll mow it, and the lawn of their elderly next-door neighbor, Eunice, as well. Sometimes he gets up at 4:30 A.M.—an hour earlier than necessary—if Larry, his half uncle, needs a ride to work. Larry, who lives in a rented apartment two miles from the Mertens and drives an old clunker that breaks down regularly, has been married and divorced several times and has paid a lot of money for child support over the years. He is a security guard at a tire company and makes five dollars an hour. "If he doesn't get to work, he'll lose his job," Kenny says. In addition, Kenny helps his half brother Bob, who is also divorced and paying child support, with lifts to work and with loans.

Around 7:30 P.M., Kenny, who has changed into a clean T-shirt and a pair of old jeans, fixes dinner for himself and his two sons. Dinner is often macaroni and cheese, or spaghetti with store-bought sauce or stewed tomatoes from Bonita's mother's garden. He doesn't prepare salad or a separate vegetable ("Sauce or stewed tomatoes is the vegetable," he says); dessert, which tends to be an Iowa brand of ice cream, Anderson Erickson, is a rare luxury. Kenny takes the boys out for Subway sandwiches whenever he gets "a hankering" for one. Once a week—most likely on Friday, when he gets paid—he takes them out for dinner, usually to McDonald's. "It's easier than cooking," Kenny says.

Because Bonita works the evening shift, Kenny spends more time with his sons than most fathers do; because she doesn't drive, he spends more time behind the wheel. Christopher, a short, trim, cute boy with hazel eyes and brown hair, is one badge away from becoming an Eagle Scout, and Kenny drives him to many Scouting activities. This summer, Kenny drove Eunice, who is 85, to the hospital to visit her 90-year-old husband, Tony, who had become seriously ill in August. After Tony's death, on September 12th, Kenny arranged for the funeral—choosing the casket and the flowers, buying a new shirt for Tony, and chauffeuring the boys to the private viewing at the funeral home. "Everyone was real appreciative," he says.

At around eight-thirty on evenings free from special transportation duties, Kenny unwinds by watching more television, playing solitaire, dozing again, and drinking his third Pepsi of the day. (He is a self-described "Pepsiholic.") Around nine-fifty, he drives two miles to the Luther Park nursing home for Bonita.

Bonita Merten leaves the house before 1 P.M., carrying a 16-ounce bottle of Pepsi (she, too, is a Pepsiholic), and catches the bus to work. She is dressed in her navy-blue uniform and white shoes. Since the uniforms cost 33 dollars, Bonita considers herself lucky to have been given a used one by a nurse's aide who quit, and she bought another, secondhand, for 10 dollars. Luther Park recently announced a mandatory change to forest-green uniforms, and Bonita does not look forward to having to shell out for new attire.

Bonita clocks in before one-forty-five, puts her Pepsi in the breakroom refrigerator, and, with the other evening aides, makes rounds with the day aides. She and another aide are assigned to a wing with 20 long-term residents. "The residents have just been laid down on top of their beds before we get there," Bonita says. "First, I change water pitchers and give the residents ice—got to remember which ones don't want ice, just want plain water. We pass out snacks—shakes fortified with protein and vitamins, in strawberry, vanilla, or chocolate. They need the shakes, because they ordinarily don't want to eat their meals. While I'm doing that, the other aide has to pass out the gowns, washrags, and towels, and the Chux—great big absorbent pads—and Dri-Prides. They're adult snap pants with liners that fit inside them. We don't call them diapers because they're not actually diapers, and because residents got their pride to be considered."

At three-thirty, Bonita takes a 10-minute break and drinks some Pepsi. "We start getting the residents up and giving showers before our break and continue after," Bonita says. "Each resident gets two showers a week, and it works out so's I have to shower three patients a day."

One aide eats from four-thirty to five, the other from five to five-thirty. Until August 1st, Bonita bought a two-dollar meal ticket if she liked what was being offered in the employees' dining room. When the meal didn't appeal to her—she wouldn't spend the two dollars for, say, a turkey sandwich and a bowl of cream-of-mushroom soup ("I don't like it at all")—she either bought a bag of Cheetos from a vending machine or skipped eating altogether. On August 1st, the nursing home reduced meal tickets to a dollar. "Even a turkey sandwich is worth that much," she says.

The residents eat at five-thirty, in their dining room. "We pass trays and help feed people who can't feed themselves," Bonita says. "Sometimes we feed them like a baby or encourage them to do as much as they can." At six-thirty, Bonita charts their meals—"what percent they ate, how much they drank. They don't eat a whole lot, because they don't get a lot of exercise, either. We clear out the dining room and walk them or wheel them to their rooms. We lay them down, and we've got to wash them and position them. I always lay them on their side, because I like lying on my side. I put a pillow behind their back and a blanket between their legs. We take the false teeth out of those with false teeth, and put the dentures into a denture cup for those that will let us. A lot of them have mouthwash, and we're supposed to rinse their mouth. We're supposed to brush their teeth if they have them. After everyone is down, we chart. We check off that we positioned them and if we changed their liners. I'm supposed to get a 10-minute evening break, but I hardly ever take it. Charting, I'm off my feet, and there's just too much to do. Often we're short—I'll be alone on a hall for a few hours. The last thing we do is make rounds with the shift coming in. I clock out by nine-forty-five. Ninety-nine percent of the time, Kenny picks me up. When I had different hours and he'd be bowling, his half brother Bob picked me up, or I took a cab for five dollars. The bus is one dollar, but it stops running by seven o'clock."

Bonita has worked all three shifts at Luther Park. The evening shift currently pays 50 cents an hour more than the day shift and 50 cents less than the night shift, but days and nights involve more lifting. (In moving her patients, Bonita has injured her back more times than she can remember, and she now wears a wide black belt with straps which goes around her sacroiliac; she also uses a mechanical device to help carry heavy resident, between their wheelchairs and their beds.) Bonita's 1994 earnings from Luther Park were only 869 dollars higher than her 1993 earnings, reflecting an hourly increase in wages from six dollars and fifty cents to six-sixty-five and some overtime hours and holidays, for which she is paid time and a half. This July 1st, she received the grandest raise that she has ever had in her life—75 cents an hour—but she believes there is a hold-down on overtime, so she doesn't expect to earn substantially more in 1995. Luther Park gives her a ham for Easter, a turkey for Thanksgiving, 10 dollars for her birthday, and 20 dollars for Christmas.

Bonita rarely complains about working at the nursing home. "I don't mind emptying bedpans or cleaning up the residents' messes," she says. She regards her job, with its time clocks, uniforms, tedious chores, low wages, penny-ante raises, and Dickensian holiday rewards, as "a means to a life."

Bonita and Kenny Merten and their two sons live in a statistical land above the lowly welfare poor but far beneath the exalted rich. In 1994, they earned $31,216 between them. Kenny made $17,239 working for Bonnie's Barricades; Bonita made $13,977 at Luther Park. With an additional $1,212 income from other sources, including some money that Kenny withdrew from the retirement plan of a previous employer, the Mertens' gross income was $32,428. Last year, as in most other years of their marriage, the Mertens spent more than they earned.

The Mertens' story is distinctive, but it is also representative of what has happened to the working poor of their generation. In 1974, Kenny Merten was making roughly the same hourly wage that he is today, and was able to buy a new Chevrolet Nova for less than 4,000 dollars; a similar vehicle today would cost 15,000 dollars—a sum that even Kenny, who is far more prone than Bonita to take on debt, might hesitate to finance. And though Kenny has brought on some of his own troubles by not always practicing thrift and by not always following principles of sound money management, his situation also reflects changing times.

In the 1960s, jobs for high school graduates were plentiful. Young men could easily get work from one day to the next which paid a living wage, and that's what Kenny did at the time. By the mid-80s, many of these jobs were gone. In Des Moines, the Rock Island Motor Transit Company (part of the Chicago, Rock Island & Pacific Railroad) went belly up. Borden moved out of the city, and so did a division of the Ford Motor Company. Utility companies also began downsizing, and many factory jobs were replaced by service-industry jobs, which paid less. Although there is a chronic shortage of nurse's aides at Luther Park, those who stay are not rewarded. After 15 years of almost continuous employment, Bonita is paid 7 dollars and 40 cents an hour—55 cents an hour more than new aides coming onto the job.

Working for one employer, as men like Kenny's father-in-law used to do, is a novelty now. Des Moines has become one of the largest insurance cities in the United States, but the Mertens don't qualify for white-collar positions. Civil-service jobs, formerly held by high-school graduates, have become harder to obtain because of competition from college graduates, who face diminishing job opportunities themselves. Bonita's 37-year-old brother, Eugene, studied mechanical engineering at the University of Iowa, but after graduation he wasn't offered a position in his field. He went to work for a box company and later took the United States Postal Service exam. He passed. When Bonita and Kenny took the exam, they scored too low to be hired by the Post Office.

Although 31 percent of America's four-person families earned less in 1994 than the Mertens did, Kenny and Bonita do not feel like members of the middle class, as they did years ago. "There ain't no middle class no more," Kenny says. "There's only rich and poor."

This is where the $32,428 that the Mertens grossed last year went. They paid $2,481 in federal income taxes. Their Iowa income-tax bill was $1,142, and $2,388 was withheld from their paychecks for Social Security and Medicare. These items reduced their disposable income to $26,417. In 1994, Bonita had $9.64 withheld from her biweekly paycheck for medical insurance, and $14.21 for dental insurance—a $620.10 annual cost. The insurance brought their disposable income down to $25,797.

The highest expenditures in the Mertens' budget were for food and household supplies, for which they spent approximately $110 a week at various stores and farmers' markets, for a yearly total of $5,720. They tried to economize by buying hamburger and chicken and by limiting their treats. (All four Mertens like potato chips.) Kenny spent about eight dollars per working day on breakfast (two doughnuts and a Pepsi), lunch (a double cheeseburger or a chicken sandwich) and sodas on the road—an additional $2,000 annually. His weekly dinner out at McDonald's with his sons cost between 11 and 12 dollars—600 dollars a year more. Bonita's meals and snacks at work added up to about 300 dollars. Kenny sometimes went out to breakfast on Saturday—alone or with the boys—and the meals he and his sons ate at McDonald's or Subway and the dinners that all four Mertens ate at restaurants like Bonanza and Denny's probably came to another 600 dollars annually. David and Christopher's school lunches cost a dollar-fifty a day; they received allowances of 10 dollars a week each, and that provided them with an extra 2 dollars and 50 cents to spend. The money the boys paid for food outside the house came to 500 dollars a year. The family spent a total of about $9,720 last year on dining in and out; on paper products and cleaning supplies; and on caring for their cats (they have two). This left them with $16,077.

The Mertens' next-highest expenditure in 1994 was $3,980 in property taxes and payments they made on a fixed-rate, 30-year, 32,000-dollar mortgage, on which they paid an interest rate of 8.75 percent. This left them with $12,097.

In April of 1994, Kenny's 1979 Oldsmobile, with 279,000 miles on it, was no longer worth repairing, so he bought a 1988 Grand Am from Bonita's brother Eugene for 3,000 dollars, on which he made four payments of 200 dollars a month. The Grand Am was damaged in an accident in September, whereupon he traded up to an 11,000-dollar 1991 Chevy Blazer, and his car loan payments increased to $285 a month. Bonita has reproached Kenny for what she regards as a nonessential purchase. "A man's got his ego," he replies. "The Blazer is also safer—it has four-wheel drive." The insurance on Kenny's cars cost a total of $798, and he spent 500 dollars on replacement parts. Kenny figures that he spends about 20 dollars a week on gas, or about $1,040 for the year. After car expenses of $2,338 and after payments on the car loans of $1,655, the Mertens had $8,104 left to spend. A 10-day driving vacation in August of last year, highlighted by stops at the Indianapolis Motor Speedway, Mammoth Cave, in Kentucky, and the Hard Rock Cafe in Nashville, cost 1,500 dollars and left them with $6,604.

The Mertens' phone bill was approximately 25 dollars a month: the only long-distance calls Bonita made were to her mother and to her youngest brother, Todd, a 33-year-old aerospace engineer living in Seattle. She kept the calls short. "Most of our calls are incoming, and most of them are for Christopher," Bonita says. The Mertens' water-and-sewage bill was about 50 dollars a month; their gas-and-electric bill was about 150 dollars a month. "I have a hard time paying them bills now that the gas and electric companies have consolidated," (Kenny says. "Before, if the gas was 75 dollars and the electric was 75 dollars, I could afford to pay one when I got paid. My take-home pay is too low to pay the two together." After paying approximately 2,700 dollars for utilities, including late charges, the Mertens had a disposable income of $3,904.

Much of that went toward making payments to a finance company on two of Kenny's loans. To help pay for the family's 1994 vacation, Kenny borrowed 1,100 dollars, incurring payments of about 75 dollars a month for two years and three months, at an interest rate of roughly 25 percent. Kenny was more reluctant to discuss the second loan, saying only that it consisted of previous loans he'd "consolidated" at a rate of about 25 percent, and that it cost him 175 dollars a month in payments. Also in 1994 he borrowed "a small sum" for "Christmas and odds and ends" from the credit union at Bonnie's Barricades; 25 dollars a week was deducted from his paycheck for that loan. Payments on the three loans—about 4,300 dollars last year—left the Merten family with a budget deficit even before their numerous other expenses were taken into account.

Except in a few small instances (according to their 1994 Iowa income-tax return, Bonita and Kenny paid H & R Block 102 dollars to prepare their 1993 return, and they gave 125 dollars to charity), it isn't possible to determine precisely what the rest of the Mertens' expenditures were in 1994. Several years ago, Kenny bounced a lot of checks, and he has not had a checking account since. Kenny exceeded the limits on both of their MasterCards a few years ago, and the cards were cancelled. Bonita has a J. C. Penney charge card but says, "I seldom dust it off." Now and then, Bonita went to a downtown outlet store, and if a dress caught her fancy she might put it on layaway. On special occasions, she bought inexpensive outfits for herself and for Kenny. Before last year's summer holiday, she spent seven dollars on a top and a pair of shorts, and during the trip Kenny bought a 75 dollar denim jacket for himself and about 50 dollars' worth of T-shirts for the whole family at the Hard Rock Cafe. One consequence of Kenny's having had polio as a child is that his left foot is a size 5½ and his right foot a size 7. If he wants a comfortable pair of shoes, he has to buy two pairs or order a pair consisting of a 5½ and a 7. Often he compromises, buying sneakers in size 6½. David wears T-shirts and jeans as long as they are black, the color worn by Garth Brooks, his favorite country singer. Christopher is partial to name brands, and Bonita couldn't say no to a pair of 89 dollar Nikes he coveted last year. The Mertens spent about 700 dollars last year on clothing, and tried to economize on dry cleaning. "I dry-clean our winter coats and one or two dresses, but I avoid buying anything with a 'Dry-clean only' label," Bonita says.

The Mertens' entertainment expenses usually come to a thousand dollars a year, but that amount was exceeded in 1994 when Kenny bought a mountain bike for every member of the family. The bikes (Bonita has yet to ride hers out of the driveway) cost 259 dollars apiece, and Kenny made the final payments on them earlier this year. This July, David rode Kenny's bike to the hardware store, and it was stolen while he was inside. Kenny yelled at David; Bonita told Kenny he was being too hard on him, and Kenny calmed down.

Bonita and Kenny don't buy books or magazines, and they don't subscribe to newspapers. (They routinely borrowed Eunice and Tony's Des Moines *Register* until Tony's death, when Eunice cancelled it.) They rarely go to the movies—"Too expensive," Kenny says—but regularly rent movies and video games, usually at Blockbuster. For amusement, they often go to malls, just to browse, but when they get a serious urge to buy they go to antique stores. Kenny believes in "collect-ibles." His most treasured possession is an assortment of Currier & Ives dishes and glasses.

The Mertens have never paid to send a fax, or to send a package via Federal Express, and they aren't online: they have no computer. They even avoid spending money on postage: Kenny pays his bills in person. Bonita used to send out a lot of Christmas cards, but, she says, "I didn't get a whole lot back, so I quit that, too." They spend little on gifts, except to members of Bonita's family.

Kenny knows how much Bonita loves red roses. Twenty-two years ago, he gave her one red rose after they had been married one month, two after they had been married two months, and continued until he reached 12 red roses on their first anniversary. He also gave her a dozen red roses when she had a miscarriage, in 1973, "to make her feel better." To celebrate the birth of David and of Christo-pher, he gave her a dozen red roses and one yellow one for each boy. And Kenny gives Bonita a glass rose every Christmas.

On a Sunday evening this summer, the four Mertens went to Dahl's, their supermarket of choice in Des Moines. They bought four rolls of toilet paper (69 cents); a toothbrush (99 cents); a box of Rice Krispies (on sale for $1.99); eight 16-ounce bottles of Pepsi ($1.67); a gallon of 1-percent milk ($2.07); a large package of the least expensive dishwasher detergent ($2.19), the Mertens having acquired their first dishwasher in 1993, for 125 dollars; two jars of Prego spaghetti sauce ($3); a box of Shake 'n Bake ($1.99); two rolls of film ($10.38), one for Kenny, who owns a Canon T50 he bought for 125 dollars at a pawnshop, and one for Christopher to take to Boy Scout camp in Colorado; a battery ($2.99) for Christopher's flashlight, also for camp; a pound of carrots (65 cents); a green pepper (79 cents); some Ziploc bags ($1.89); a Stain Stick ($1.89); a box of 2000 Flushes ($2.89); a package of shredded mozzarella ($1.39) to add to some pizza the Mertens already had in the freezer; and 12 cans of cat food ($3). Bonita bought one treat for herself—a box of toaster pastries with raspberry filling ($2.05). Christopher asked for a Reese's peanut-butter cup (25 cents), a bottle of Crystal Light (75 cents), and a package of Pounce cat treats ($1.05). All three purchases were O.K.'d.

David, who is enchanted by electrical fixtures, was content to spend his time in the store browsing in the light-bulb section. He was born with a cataract in his left eye, and the Mertens were instructed to put drops in that eye and a patch over his "good" right eye for a few years, so that the left eye wouldn't become lazy. Sometimes when they put the drops in, they told David to look up at a light. Today, David's main obsession, which apparently dates back to the eyedrops, is light. "We'd go someplace with David, and if there was a light with a bulb out he'd say, 'Light out,'" Bonita recalls. "We'd tell him, 'Don't worry about that,' and pretty soon he was saying, 'Light out, don't worry about that.'"

At 20, David looks 15. A lanky young man with copper-colored hair, hearing aids in both ears, and eye-glasses with thick lenses, he attends Ruby Van Meter, a special public high school for the city's mentally challenged. He reads at a fifth-grade level, and he doesn't read much. For years, the Mertens have been applying—without success—for Supplemental Security Income for David. In June of this year, when his application for S.S.I. was once again turned down, the Mertens hired a lawyer to appeal the decision. David has held a series of jobs set aside for slow learners (working, for instance, as a busboy in the Iowa state-house cafeteria and in the laundry room of the local Marriott hotel), but he says that his "mood was off" when he was interviewed for several possible jobs this summer, and he drifted quietly through his school vacation. He will not be permitted to remain in school past the age of 21. If David could receive monthly S.S.I. checks and Medicaid, the Mertens would worry less about what will happen to him after they are gone. They have never regarded David as a burden, and although he has always been in special-education classes, they have treated him as much as possible the way they treat Christopher. Say "special ed" to Bonita, and she will say, "Both my boys are very special."

The Dahl's bill came to $44.75. When Kenny failed to take money out of his pocket at the cash register, Bonita, looking upset, pulled out her checkbook. She had expected Kenny to pay for the groceries, and she had hoped that the bill would be 40 dollars or less. But Kenny was short of money. "Aargh," Bonita said, softly.

Bonita didn't want to write checks for groceries, because she has other ideas about where her biweekly paychecks—about 400 dollars take-home—should go. Most of her first check of the month goes toward the mortgage—$331.68 when she pays it before the 17th of the month, $344.26 when she doesn't. Bonita likes to put aside the second check for the two most important events in her year—the family's summer vacation and Christmas. In theory, Kenny is supposed to pay most of the other family expenses and to stick to a budget—a theory to which he sometimes has difficulty subscribing. "I don't like to work off a budget," he says. "I think it restricts you. My way is to see who we have to pay this week and go from there. I rob Peter to pay Paul and try to pay Peter back." In practice, Kenny rarely pays Peter back. With his take-home pay averaging about 235 dollars a week, he can't.

When a consumer counselor, who does not know the Mertens, was questioned about the family's current financial predicament—specifically, their 1994 income and expenditures—she made numerous recommendations. Among her suggestions for major savings was that the Mertens cut their food bills dramatically, to 5,400 dollars a year. She proposed stretching the Mertens' food dollars by drastically curtailing their eating out and by buying in bulk from the supermarket. She said that Kenny should get rid of his high-interest loans, and use the money he was spending on usurious interest to convert his mortgage from 30 years to 15. The way Kenny and Bonita were going, the counselor pointed out, they would not finish paying off their current mortgage until they were 79 and 77 years old, respectively. The Mertens' principal asset is 8,000 dollars in equity they have in their house. If the Mertens wanted to retire at 65, they would need more than what they could expect to receive from Social Security.

The counselor had many minor suggestions for economizing at the grocery store. The Mertens should buy powdered milk and mix it with one-percent milk instead of buying two-percent milk. They should cut down even further on buying meat; beans and lentils, the counsellor observed, are a nutritious and less costly form of protein. She recommended buying raisins rather than potato chips, which she characterized as "high-caloric, high-fat, and high-cost."

The counsellor had one word for the amount between 1,500 and 2,500 dollars—that the Mertens spent on vacations: "outlandish." Their vacations, she said, should cost a maximum of 500 dollars a year. She recommended renting a cabin with another family at a nearby state park or a lake. She urged the Mertens to visit local museums and free festivals, and go on picnics, including "no-ant picnics"—on a blanket in their living room.

Kenny and Bonita were resistant to most of the suggestions that were passed on to them from the counsellor, who is funded mainly by creditors to dispense advice to those with bill-paying problems. According to Kenny, buying a dozen doughnuts at the supermarket and then taking breakfast to work would be "boring." Bonita says she tried powdered milk in the mid-80s, when Kenny was unemployed, and the kids wouldn't drink it. She does buy raisins, but the boys don't really like them. Bonita and Kenny both laugh at the prospect of a no-ant picnic. "Sitting on the living-room carpet don't seem like a picnic to me," Bonita says.

Bonita surmises that the counselor hasn't experienced much of blue-collar life and therefore underestimates the necessity for vacations and other forms of having fun. "We couldn't afford vacations in the 80s, and if we don't take them now the kids will be grown," she says. Kenny reacted angrily to the idea of the boys' eating dried beans and other processed foods. "I lived on powdered milk, dried beans, surplus yellow cheese, and that kind of stuff for two years when I was a kid," he says. "I want better for my boys."

Kenny acknowledges that he tried to confine his responses to the consumer counsellor's minor suggestions, because he realizes that her major recommendations are sound. He also realizes that he isn't in a position to act on them. He dreams of being free of debt. He has tried a number of times to get a 15-year mortgage, and has been turned down each time. "We both work hard, we're not on welfare, and we just can't seem to do anything that will make a real difference in our lives," he says. "So I save 10 dollars a bowling season by not getting a locker at the alley to store my ball and shoes, and have to carry them back and forth. So I save 25 dollars by changing my own oil instead of going to Jiffy Lube. So what? Going out to dinner is as necessary to me as paying water bills."

Kenneth Deane Merten was born poor and illegitimate to Ruby Merten in her mother's home, outside Des Moines, on October 5, 1944; his maternal relatives declined to reveal his father's name, and he never met his father. Ruby Merten went on to marry a soldier and had another son, Robert. She divorced Bob's father, and later married Don Summers, a frequently unemployed laborer, with whom she had three more children. "Mr. Summers was so mean he made me stand up all night in the bed when I was eight years old," Kenny recalls. He has never hit his own sons, because "I know what it done to my life and I don't want it to get passed down." The family often moved in haste when the rent was due. Kenny attended eight or ten schools, some of them twice, before he completed sixth grade.

Kenny's mother died of cancer at 27, when he was 14. The three younger children stayed with Don Summers and a woman he married a month later. Kenny and Bob went to live with their maternal grandparents, and their lives became more stable. Even so, Kenny's school grades were low. "I had a hard time with math and science," he says. "Coulda been because of all the early moving around. I ain't stupid." He spent his high-school years at Des Moines Technical High School and graduated in 1964, when he was almost 20.

Two days later, he found a job as a shipping clerk for *Look* magazine. He kept the job until 1969, and left only when it became apparent that the magazine was cutting back its operations. He drove a cab from 1969 to 1972, drank too much, and did what he calls "some rowdy rambling." He had put much of that behind him when he got a job as a factory worker at EMCO Industries, a manufacturer of muffler parts and machinery bolts, in the fall of 1972, shortly before he met Bonita.

Bonita Anne Crooks was born on October 7, 1946, in Harper, Iowa. Her father, Cloyce Crooks, was employed all his working life by the Natural Gas Pipeline Company; his wife, Pauline, stayed home to take care of Bonita and her three younger brothers. Bonita was required to do chores, for which she was paid, and to deposit those earnings in a bank. She took tap-dancing lessons, wore braces on her teeth, and often went with her family on vacation to places like California and Texas. "Kenny's growing up was a lot worse than mine," she says. In 1965, Bonita graduated from a Catholic high school and became a nurse's aide, while living at home and continuing to bank her money. In 1971, she moved to Des Moines, and the following year she got a job as a keypunch operator for a large insurance company. Keypunching, however, proved too difficult for her (she couldn't combine accuracy with high speed), and she soon transferred within the company to a lower-paying position—that of a file clerk.

Bonita met Kenny in October 1972 on a blind date that had been arranged by a friend of hers. "I had been jilted by a younger man, and I knew Kenny was meant for me on our first date, when he told me he was born on October 5, 1944—exactly two years and two days earlier than me," Bonita says. She and Kenny fell in love quickly and were married in a traditional ceremony at a Catholic church in Harper on June 30, 1973. The newlyweds set off for Colorado on their honeymoon, but Kenny's car, a secondhand 1966 Pontiac Bonneville convertible, broke down, and the couple ended up in the Black Hills of South Dakota. When they were courting, Kenny had asked Bonita what sort of engagement ring she wanted. She had declined a "chunky" diamond, and said that matching wedding bands would suffice. "I suspected Kenny had debts," Bonita says. "I just didn't know how many he had until we got home."

The couple moved into a modest two-bedroom house. Bonita kept her file-clerk job after David's birth, in April 1975, but when she became pregnant with Christopher, who was born in November 1979, her doctor ordered her to bed. From the window of her bedroom, Bonita could see the Luther Park nursing home being built "kinda like next to my back yard." She didn't return to the insurance company, because her pay couldn't cover the cost of daytime care of two children. Kenny was working days at EMCO, so in June 1980 Bonita took a job on the 3-to-11 P.M. shift at Luther Park. She earned more there than she had as a file clerk. On some nights, Kenny drove a cab. He needed two jobs, because he regularly spent more than he and Bonita earned, just as he had overspent his own pay when he was single. Every year or two, he bought a new car. "I shouldn't have bought those new cars, but life with Don Summers made me feel completely insecure," he says. "Driving new cars gave me a sense of self-worth."

Kenny lost his job at EMCO at the end of 1983. He says that he had asked his supervisor for permission to take some discarded aluminum parts, and that permission was granted. But as he was driving off EMCO's premises with the parts in the bed of his pickup he was accused of stealing them. His supervisor then denied having given Kenny permission to take the parts. A demoralized Kenny didn't seek a new job for a year. He had already stopped driving the cab—after being robbed twice—and had started mowing lawns part time in the spring and summer, and doing cleanup work and shovelling snow in the fall and winter. Kenny's business failed—"There were too many unemployed guys like me out there." Many of his prized belongings were repossessed, among them a Curtis-Mathes stereo console. For two weeks in the summer of 1984, the Mertens were without gas or electricity or telephone service. They went on food stamps. Bonita felt guilty about going to work in air-conditioned surroundings while her husband and children were at home in the heat. Kenny felt humiliated when Bonita's parents visited their dark, sweltering house over the Fourth of July weekend. While Kenny has done better financially than most of his side of the family, it pains him that he hasn't done as well as Bonita's brothers, and that they regard him as a spendthrift and an inadequate provider. "When they get down on Kenny, I feel like I'm caught between a rock and a crevice," Bonita says.

Kenny's starting salary at EMCO had been seven dollars an hour. By the time he was terminated, it was eight-ninety-five an hour. In 1985, he found several jobs he liked, but none paid more than seven dollars an hour. One such job was with Bob Allen Sportswear, and he kept it until 1987, when he was let go during the off-season. He occasionally filed unemployment claims, and the family qualified for food stamps and received some groceries from food banks. During the rocky period between 1984 and 1988, Kenny tried to continue making payments on bills that he owed, in order to avoid having to declare bankruptcy, but his debts grew to the point where they exceeded his assets by "I think 12 or 13 thousand dollars"; his creditors—mostly finance companies—got fed up with him, and then he had no choice. The Mertens were able to keep their house and their '79 Olds. Going on food stamps didn't embarrass them—the boys had to eat, and they went off food stamps whenever Kenny had a new job—but the bankruptcy filing was published in the newspaper and made Bonita feel ashamed.

In 1989, after seeing an ad on television, Kenny enrolled in electronics courses at a local vocational school and borrowed 7,200 dollars to pay for his studies. His deficiency in math came back to haunt him, and he eventually dropped out. While at school, he had heard of an opening as a janitor at Ryko Manufacturing, an Iowa manufacturer of car washes. He eventually moved up to a factory job, working full time at Ryko in the early 90s for three years. Those years were happy ones. He got regular raises, and during the April-to-December busy season he earned a lot of overtime. In the summer of 1991, the Mertens flew to Seattle to visit Bonita's brother Todd. They had just enough money to cover one plane fare, and asked Bonita's brother Eugene to lend them the money for the three other tickets. Bonita took three months off that year; by then, she had worked full time at Luther Park for 11 straight years and needed a break. Kenny was proud to be the family's main provider, and wanted Bonita to stay home and take it easy.

In February 1993 Ryko fired Kenny Merten. His supervisors said that the work he did on the assembly line was neither fast enough nor of a sufficiently high quality. He was earning 11 dollars and 80 cents an hour—almost 30,000 dollars a year including overtime—when he was terminated. "In today's job market, first-rate companies like Ryko can afford to be selective," he says. "They want to hire young men."

Around the same time, Luther Park announced that it intended to expand. The nursing home offered the Mertens 39,000 dollars for the house they had lived in for 18 years. Kenny and Bonita accepted the offer, and were allowed to stay on, free of charge, for six months while they went house hunting. After they sold their house, it became apparent that they had been using it to supplement their income. The house they had bought for 14,800 dollars had appreciated handsomely in value, but they had kept re-mortgaging, and now they owed 29,000 dollars on it. As a result, they netted only 10,000 dollars from the sale. The purchase price of the Mertens' new home was 40,000 dollars. They spent 2,000 dollars from the sale of the old house on improvements to their new home, and this reduced the amount of the down payment they were able to afford to 8,000 dollars.

Kenny attempted to return to work at several of the companies where he had previously been employed, but they weren't hiring. It took him five months to find his current job with Bonnie's Barricades—far more arduous work, at lower wages than he had been paid at EMCO more than 20 years earlier. "I know I'll never be able to earn 11.80 an hour again," he says. "The most I can hope for is a seven-dollar-an-hour job that doesn't involve swinging sandbags. Maybe if I can come home less tired at the end of the day, I can handle an evening job."

This year did not get off to a good start for Kenny. In January, he hocked two rings that Bonita had given him for a hundred dollars, in order to pay a utility bill. Then, three months later, true to form, Kenny spotted two rings at a local pawnshop that he wanted Bonita to have—a 199-dollar opal ring and a 399-dollar diamond-cluster ring. He asked the pawnshop owner to take the two rings out of the showcase and agreed to make periodic 20 dollar payments on them until they were paid off.

Kenny was not worried about how he would pay for the rings, or how he would pay for the family's annual summer vacation. In September of last year, a few days after the Mertens returned from that summer's driving trip, his Grand Am was rear-ended. After the collision, in which Kenny hurt his back, he hired a lawyer on a contingency basis. The young man who had caused the accident had adequate insurance, and Kenny expected to be reimbursed for medical bills and lost wages. (He hadn't been permitted to lift heavy objects for several weeks.) He also expected the insurance company to pay a sizable sum—10 or 15 thousand dollars—for pain and suffering. Kenny's lawyer told him that he could expect the insurance company to settle with him by March. When the insurance money failed to arrive that month, Kenny's lawyer told him to expect an offer in April, then in May, and then in June. In early July, the lawyer said that he could get Kenny 6,500 dollars by the end of the month just in time to save the Mertens' summer vacation. The insurance payment and the annual vacation had been the focus of Bonita's attention for seven months. "If you don't go on vacation, a year has gone by with nothing to show for it," she says.

Bonita wanted the family to travel to Seattle to visit Todd because he had a new home and she was eager to see it. The Mertens made meticulous plans for a driving trip to the state of Washington. They decided they would get up at 4 A.M. on Saturday, August 5th, and drive to Rapid City, South Dakota. They would visit Mt. Rushmore, and Kenny, who has an eye for landscapes, would take photographs of the Devils Tower, in Wyoming, at sunrise and sunset. They would arrive at Todd's home on Wednesday, August 9th, spend a few days there, and return to Des Moines, by way of the Mall of America, in Bloomington, Minnesota, on August 19th. Both Bonita and Kenny had arranged with their employers to take one week off with pay and one without.

Six days before their departure, however, their lawyer called with crushing news; the insurance payment would not be arriving until September. The following evening, Bonita injured her shoulder lifting a patient at the nursing home, but she was still determined to have her vacation. Although Kenny was behind on almost all his bills—he had just borrowed 75 dollars from David to pay a water bill—he went to a bank and to his credit union on August 2nd to borrow 2,500 dollars to cover the cost of the vacation, figuring he would pay off this newest loan from the insurance money in September. On the evening of August 2nd, Bonita reinjured her shoulder while helping another aide transfer a resident from her wheelchair to her bed.

Both the bank and the credit union turned Kenny down. Not only did he have too much outstanding debt of his own but he had also cosigned a loan on his half brother Bob's car. Without being able to borrow, the Mertens could not go on vacation. To make matters worse, Luther Park had sent Bonita to a doctor, and he informed her that she would require physical therapy three times a week for the next two weeks. The vacation would have to be cancelled. "When Kenny told me he'd been turned down for the loan, his jaw dropped about two inches," Bonita recalls. "Kenny was so shocked and disappointed for me that I couldn't be disappointed for myself."

The Mertens have had their share of disappointments, but they don't stay down long. On the morning they had set aside to pack for their trip, Bonita baked banana bread. That evening, after she finished work, Kenny took the whole family out to dinner. From there they drove to Blockbuster and bought two videos—"Sister Act 2" (David had loved the original) and a Beatles movie. They also rented two movies, and a video game that Christopher wanted. The boys spent the following week at their grandmother's. During the second vacation week, Bonita took David to the Iowa State Fair, in town. "Me and David really had fun together," she says.

Both Mertens spent a little money during the two weeks that they didn't go out West. Bonita made a payment to Fingerhut on a shelf that she had bought for David's room and on a game that she had bought him, and she finished paying Home Interiors for some mirrors, sconces, and a gold shelf that she had bought for her bedroom. "When I buy this stuff, I can see Kenny getting a little perturbed, but he doesn't say anything," she says. Later in August, the front brakes on Kenny's Blazer failed, and replacement parts cost about a hundred dollars. The labor would have cost him twice that much, but Eunice, the next-door neighbor, gave him some furniture that she no longer needed, and he bartered the furniture with a friend who is an auto mechanic. Kenny and Bonita agreed that driving with faulty brakes through the mountains on their way West would have been dangerous, so it was a blessing in disguise that they had been forced to remain at home.

On Friday, September 22nd, Kenny, feeling unusually fatigued, decided to take the day off from work. After lunch, he drove Bonita to their lawyer's office. The insurance company had agreed to pay Kenny 7,200 dollars. The lawyer would get a third—2,400 dollars—and Kenny owed 1,200 dollars in medical bills, so he would net 3,600 dollars. He had wanted more—to pay off more of his debts and bills—but this was three days after Bonita's lucky potato strike, and she was feeling optimistic. She persuaded Kenny to put the agony of waiting behind them and to accept the offer. The next day, Kenny drove Bonita, David, and Christopher to the pawnshop. The proprietor, Doug Schlegel, was expecting them. At the cash register, Doug handed Kenny a small manila envelope with the opal ring inside. "Hey, Kiddo!" Kenny called out to Bonita as he removed the ring from the envelope. "Come here!"

Bonita tried to kiss Kenny, but he quickly moved away. "I love you," she said. After Bonita finished working the opal ring down the third finger of her left hand, checking to see whether it fitted properly, Doug told her, "You don't want to let it sit in the sun or put it in hot water."

"I know," Bonita said. "Opals are soft and touchy. They're my birthstone. I have one I bought for myself, but this is lots prettier."

Once the Mertens were back in the Blazer, Bonita asked Kenny, "Is the opal my birthday present?" Her 49th birthday was coming up in two weeks.

"It's a prebirthday present," Kenny replied. He didn't mention his plan to give her the more expensive ring—the one with the diamond cluster—for Christmas, provided he could make the payments in time.

"Thank you, Kenny. I love you," Bonita said.

"Sure," Kenny said. "You love to pick on me and drive me crazy."

Bonita touched Kenny's hand. "Leave me alone, I'm driving," he told her. When Kenny stopped at a red light, Bonita said, "You're not driving now." But the light suddenly turned green. Throughout the fall, Kenny Merten refused to fret over the very real possibility that he would have to file for bankruptcy again if he didn't get his financial house in order. He was thinking only as far ahead as Christmas—imagining himself putting the box that held the diamond-cluster ring for Bonita under the tree in their living room and marking it "Open this one last." Kenny predicts that when his brothers-in-law see the ring they will surely disapprove, but he doesn't care. "The rings shouldn't be in the budget, but they are," he says.

Kenny's mother's short life left him with a determination to marry once and to make that marriage succeed—something that few of his relatives have done. Bonita has often said that one reason she loves Kenny is that he surprises her every once in a while.

"Diamonds are a girl's best friend, next to her husband," Kenny says. "And Bonita's worth that ring, every bit of it. After all, she puts up with me."

The Working Poor

DAVID K. SHIPLER

Over the life of a 30-year home mortgage of $100,000, the difference in payments between interest rates of 8% and 10.5% is over $65,000. In other words, when a person takes out a loan at the higher interest rate (the "subprime" rate) they will end up paying $65,000 more than the borrower who has a lower interest rate. Unfortunately, these subprime loans are often the only loans available to lower-income borrowers. In the following selection, David Shipler demonstrates how credit card companies operate in a similar fashion, resulting in high credit card debt for the most vulnerable. As you read this selection, think about the issue of personal responsibility versus corporate responsibility. Are credit card companies to blame? How would the different theoretical perspectives explain the problem of credit card debt?

High interest may be the most ubiquitous trap for low-wage workers. Married, Ann was in the middle class, with all the perks of easy credit. Divorced, she sank rapidly, and for a while, the only barriers between her and utter destitution were four thin pieces of plastic: one from Discover, another from Citibank, and two from Sears. As the balances ran up, she restricted the use of her cards to essentials such as car repairs or purchases that she could justify as contributions to her children's physical health and intellectual well-being: a set of cross-country skis, a computer for Sandy, who later won full financial aid at Dartmouth. "Credit cards went for things like a bicycle," she insisted, "not for potato chips or little Barbie dolls, but things like books, for things that would make them larger and their lives larger, that would contribute to their growing."

The current moment always chafed against the uncertain future. "Christmas was always huge in gift giving," she confessed, "because I thought there may not be a next year."

"Each year you said we can't do it again," added Sandy as he stared at his laptop in the living room.

Ann's relatives were critical of her. "If we decided to splurge and get a box of raspberries in the middle of the winter, that would be just unforgivable, because we didn't have the means to do that," she said. "We shouldn't have those kinds of choices. And I often hear people say, 'Well, look at them, I think they're on welfare. They have food stamps. What are they doing with a television?' I know from the everyday grind of not knowing what's going to happen next that people need some way to relieve that pressure and that pain—and it is pain. Some of us can do it in healthy ways, like putting cross-country skis on a credit card—and that's not very responsible, but it's pretty healthy." She laughed, but not merrily.

The real price was reflected in those bills with the snowballing balances. Since her credit rating was not exactly AAA, she was being charged up to 23.999 percent interest. What's more, while she was faithfully paying the finance charge and minimum almost every month, she did not always get her salary in time to meet the deadline; as a result, she gradually realized, the card companies were adding late fees to her principal, then charging the exorbitant interest on that ever-growing principal. Long after she stopped using the cards, the balance continued to rise.

This has become a chronic problem across the country as lenders search credit records for minor delinquencies to label them "subprime." If you're in that category you get charged higher fees and interest, but you may not know it, because few states require lenders to reveal the score that determines a consumer's credit rating, even when the borrower sees his credit report. The score, running from a low of 375 to a high of 900, is based on five factors: punctuality of payment, the amount of debt, how long credit has been used (the longer the better), how much new credit has been requested (the less the better), and whether the borrower uses a mixture of credit (mortgages and auto loans are preferred over credit cards). Often, the lenders get the facts wrong, of course, and it's to their advantage. Subprime lending grew from about $37 billion to $370 billion from 1991 to 1999, with major banks among the culprits, according to *Consumer Reports.* In the 1990s, the magazine reported, lenders "relaxed the old standards of sound lending by luring consumers into debt waters well over their head, but they didn't relax the old strict standards of loan repayment. The result: Easy-money lenders point fingers at the subprime class they helped create, then punish those borrowers with significantly higher interest rates and fees. College students—and now even 16-year-olds—are a new target for subprime lenders."

Sandy Brash, an Ivy League student with no money at all, "gets an offer a day, at least," said his mother. Because of the aggressive soliciting and the easy credit, even teenagers were declaring bankruptcy, a financial counselor told Ann. She found the notion of bankruptcy abhorrent. She sat one day at the dining room table in her shabby, $400-a-month apartment, her head in her hands, compiling the modest figures for her tax return and tracking her expenses. On a pad of white lined paper, she had written lists of numbers, none of them very large. "I don't know," she said. "I don't even feel like trying; I feel that hopeless. There's no way out of this." Many people get out by declaring bankruptcy, I said. "It sounds like taking welfare, and I don't want to do it," she retorted. "I just want to pay what I owe." Her voice rose onto a high note of anxious melancholy. "But I can't do it with these kinds of rates. I knew that it was gonna take me about an extra thousand dollars a year to get the kids by over those growing years, but I just couldn't find a way around it. And so I did it. And I knew I'd have to pay the piper. So. There it is."

In one respect, Ann was typical of the low-wage working people I spoke with across the country—in New Hampshire towns, North Carolina fields, and Los Angeles housing projects. They were white and black, Latino and Asian, native-born and newly arrived in America, and they were not gripped by rage. Ann did not point a finger of blame. She did not make sweeping criticisms of society at large. "I got myself into this, I made the choices," she said plainly. "In spite of the fact that the credit card companies are taking advantage of people, that they're really awful in charging such awful interest rates, I made the choice of using them. I haven't used them in a couple of years. And plus I can't answer the phone" She did not answer the phone because she hated to hear the bill collectors. "They have all kinds of tones of voices," she said. They left alarming messages on the answering machine, like, "Call this number immediately."

Always when she talked this way she then apologized for "complaining." But I was an instigator in her complaints, I suppose, for I kept asking questions. What does this feel like? What do you think about? How foreign does the zone along the edge of poverty seem to someone who grew up in middle-class comfort? "Nobody really wants to know that sometimes $2 is a significant amount, and $25 always is tremendous," she said, as if this condition still amazed her as well. "Tell me it's not true for ordinary, everyday people. Is it the same? I mean, normal life"—she gave a despairing laugh—"before life was like this. I can't remember. I can't remember what it was like. I mean, every day and every night when I'm trying to fall asleep, there's this worry hanging. Is the car gonna make it through because I haven't maintained it properly? How am I gonna get this? I know I have to do this. How am I gonna get it done? How am I gonna stretch to get these bills paid? If one extra thing happens—."

In May, three months before her car lease expired, her ex-husband's $100-a-week child support payments were scheduled to end because Sally would turn eighteen. It was a deadline of sorts, and Ann finally conceded that bankruptcy had to be considered. It went against her grain, but she couldn't make the numbers add up another way. She then discovered that she was too poor to declare bankruptcy; she would need $700 for the lawyer and $200 as a filing fee. She went to a financial counselor instead.

The counselor was accustomed to working with credit card companies to lower the interest rate to zero if the principal could be paid off in regular installments. But Ann turned out to be too poor for that option as well; looking at her low income, her expenses, and her complete lack of assets, the counselor told her that she would not be able to make the payments. So he advised her to stop paying her credit card bills, pay the rent and electricity first, save the money for bankruptcy, and file when she had enough. Gritting her teeth to "put the moral question aside," as she described it, she stopped paying the credit card bills in March, took sums out of her food money, saved for seven months, and finally in October had pulled together the $900 required to file. It was no cause for celebration. "I take home about $860 every two weeks," she explained. "One half of the biweekly check goes to rent, the other half to the car. Then there are utilities and transportation costs to get back and forth to work. I can't replace underwear. We're not having Christmas this year, though we will try to have a meal. I'm sorry, I don't mean to complain."

On the surface, it seems odd that an interest rate can be determined by the condition of an apartment, which in turn can generate illness and medical bills, which may then translate into a poor credit rating, which limits the quality of an automobile that can be purchased, which jeopardizes a worker's reliability in getting to work, which limits promotions and restricts the wage, which confines a family to the dilapidated apartment. Such are the interlocking deficits of poverty, one reinforcing the other until an entire structure of want has been built. Such was the prison of Lisa Brooks.

She was only twenty-four, but a blemish of weariness tainted her youthful face, and her blond hair was stringy with the carelessness of stress. She worked hard and well as a caretaker at a halfway house for mentally ill adults. She was good with them, kind and firm, but she was paid only $8.21 an hour, which put her and her four children a couple of thousand dollars a year below the federal poverty line.

She lived in a rough section of Newport, New Hampshire, in the kind of housing shown by recent studies to cause and exacerbate asthma in children. Lisa had never noticed any mold, mites, mouse droppings, or roaches, which have been linked to asthma. But she did notice that her nine-year-old son, Nicholas, got worse after they moved into a damp, drafty apartment in an old wooden house on Beech Street.

Nicholas, home with his blind grandmother, had sudden trouble breathing on two occasions. She called 911, and each time an ambulance whisked him to a hospital, once to Claremont and once to New London. In each emergency room, he was treated with oxygen and steroids. But the family's health insurance, for which Lisa paid $97 every two weeks, refused to cover the ambulance charges of $240 and $250, arguing that the doctor had never obtained the proper authorization. Lisa did not understand the insurance rules and procedures and did not know how to appeal. "I fought with the doctor's office and the insurance company," she complained, "and they still said no matter what, I had to pay for it."

She could not pay immediately or all at once, for she operated close to the edge of insolvency. So the charges went onto her credit report. When she tried to move to decent housing by applying for a loan to buy a mobile home, she was denied because her credit record showed the overdue ambulance bills. When she tried to buy a more reliable car, which she needed to get to work, she was also denied. So when her 1989 Dodge Caravan developed fatal electrical problems, she had no choice but to go to a used-car lot that didn't do credit checks but charged her 15.747 percent interest. She paid $5,800 for a 1995 Plymouth Neon that had 82,000 miles, a bad alternator, and other troubles that cost $100 to $200 a month to repair.

On the day Lisa told me about her high-interest loan, I happened to receive an unsolicited offer from my insurance company of an auto loan at 7.5 percent, less than half of her rate. I didn't need the loan, and that's why my rate was so low. In a free market economy, people are like corporations issuing bonds: the less secure they are financially, the more interest they have to pay when they borrow.

CHAPTER 4

Discrimination/Racism/Stigma

In 2005 median household income for Whites was $50,984, Native Americans $33,627, Latinos $35,967, and African Americans $30,858. While the official poverty rate by race/ethnicity follows that pattern, the rates for non-Whites is almost three times the rate for Whites (the rate for Whites in 2005 was 8.3 percent, for Native Americans 25.3 percent, Latinos 21.8 percent, and African Americans 24.9 percent).

The relatively high poverty rates for African Americans, Latinos, and Native Americans is associated with various forms of institutional discrimination such as attending underfunded schools, living in areas of concentrated poverty, being disproportionately employed in the lowest segment of the labor market where pay is at or near the minimum wage, and relatively high unemployment. For example, the unemployment rate for African Americans is consistently at least twice the rate for Whites.

Historically, African Americans have been the largest racial/ethnic minority and have experienced the greatest social and economic discrimination. But the demographics of minorities are changing in the United States with the recent waves of immigrants from Latin America and Asia. Since 2000: (1) Latinos outnumber African Americans (in 2005, there were 44.3 million Latinos and 36.7 million Blacks); (2) one out of eight residents is foreign-born; (3) there may be as many as 12 million undocumented people in the United States. Immigrants enter at the bottom of society's stratification system, doing society's "dirty work" for low wages and few if any benefits. Moreover, because of the 1996 welfare reform passed by Congress, all legal immigrants are cut off from food stamps, and those who entered the country after the welfare bill was signed are ineligible for federal programs such as Supplemental Security Income and state-run programs such as temporary welfare and Medicaid. One consequence is the lack of health care—a study by the Center on Budget Priorities found that nationally 46 percent of immigrant children who were not citizens lacked health insurance in 1999, compared to 20 percent of children whose parents were native-born (Scher, 2001).

Closely related to discrimination is the concept of stigma. A **stigma** is an attribute that is socially devalued and disgraced. Sociologist Erving Goffman describes it this way in his classic *Stigma*:

> While the stranger is present before us, evidence can arise of his possessing an attribute that makes him different from others in the category of persons available for him to be, and of a less desirable kind—in the extreme, a person who is quite thoroughly bad, or dangerous, or weak. He is thus reduced in our minds from a whole and usual person to a tainted, discounted one. Such an attribute is a stigma, especially when its discrediting effect is very extensive; sometimes it is also called a failing, a shortcoming, a handicap. (Goffman, 1963:3)

People with stigmas have what Goffman called a spoiled identity and this spoiled identity has negative consequences:

> By definition, of course, we believe the person with a stigma is not quite human. On this assumption we exercise varieties of discrimination, through which we effectively, if often unthinkingly, reduce his life chances. We construct a stigma-theory, an ideology to explain his inferiority and account for the danger he represents, sometimes rationalizing an animosity based on other differences such as those of social class. (Goffman, 1963:5)

Goffman (1963) classifies social stigmas into three major categories. "Tribal identities" refer to stigmas involving nationality, ethnicity, race, and religion. "Abominations of the body" include physical deformities such as disabilities, physical unattractiveness, and diseases (HIV-AIDS). The final type involves stigmatizing "blemishes of individual character" such as mental disorder, criminality, drug addiction, homosexuality, and impoverishment. Various groups in society are singled out by the majority and defined as different and abnormal, justifying their discrimination against them as "inferiors." These "others" are not only different, they are also deficient. Thus, their identity is negatively evaluated and stereotyped—i.e., stigmatized.

THE STIGMATIZING OF THE IMPOVERISHED

According to a survey conducted in early 2001, about half of Americans believe that poverty is a combination of biological and cultural factors (National Public Radio, 2001). In effect, many Americans believe that poverty is a self-inflicted condition resulting from personal factors such as a lack of effort and/or ability (Chafel, 1997). The poor, in this view, are not only lazy but they are dependent on government welfare—characteristics that Americans despise. Young, poor women are especially stereotyped, stigmatized, and demonized. They are reviled for having children out-of-wedlock (a "culture of illegitimacy"), for transmitting negative values, and their single-parent family structure is blamed for fostering violence, crime, school failure, and for passing their poverty on to the next generation—all traits fitting with the culture of poverty (Sidel, 1996:167).

> Poor, single mothers . . . are being portrayed as the ultimate outsiders—marginalized as nonworkers in a society that claims belief in the work ethic, marginalized as single parents in a society that holds the two-parent, heterosexual family as the desired norm, and marginalized as poor people in a society that worships success and material rewards. (Sidel, 1996:6–7)

THE CONSEQUENCES OF STIGMATIZING THE IMPOVERISHED

Foremost, when most of society rejects the poor, believing that they are not only different but that they are inferior, or in Goffman's words, "not quite human," many of the poor internalize these negative stereotypes, thus feeling shame, humiliation, and disgrace for who they are. In effect, they accept society's definition and blame themselves for their failure, resulting in a self-fulfilling prophecy.

There are several other related consequences of demonizing the poor, especially poor mothers. The poor are viewed as deserving of their fate because it is their fault. Thus, the poor are seen as undeserving of government programs such as food stamps, housing subsidies, and Head Start for their children. As David Boaz, executive vice-president of the Cato Institute, a libertarian organization, put it: "We've made it possible for a teenage girl to survive with no husband and no job. . . . If we had more stigma and lower benefits, might we end up with 100,000 bastards every year rather than a million children born to alternative families?" (Sidel, 1996:6). This type of logic justified the 1996 welfare legislation that dismantled AFDC, which is discussed in Part V of this book. This "solution" to the problem of poverty assumed the reasons for poverty were within the poor, not in the structure of society. In this way, society is absolved of blame, and solutions are aimed at changing poor people rather than changing society. Finally, the stereotyping and stigmatizing of the poor (or any other minority group), assumes that the poor are a homogeneous group, when they are actually very heterogeneous, differing widely in personal characteristics and circumstances.

NOTES AND SUGGESTIONS FOR FURTHER READING

Albelda, Randy, and Ann Withorn (Eds.) (2002). *Lost Ground: Welfare Reform, Poverty, and Beyond.* Cambridge, MA: South End Press.

Bray, Rosemary L. (1998). *Unafraid of the Dark.* New York: Random House.

Brunious, Loretta J. (1998). *How Disadvantaged Adolescents Socially Construct Reality: Do You Hear What I Hear?* New York: Garland.

Chafel, Judith A. (1997). "Societal Images of Poverty." *Youth and Society* 28 (June):432–463.

Coles, Robert, Randy Testa, and Michael Coles (Eds.) (2001). *Growing Up Poor: A Literary Anthology.* New York: The New Press.

Fair, Bryan K. (1997). *Notes of a Racial Caste Baby: Color Blindness and the End of Affirmative Action.* New York: New York University Press.

Goffman, Erving (1963). *Stigma: Notes on the Management of Spoiled Identity.* Englewood Cliffs, NJ: Prentice-Hall.

Harrington, Michael (1963). *The Other America: Poverty in the United States.* Baltimore: Penguin Books.

Hartman, Chester W., Bill Bradley, and Julian Bond (1997). *Double Exposure: Poverty and Race in America.* New York: M. E. Sharpe.

Heatherton, Todd F., Robert E. Kleck, Michelle R. Hebl, and Jay G. Hull (Eds.) (2000). *The Social Psychology of Stigma.* New York: The Guilford Press.

hooks, bell (2000). *Where We Stand: Class Matters.* New York: Routledge.

Katz, Jane (Ed.) (1995). *Messengers of the Wind: Native American Women Tell Their Stories.* New York: Ballantine Books.

National Public Radio (2001). "Poverty in America." Retrieved from http://search1.npr.org/search97cgi/

Quadagno, Jill (1994). *The Color of Welfare: How Racism Undermined the War on Poverty.* New York: Oxford University Press.

Sennett, Richard, and Jonathan Cobb (1973). *The Hidden Injuries of Class.* New York: Random House Vintage Books.

Waxman, Chaim I. (1977). *The Stigma of Poverty: A Critque of Poverty Theories and Policies.* New York: Pergamon Press.

Wray, Matt, and Annalee Newitz (Eds.) (1997). *White Trash: Race and Class in America.* New York: Routledge.

Zuccino, David (1997). *Myth of the Welfare Queen.* New York: Scribner's.

The Dynamics of Welfare Stigma

ROBIN ROGERS-DILLON

In this selection, Assistant Professor of Sociology at Queens College Robin Rogers-Dillon interviews 10 divorced/separated women who use public assistance. They are White, Latina, and African American, and they came from different social class backgrounds before their divorce/separation. As you read this selection, consider the following questions: What is the difference between those recipients who came from middle-class families and those who came from families that had received public assistance at some time? What does this difference say about the culture of poverty argument (regarding the cyclical nature of poverty)? What were some of the strategies women used to avoid the stigma of food stamps? Can you think of a possible alternative to food stamps, something that could help lessen the stigma of using them?

THE EXPERIENCE OF WELFARE STIGMA

The women in this study described going on to welfare in terms of necessity. The stigma of receiving welfare was almost meaningless in the face of pressing needs for food, shelter, and other goods. Most of the respondents reported that going on to welfare was not a difficult decision to make, with no job or child support, they had no other options.

> *It is instinctive. You don't have to think about there is a crumb and I'm hungry, go get it. It's survival. You do what you have to do. It is demeaning. I hate it. (Diane, white, poor during marriage)*

> *No other options. No more money could I get, (. . .) no more things could I sell. I didn't have anything left to sell, so it is either welfare or no fare, you know? (Erica, African American, middle class during marriage)*

Though the stigma of welfare was not a deterrent to applying for assistance, respondents were very aware of the stereotypes of welfare recipients. They saw

SOURCE: Robin Rogers-Dillon, "The Dynamics of Welfare Stigma," *Readings in Sociology,* 3rd ed., Garth Massey (Ed.) (New York: W. W. Norton, 2000), pp. 255–263. By permission of the author.

the public's image of most welfare recipients as one of lazy, baby-making women living off of other people's labor.

> Well [people think] that's another welfare case, you know. She's lazy. Basically that's what I hear. I hear a lot that you know, they're lazy, they don't wanna do nothing and all this kind of stuff, (. . .) A lot of men have like a stigma about women being on DPA. And a lot of them think that, you know, you lazy and you not trying to do better, all that kind of stuff. Then [I] feel a lot of times I wouldn't even let them know. (Jenny, African American, working class during marriage)

> I mean when you're on welfare you really supposed to be looking for a man, you know? It's like come and take me. (. . .) Well, [people think] you're staying home all day making more babies. (Erica, African American, middle class during marriage)

Kim, the 18-year-old daughter of a respondent, spoke about her own feelings towards public assistance recipients, before her mother became one:

> I think if someone had said they were on welfare to me, my immediate reaction would have been to the people, they are lazy and they are unmotivated and they are not as smart and they didn't get a good education and they are bleeding the government and they are bleeding us. (Kim, white, formerly middle class)

Kim's description illustrates how powerfully negative the image of welfare recipients can be.

Many of the respondents felt the need to defend themselves against unflattering assumptions that they felt others made about them based on their status as welfare recipients. For example, Erica, who only has one child, feels that by virtue of being on welfare she must defend herself against accusations that women on welfare have many children. She feels that she must distance herself from this image of the "welfare mother" even though it does not accurately reflect her situation.

> To be honest, I'm going to tell you, frankly as far as men feel about it, men feel women on welfare have a lot of children. They are promiscuous. As far as being in the African American community, it's like if you have a lot of children, forget it. Because it's like everybody is looking for a dad. And I'm not looking for a damn daddy. (Erica, African American, middle class during marriage)

The stereotype of the "welfare mother" exists apart from the actual situations of the women in this study and each of the women had to face this stereotype, but they did so in different contexts. The meaning of welfare was different for each woman, and it was shaped by her life history. For example, for Lynn, a young woman who had only a brief marriage and knew a number of other women on public assistance, welfare held little symbolic meaning, and it gave her the opportunity to go back to school.

> You know, I was like I was supposed to get this degree. . . . Not that I don't wanna get off [welfare] and be independent. (Lynn, African American, poor during marriage)

In contrast, for Lisa, a middle-aged woman who had never been poor before her divorce, food stamps symbolized her fall from the middle class and were imbued with the pain of having lost her marriage, middle class standing and the future for which she had worked for twenty years. Lisa describes trying to make sense of her unexpected entrance into the welfare system in the following way:

> I think it's [her feelings of humiliation over receiving welfare] probably a reaction to where I am now, which is not at all where I expected to be. It's interesting, like the first time I went in there, I was talking to the first in-take person, I just broke down and sobbed. I said I can't believe I'm here. I can't believe it. And she said to me. . . . She was actually very nice about it. She said to me, "Lisa, you don't understand." She said, "More and more over the last five years we've had more women who were wives or ex-wives of doctors and lawyers and very successful business-men come in and say those exact words." You just cannot believe that, I guess, that your life has taken such a major turn. (Lisa, white, middle class during marriage)

Being on welfare simply does not make sense to Lisa. Similarly, Erica, an African American woman who had surpassed her parents' economic position during her marriage, now bitterly compares her position to theirs:

> . . . and it was like my parents are so successful and not having any damn problems and that was a big thing, that it was just me. It was a total admission of failure, you know? (Erica, African American, middle class during marriage)

Another formerly middle class woman, Amy, who recently separated from her husband, explained to me how welfare benefits should be used. In the course of her explanation, it became evident that Amy was struggling to come to terms with her new economic position. Amy sounded confident and assertive as she discussed what welfare recipients should do in the abstract, but toward the end of her statement Amy's focus shifted to her own situation and her voice trailed off until it was almost inaudible:

> I think that anyone who is eligible [for welfare benefits] should be able to receive it if they chose to, but I don't think they—that you should look at that [welfare] as something that you are always going to get. You should always look to the future and see that you've got to get off it. This is just, for me this is just kind of a stopgap thing to get me through where I can afford . . . something. . . . I don't know what . . . just to manage. (Amy, white, middle class during marriage)

The fall from the middle class created tremendous confusion and anxiety for Linda, Erica and Amy. Respondents who came from families that had received public assistance at some time, on the other hand, did not experience the same kind of confusion. This is not to say that being on welfare was necessarily any easier, or even more acceptable, for them. For example, Diane, who had a very difficult relationship with her mother, a welfare recipient herself, saw receiving welfare as being a part of a painful legacy:

> She [her mother] probably expected me to continue the legacy of raising children on welfare and doing nothing with my life. If I did anything other than that she would probably be very disappointed with herself. (Diane, white, poor during marriage)

In contrast, Sally, whose mother had also been on welfare, was able to use her mother's experiences, and those of other family members who had received welfare, to legitimate her own use of welfare:

> Public assistance is not a taboo. I mean my mother was on it when she needed to be, when she was separated from my father and she had lost her two businesses she went on public assistance.

She went to college when she was on public assistance and once she got a job she got off of it. So, that's the way I saw it. You use it until, you know, you have an income. (Sally, Latina, poor during marriage)

As the last two examples illustrate, former class status, while important, did not define how respondents experienced being on welfare. Rather, a combination of the respondent's social locations and personal histories seem to have shaped their feelings about being on welfare. The specific ways in which class, race and personal histories influenced the respondents' construction of personal identity is beyond the scope of this paper. The findings in this study, however, do suggest that the effects of personal background on welfare recipients' experiences of stigma and construction of personal identities may be fertile ground for further research.*

FOOD STAMPS AND STIGMA MANAGEMENT

Food stamps are highly visible stigma symbols, they instantly, and very publicly, reveal the user's economic position and status as a welfare recipient. Even respondents who stated that receiving welfare was nothing to be ashamed of bristled over having their status as public assistance recipients revealed in the course of their daily activities and without their consent. The women often talked about having lost their privacy and about being frustrated that other people "know their business." For example, Diane explained why she dislikes the objects that mark her as a welfare recipient:

Food stamps and that little stupid blue health pass card they give you is just another way of labeling you. Your status is reduced now. You're not who you walked in as because now they see that you're less than in their mind, you're a welfare recipient. (Diane, white, poor during marriage)

Being labeled as a welfare recipient is extremely painful for Diane, and she generally tries to keep her status as a welfare recipient a secret. But this is not always possible, as the following story illustrates.

When I moved here, I figured a new neighborhood, nobody knows my business. . . . The building I moved up out [of] in West Philly, everybody was on welfare. . . . [I]t was that kind of building. Everybody had food stamps and money problems and the whole bit. When I moved here I thought, oh good, this . . . I mean there's a lot of poor people but they don't know my business. They don't know me and I can come in with some anonymity and it didn't work, because my landlord told everybody, oh the girl that's moving in she's on Section 8. He lives six houses down. So everybody knew my business and I felt so like . . . With my mask and I couldn't even put it on, you know? (Diane, white, poor during marriage)

It is particularly hard for Diane to avoid being revealed as a welfare recipient when she uses food stamps:

*See David Snow and Leon Anderson's *Down on Their Luck* (1993), especially chapter 7, for a discussion of some of the ways homeless street people construct and negotiate their personal identities in light of their stigmatized social identities.

One day I was in the store and the lady needed change. You have to pay five. . . . There's five, tens and ones. And she said, I need change. I need some ones. And the girl several registers down said, I just gave you ones. And she said, For food stamps! I couldn't crawl small enough and close enough to the ground I felt so bad. (Diane, white, poor during marriage)

Many of the respondents described feeling awkward using food stamps in front of particular people or groups of people. For example, Gina, who was raised in a working class family, talked about how she feels more hesitant to use food stamps in white neighborhoods. In her description, the social audience and situation in grocery stores outside of the inner city create a stigma that she does not feel when she shops in inner city neighborhoods:

Sometime I go and I don't shop in, say the inner city neighborhoods, my girlfriend and I we'll get in her car and we'll drive out to say a white neighborhood to go shopping—Super Fresh, or you know things like that and sometimes you are afraid, you don't want other people to see you pulling out food stamps. (Gina, African American, poor during marriage)

Another respondent, Lisa, avoids being seen by people who know her by shopping in a grocery store outside of her neighborhood:

When I know I have to go shopping now I go to another store altogether. . . . [Normally] I would go to the Acme here. I've been going there for 16 years. Most of the people, the checkers, know me. Most of them have seen my kids grow up. Whereas if I go to the other one they don't know me and I am just kind of a face in the crowd. I don't know how to put this equation together. If you know what I mean. And I don't know whether it's something I perceive or if it's wished that when I pay with food stamps it's almost like I'm a nonentity. But I don't know if they're really reacting to me that way or if I choose to. . . . They sit there looking at me that way. (Lisa, white, middle class during marriage)

Several of the women in this study were also concerned with how their children managed their use of food stamps. Pam, a young woman who had been raised in a working class family and was homeless for a time after escaping an extremely violent marriage, explains that she tries to teach her son to be discreet when he uses food stamps:

My oldest son, with the food stamps, he thinks it's like hey! And I told him, this is nothing you wanna, he wants to get food stamps and go to the corner store and buy some chips, a bag of chips and a soda. And I tell him no, it's not a thing like that. . . . It is like our family secret. . . . They can remember when we was in the shelter and so I tell them this is just like that. We just have to go through, but it's not something we want to make flyers and put out and make everybody know. (Pam, African American, poor during marriage)

In contrast, Jenny, who is also from a working class background, has tried to teach her daughter not to feel awkward about using food stamps:

So I learned in fact she [her daughter] felt funny about it especially when I would send her to the store with food stamps or whatever. You know, I didn't know it but she told me she was ashamed to use them. I thought the kid was just being lazy about going to the store. . . . But when she found out some kind of way that some of her friends were on DPA—so like now she is starting to understand that we're not the only ones in this boat, you know. (Jenny, African American, working class during marriage)

Though Pam and Jenny view food stamps differently, they have both had to teach their children how to manage food stamps and the information that food stamps convey.

Food stamps convey a degraded social status, and yet they also provide essential goods. Respondents disliked the social meaning of food stamps, but most also found food stamps helpful for budgeting and getting through the month. When I asked the women if they thought that food stamps should be replaced with cash, almost all said no. For the respondents, balancing the practical advantages of food stamps with potentially negative social consequences was a central task.

The Avoidance Strategy

Because of their power to discredit, almost all of the women in this study could think of times when they had chosen not to use food stamps. Using cash rather than food stamps was a common strategy used by respondents to avoid being labeled as welfare recipients. For example, Pam reported:

> One time I was with a friend, it was as guy, not my boyfriend but it was a friend and we was in the Acme and I felt so bad afterward because I only had a couple of dollars, you know green dollars, but I felt the way that I didn't want him to know that I was receiving public assistance. (Pam, African American, poor during marriage)

Similarly, Sally, a young woman whose mother had also received welfare, reported that she had chosen not to use food stamps when she recognized a person in the grocery store:

> I think someone was in line that was a parent of my son's [friend] . . . something like that, and I don't like them knowing my business. (Sally, Latina, poor during marriage)

Diane chose not to use food stamps to preserve an image of herself in front of two men that she did not even know:

> And then one time I was shopping and there were two good looking, really good looking guys—a couple of years ago when I was really thin. And they were making little comments about me. And I was going on a picnic with my then best friend Judy, who was the one on welfare, single parent and section 8 too. And I wouldn't pay with my food stamps. I paid in cash because I didn't want them to get a different idea of me. And she got on my case all the way to the car, all the way to the park. She said, that was so stupid. Why would you do that? I said, Judy, everybody was looking at me. They noticed me and I didn't want them to think any less of me, so, you know, I paid cash instead of stamps. Now, I know I'm going to suffer at the end of the month for doing that, but I did it. (Diane, white, poor during marriage)

Terri, who lives in an area where food stamps are common, often avoids being publicly discredited altogether by sending her boyfriend to the grocery store with her food stamps rather than going herself.

> I don't go to the store. I send my boyfriend. I call him and he says "I don't care [about using food stamps], I'll go." Then he goes to the store. (Terri, Latina, poor during marriage)

Using food stamps in the grocery store brought the women's status as welfare recipients into sharp focus. In front of specific social audiences, such as boyfriends, neighbors, et cetera, being labeled as a welfare recipient was particularly trouble-some to the respondents. In order to avoid being discredited in these situations, respondents employed several strategies: using cash rather than food stamps, shopping in different neighborhoods, and sending someone else to the grocery store. These strategies, especially using cash rather than food stamps, are difficult to sustain. The respondents had to choose carefully in which situations being dis-credited outweighed the relative hardships of an avoidance strategy. The calcula-tions made by respondents highlights the dynamic nature of welfare stigma; if welfare stigma were static, then there would be no need to employ strategies that can only be used sporadically.

The Recasting Strategy

Recasting welfare in a more positive light was another strategy used by respon-dents to manage welfare stigma. Though they could not eliminate the negative public images of welfare recipients, respondents could, and did, recast welfare in a more positive light for themselves. Knowing that other people used or accepted food stamps helped some of the respondents to view their own use of food stamps more positively. In a striking example of recasting welfare, Lynn "discovered" (incorrectly) that food stamps were legal tender outside of the United States:

> And as I found out from my sister, she is really intelligent. She's been around and everything. She told me she's taken her food stamps outside the United States and used them because you can. . . . She said they are legal tender just like money. I was shocked, you know. She was like with somebody important. And she went to the store and pulled out food stamps. I was like, oh my god. I was like, you go girl. I didn't know that. . . . It's just to know that . . . to know that they're legal tender elsewhere. (Lynn, African American, poor during marriage)

Hearing that her sister was able to use food stamps outside of the United States helped Lynn to view food stamps as being legitimate, "just like money" in every way. Similarly, seeing her sister use food stamps in front of "someone important" helped Lynn to be less ashamed about using food stamps herself. In a similar story, Jenny, an African American respondent, explained that seeing white people use food stamps helped her to view food stamps as being legitimate and nothing to be embarrassed about:

> I was pretty much embarrassed. . . . Then I seen some of the white people around here with them, I said, "oh well that's it." So now it didn't bother me. (Jenny, African American, working class during marriage)

Sally, a young Latina woman, was able to construct a positive image of welfare recipients based on her own experiences:

> The only images [of welfare recipients] I had were of my mother or my family members and I knew that they were on the system because they needed to be on the system. (Sally, Latina, poor during marriage)

The positive image of welfare recipients that Sally gained from her family helped her to legitimate being on welfare herself.

Lisa and Erica, two formerly middle class respondents, framed their being on welfare as a consequence of larger social forces. Lisa was able to depersonalize and manage the stigma of welfare by seeing her economic decline as being, in part, a result of an economic recession.

> There's so many people in unemployment and then on the welfare when unemployment runs out. Many of them have no alternative but to go on welfare whether it's food stamps or, you know, total assistance. And again that's not through any fault of their own. And I don't know what the proportions are, but my guess is there's probably a whole lot bigger numbers of people on some form of public assistance now as a direct result. I mean, I call it a depression. (Lisa, white, middle class during marriage)

Lisa also viewed being on welfare as the result of her divorce and of unjust divorce laws:

> I think with the divorce rate coming up, a lot of women . . . the divorce laws totally inadequate, totally inadequate. Leaves a lot of women who otherwise would still be in whatever marriage. Leaves them out on a limb because the laws aren't there to protect their interests and their children's interest. (Lisa, white, middle class during marriage)

Erica viewed her entrance onto welfare as the combined result of her divorce, economic hard times and racism. During her marriage Erica had achieved a middle class household income of around $40,000. After her husband left, Erica struggled financially but survived. She supported herself and her son for several years before she lost her job when the hospital at which she worked was sold:

> I'm going to be honest and tell you. Being African American, there's a lot of us who are out of work and there is a lot of us who are. . . . If we're getting the assistance ourselves [or] we know somebody who say getting assistance and it is not the big embarrassment that it might be, other people, you know. And you're the last hired, first fired. You tend to have to find stopgap measures. (Erica, African American, middle class during marriage)

One interesting aspect of the recasting strategy is that there seemed to be a class pattern to it. Formerly working and lower class respondents, such as Lynn, Sally, and Jenny, tended to recast welfare itself in a positive light, seeing it as a legitimate form of income. In contrast, formerly middle class respondents, such as Lynn and Erica, emphasized the larger social forces, such as economic hard times combined with racial and gender inequality, that made their receipt of welfare inevitable. Seeing their being on welfare as the inevitable outcome of social inequality, the middle class women were able to deflect some of the stigma of welfare. In both of these strategies, the respondents redefined the meaning of their being on welfare in a more positive light.

Sunset Trailer Park

ALLAN BÉRUBÉ WITH FLORENCE BÉRUBÉ

Many have heard the term "trailer trash" and the stereotypes that go along with that term. On the Internet, one can find thousands of websites and even items for sale under the term "trailer trash." Thinking sociologically, where do these stereotypes come from, and how do they affect the people that they supposedly "describe"? In this essay, Allan Bérubé talks with his mother about growing up as part of a white, working-class family in the Sunset Trailer Park in Bayonne, New Jersey. In his essay, Bérubé talks about the two conflicting stereotypes of trailer park life in the popular culture of the 1950s. Do these same stereotypes exist today? What type of social hierarchy existed within the park? Do these hierarchies exist in all types of neighborhoods? Do people "naturally" rank each other, regardless of social class? What are the inevitable effects of such hierarchies?

"I cried," my mother tells me, "when we first drove into that trailer park and I saw where we were going to live." Recently, in long-distance phone calls, my mother—Florence Bérubé—and I have been digging up memories, piecing together our own personal and family histories. Trailer parks come up a lot.

During the year when I was born—1946—the booming, postwar "trailer coach" industry actively promoted house trailers in magazine ads like this one from the *Saturday Evening Post*:

Trailer Coaches Relieve Small-Home Shortage Throughout the House-Hungry Nation

Reports from towns and cities all over the United States show that modern, comfortable trailer coaches—economical and efficient beyond even the dreams of a few years ago—are playing a major part in easing the need for small-family dwellings. Returning veterans (as students or workers), newlyweds, and all others who are not ready for—or can't locate—permanent housing, find in the modern trailer coach a completely furnished (and amazingly comfortable) home that offers the privacy and efficiency of an apartment coupled with the mobility of an automobile.

SOURCE: Allan Bérubé with Florence Bérubé, "Sunset Trailer Park," in *White Trash*, Matt Wray and Annalee Nevitz (Eds.) (New York: Routledge, 1997), pp. 15–20. Reproduced by permission of Routledge, Inc., part of the Taylor and Francis Group.

When I was seven, my parents, with two young children in tow, moved us all into a house trailer, hoping to find the comfort, privacy, and efficiency that the "trailer coach" industry had promised. But real life, as we soon discovered, did not imitate the worlds we learned to desire from magazine ads.

Dad discovered "Sunset Trailer Park" on his own and rented a space for us there before Mom was able to see it. On our moving day in January 1954, we all climbed into our '48 Chevy and followed a rented truck as it slowly pulled our house trailer from the "Sunnyside Trailer Park" in Shelton, Connecticut, where we lived for a few months, into New York State and across Manhattan, over the George Washington Bridge into New Jersey, through the garbage incinerator land-scape and stinky air of Secaucus—not a good sign—then finally into the Sunset Trailer Park in Bayonne.

A blue-collar town surrounded by Jersey City, Elizabeth and Staten Island, Bayonne was known for its oil refineries, tanker piers and Navy yard. It was a small, stable, predominantly Catholic city of working-class and military families, mostly white with a small population of African Americans. When we moved there, Bayonne was already the butt of jokes about "armpits" of the industrial Northeast. Even the characters on the TV sitcom *The Honeymooners*, living in their blue-collar world in Brooklyn, could get an easy laugh by referring to Bayonne. "Ralph," Alice Kramden says to her husband in one episode, "you losing a pound is like Bayonne losing a mosquito." My mom was from Brooklyn, too. A Bayonne trailer park was not where she wanted to live or raise her children.

Along with so many other white working-class families living in fifties trailer parks, my parents believed that they were just passing through. They were headed toward a *Better Homes and Gardens* suburban world that would be theirs if they worked hard enough. We moved to Bayonne to be closer to Manhattan, where Dad was employed as a cameraman for NBC. He and his fellow TV crewmen enjoyed the security of unionized, wage-labor jobs in this newly expanding media indus-try. But they didn't get the income that people imagined went with the status of TV jobs. Dad had to work overtime nights and on weekends to make ends meet. His dream was to own his own house and start his own business, then put us kids through school so we would be better off and not have to struggle so much to get by. My parents were using the cheapness of trailer park life as a stepping-stone toward making that dream real.

As Dad's job and commuting took over his life, the trailer park took over ours. We lived in our trailer from the summer of 1953 through December 1957, most of my grade school years. And so I grew up a trailer park kid.

Sunset Trailer Park seemed to be on the edge of everything. Bayonne itself is a kind of land's end. It's a peninsula that ends at New York Bay, Kill Van Kull and Newark Bay—polluted bodies of water that all drain into the Atlantic Ocean. You reached our trailer park by going west to the very end of 24th Street, then past the last house into a driveway where the trailer lots began. If you followed the drive-way to its end, you'd stop right at the waterfront. The last trailer lots were built on top of a seawall secured by pilings. Standing there and looking out over New-ark Bay, you'd see tugboats hauling barges over the oil-slicked water, oil tankers and freighters carrying their cargoes, and planes (no jets yet) flying in and out of Newark Airport. On hot summer nights the steady din of planes, boats, trucks and freight trains filled the air. So did the fumes they exhaled, which, when mixed with the incinerator smoke and oil refinery gasses, formed a foul atmospheric concoction that became world-famous for its unforgettable stench.

The ground at the seawall could barely be called solid earth. The owner of the trailer park occasionally bought an old barge, then hired a tugboat to haul it right up to the park's outer edge, sank it with dump-truck loads of landfill, paved it over with asphalt, painted white lines on it and voila!—several new trailer lots were available for rent. Sometimes the ground beneath these new lots would sink, so the trailers would have to be moved way until the sinkholes were filled in. Trailers parked on lots built over rotten barges along the waterfront—this was life on a geographic edge.

It was life on a social edge, too—a borderland where respectable and "trashy" got confused.

"Did you ever experience other people looking down on us because we lived in a trailer park?" I ask my mom.

"Never," she tells me.

"But who were your friends?"

"They all lived in the trailer park."

"What about the neighbors who lived in houses up the street?"

"Oh, they didn't like us at all," she says. "They thought people who lived in trailers were all low-life and trash. They didn't really associate with us."

In the 1950s, trailer parks were crossroads where the paths of poor, working-class and lower-middle-class white migrants intersected as we temporarily occupied the same racially segregated space—a kind of residential parking lot—on our way somewhere else. Class tensions—often hidden—structured our daily lives as we tried to position ourselves as far as we could from the bottom. White working-class families who owned or lived in houses could raise their own class standing within whiteness by showing how they were better off than the white residents of trailer parks. We often responded to them by displaying our own respectability and distancing ourselves from those trailer park residents who were more "lower-class" than we were. If we failed and fell to the bottom, we were in danger of also losing, in the eyes of other white people, our own claims to the racial privileges that came with being accepted as white Americans.

In our attempt to scramble "up" into the middle class, we had at our disposal two conflicting stereotypes of trailer park life that in the 1950s circulated through popular culture. The respectable stereotype portrayed residents of house trailers as white World War II veterans, many of them attending college on GI loans, who lived with their young families near campuses during the postwar housing shortage. In the following decades, this image expanded to include the predominantly white retirement communities located in Florida and the Southwest. In these places, trailers were renamed "mobile" or "manufactured" homes. When parked together, they formed private worlds where white newlyweds, nuclear families and retirees lived in clean, safe, managed communities. You can catch a glimpse of this world in the 1954 Hollywood film *The Long, Long Trailer,* in which Lucille Ball and Desi Arnaz spend their slapstick honeymoon hauling a house trailer cross country and end up in a respectable trailer park. (The fact that Arnaz is Cuban-American doesn't seriously disrupt the whiteness of their Technicolor world—he's assimilated as a generically "Spanish" entertainer, an ethnic individual who has no connection with his Cuban American family or community).

A conflicting stereotype portrayed trailer parks as trashy slums for white transients—single men drifting from job to job, mothers on welfare, children with no adult supervision. Their inhabitants supposedly engaged in prostitution and extramarital sex, drank a lot, used drugs, and were the perpetrators or victims of domestic violence. With this image in mind, cities and suburbs passed zoning laws restricting trailer parks to the "other side of the tracks" or banned them altogether. In the fifties, you could see this "white trash" image in B-movies and on the covers of pulp magazines and paperback books. The front cover of one "trash" paperback, "Trailer Park Woman," proclaims that it's "A bold, savage novel of life and love in the trailer camps on the edge of town." The back cover, subtitled "Temptation Wheels," explains why trailers are the theme of this book.

> Today nearly one couple in ten lives in a mobile home—one of those trailers you see bunched up in cozy camps near every sizable town. Some critics argue that in such surroundings love tends to become casual. Feverish affairs take place virtually right out in the open. Social codes take strange and shocking twists . . . 'Trailer Tramp' was what they called Ann Mitchell—for she symbolized the twisted morality of the trailer camps . . . this book shocks not by its portrayal of her degradation—rather, by boldly bringing to light the conditions typical of trailer life.

This image has been kept alive as parody in John Waters' independent films, as reality in Hollywood films such as *Lethal Weapon, The Client* and *My Own Private Idaho,* and as retro-fifties camp in contemporary postcards, posters, t-shirts and refrigerator magnets.

I imagine that some fifties trailer parks did fit this trashy stereotype. But Sunset Trailer Park in Bayonne was respectable—at least to those of us who lived there. Within that respectability, however, we had our own social hierarchy. Even today, trying to position ourselves into it is difficult. "You can't say we were rich," as my mom tries to explain, "but you can't say we were at the bottom, either." What confused things even more were the many standards by which our ranking could be measured—trailer size and model, lot size and location, how you kept up your yard, type of car, jobs and occupations, income, number of kids, whether mothers worked as homemakers or outside the home for wages. Establishing where you were on the trailer park's social ladder depended on where you were standing and which direction you were looking at any given time.

To some outsiders, our trailer park did seem low-class. Our neighbors up the street looked down on us because they lived in two- or three-family houses with yards in front and back. Our trailers were small, as were our lots, some right on the stinky bay. The people in houses were stable; we were transients. And they used to complain that we didn't pay property taxes on our trailers, but still sent our kids to their public schools.

On our side, we identified as "homeowners" too (if you ignored the fact that we rented our lots) while some people up the street were renters. We did pay taxes, if only through our rent checks. And we shared with them our assumed privileges of whiteness—theirs mostly Italian, Irish, and Polish Catholic, ours a more varied mix that included Protestants. The trailer park owner didn't rent to Black families, so we were granted the additional status of having our whiteness protected on his private property.

The owner did rent to one Chinese American family, the Wongs (not their real name), who ran a Chinese restaurant. Like Desi Arnaz, the presence of only one Chinese family didn't seriously disrupt the dominant whiteness of our trailer park. They became our close friends as we discovered that we were almost parallel families—both had the same number of children and Mrs. Wong and my mother shared the same first name. But there were significant differences. Mom tells me that the Wongs had no trouble as Asian-Americans in the trailer park, only when they went out to buy a house. "You don't realize how discriminatory they are in this area," Mrs. Wong told my mother one day over tea. "The real estate agents find a place for us, but the sellers back out when they see who we are." Our trailer park may have been one of the few places that accepted them in Bayonne. They fit in with us because they, unlike a poorer family might have been, were considered "respectable." With their large trailer and their own small business, they represented to my father the success he himself hoped to achieve someday.

While outsiders looked down on us as trailer park transients, we had our own internal social divisions. As residents we did share the same laundry room, recreation hall, address and sandbox. But the owner segregated us into two sections of his property: Left courtyard for families with children, right courtyard for adults, mostly newlyweds or retired couples. In the middle were a few extra spaces where tourists parked their vacation trailers overnight. Kids were not allowed to play in the adult section. It had bigger lots and was surrounded by a fence, so it had an exclusive air about it.

The family section was wilder, noisier and more crowded because every trailer had kids. It was hard to keep track of us, especially during summer vacation. Without having to draw on those who lived in the houses, we organized large group games—like Red Rover and bicycle circus shows—on the common asphalt driveway. Our activities even lured some kids away from the houses into the trailer park, tempting them to defy their parents' disdain for us.

We defended ourselves from outsiders' stereotypes of us as low-life and weird by increasing our own investment in respectability. Trashy white people lived somewhere else—probably in other trailer parks. We could criticize and look down on them, yet without them we would have been the white people on the bottom. "Respectable" meant identifying not with them, but with people just like us or better than us, especially families who owned real houses in the suburbs.

My mom still portrays our lives in Bayonne as solidly middle-class. I'm intrigued by how she constructed that identity out of a trailer park enclave confined to the polluted waterfront area of an industrial blue-collar town.

"Who were your friends?" I ask her.

"We chose them from the people we felt the most comfortable with," she explains. These were couples in which the woman was usually a homemaker and the man was an accountant, serviceman or salesman—all lower-middle-class, if categorized only by occupation. As friends, these couples hung out together in the recreation hall for birthday, Christmas and Halloween costume parties. The women visited each other every day, shared the pies and cakes they baked, went shopping together and helped each other with housework and baby-sitting.

"There was one woman up the street," my mom adds, "who we were friends with. She associated with us even though she lived in a house."

"Who didn't you feel comfortable with?" I ask her.

"Couples who did a lot of drinking. People who had messy trailers and didn't keep up their yards. People who let their babies run around barefoot in dirty diapers. But there were very few people like that in our trailer park." They were also the boys who swam in the polluted brine of Newark Bay, and the people who trapped crabs in the same waters and actually ate their catch.

When we first entered the social world of Sunset Trailer Park, our family found ways to fit in and even "move up" a little. Physical location was important. Our trailer was first parked in a middle lot. We then moved up by renting the "top space"—as it was called—when it became available. It was closest to the houses and furthest from the bay. Behind it was a vacant housing lot, which belonged to the trailer park owner and separated his park from the houses on the street—a kind of "no-man's-land." The owner gave us permission to take over a piece of this garbage dump and turn it into a garden. My dad fenced it in and my mom planted grass and flowers which we kids weeded. Every year the owner gave out prizes—usually a savings bond—for the best-looking "yards." We won the prize several times.

Yet the privilege of having this extra yard had limits. With other trailer park kids we'd stage plays and performances there for our parents—it was our makeshift, outdoor summer stock theater. But we made so much noise that we drove the woman in the house that overlooked it crazy. At first she just yelled "Shut up!" at us from her second-story window. Then she went directly to the owner, who prohibited the loudest, most unruly kids from playing with us. After a while we learned to keep our own voices down and stopped our shows so we, too, wouldn't be banned from playing in our own yard.

My mom made a little extra money—$25 a month—and gained a bit more social status by working for the owner as the manager of his trailer park. She collected rent checks from each tenant, handled complaints and made change for the milk machine, washers and dryers. "No one ever had trouble paying their rent," Mom tells me, adding more evidence to prove the respectability of our trailer park's residents.

Our family also gained some prestige because my dad "worked in TV" as a pioneer in this exciting new field. Once in a while he got tickets for our neighbors to appear as contestants on the TV game show *Truth or Consequences*, a sadistic spectacle that forced couples to perform humiliating stunts if they couldn't give correct answers to trick questions. Our neighbors joined other trailer park contestants who in the fifties appeared on game shows like *Beat the Clock*, *Name That Tune*, *You Bet Your Life* and especially *Queen for a Day*. The whole trailer park was glued to our TV set on nights when our neighbors were on. We rooted for them to win as they became celebrities right before our eyes. Even the putdown "Bayonne jokes" we heard from Groucho Marx, Ralph Kramden and other TV comics acknowledged that our town and its residents had at least some status on the nation's cultural map.

My dad wasn't the only trailer park resident who gained a little prestige from celebrity. There was a musician who played the clarinet in the NBC orchestra. There was a circus performer who claimed he was the only man in the world who could juggle nine balls at once. He put on a special show for us kids in the recreation hall to prove it. There was a former swimming champion who lived in a trailer parked near the water. Although he was recovering from pneumonia, he jumped into Newark Bay to rescue little Jimmy who'd fallen off the seawall and was drowning. He was our hero. And there was an elderly couple who shared a tiny Airstream with 24 Chihuahua dogs—the kind pictured in comic books as small enough to fit in a teacup. This couple probably broke the world's record for the largest number of dogs ever to live in a house trailer. You could hear their dogs yip hysterically whenever you walked by.

Trailer park Chihuahua dog collectors, game show contestants, circus performers—lowlife and weird, perhaps, to outsiders, but to us, these were our heroes and celebrities. What's more, people from all over the United States ended up in our trailer park. "They were well-traveled and wise," my mom explains with pride, "and they shared with us the great wealth of their experience." This may be why they had more tolerance for differences (within our whiteness, at least) than was usual in many white communities during the fifties—more tolerant, my mom adds, than the less-traveled people who lived in the houses.

Migrants and the Community

TOBY F. SONNEMAN

Migrant workers are believed to number around 3 million adults and children, working without health benefits. This essay is taken from a book about the lives and experiences of such workers. The author and her husband are themselves "fruit tramps," enduring low pay, low status, and back-breaking work as they travel to different regions where the fruit is ripe for picking. From the reading, migrants appear to be treated by the public in ways similar to the ways homeless people are treated. What are the similarities and differences between these two groups? How would cultural and structural theorists analyze migrant workers' life situations?

One evening, after the children in camp were asleep for the night, a few people still sat outside in the waning light of dusk, quietly talking. The screen door of one of the trailers nearby opened with a creak, and a woman poked her head out.

"Hank, would you run to the store for some bread? We ain't got enough for tomorrow's lunch."

Hank sighed and got up from his chair reluctantly. "That's about the third time today I've been up at that there Tom's Market," he complained. "I swear, those people are gettin' rich off us fruit tramps."

As he headed for his pickup, the other pickers watched him sympathetically. The little store he was driving to, only a mile and a half away, was surrounded by orchards and used mainly by pickers who didn't want to travel five miles to a larger town.

Walter shook his head. "Yeah, I bought three dollars of groceries over there today, and the man only charged me five dollars!" he quipped.

"Well, you know they jack the prices up just as soon as the fruit pickers hit town," Darlene said. "A gallon of milk is thirty cents higher once the pickers get into town. They just figure we got no choice."

"What gets me is the way some of these locals act toward you, like your money ain't as good as theirs." Travis, a small, energetic man, wrinkled his forehead in

SOURCE: Toby F. Sonneman, *Fruit Fields in My Blood: Okie Migrants in the West* (Moscow, ID: University of Idaho Press, 1992), pp. 171–175. Reprinted by permission of the University of Idaho Press.

disgust. "I went into the grocery one time, and I'd been uptown and got me sixty-five dollars worth of food stamps in my pocket. And I'm about to pay for my groceries, when this old lady says to one, 'You'd better go to the back of the line.' I said, 'Why is that?' and she said, 'Those food stamps. I had to pay for those things.' I said, 'Lady, I had to pay for 'em too, and I got every right to 'em.' Hell, I bet that old lady was drawin' her social security too!

"That makes me so blame mad!" he went on. "We're the ones that's harvesting their food and they think they're better'n us just because we have to use food stamps when there ain't no work."

Because most of the interactions between migrants and the community occur in stores, especially grocery stores, these are the main places where each group forms its opinion of the other. Most of the Okies we talked to had an active distrust of storekeepers. We never discovered if the stores really raised their prices when the pickers came to town, but many of the people we worked with believed they did. Smaller markets, which fruit pickers must often rely on because they are more rural, always had higher prices than stores in town, because of various economic factors. Because pickers frequented these stores in such great numbers, they often felt that they were being taken advantage of because of their needs.

Fruit pickers are especially sensitive to the attitudes of grocery-store clerks. They often feel negatively judged for the work they do—yet this is the very work that the grocery business profits from.

"Those storekeepers look down on us fruit tramps," Darlene told us. Her strong voice had a bitter edge. "You know how when they give you your change back, whenever you got dirty hands from workin' in the fields, they hold their hand six or eight inches from yours and drop your money down into it."

"Yeah," agreed Thelma, a mild-mannered woman who was married to Travis. "Or they lay the money on the counter, like they'd catch something awful if they touched you."

This particular experience of the clerk not putting the change in the fruit picker's hand is one I heard complaints of often, and I experienced it personally. The implication that fruit pickers are too dirty to touch is especially damaging to a picker's pride.

"It's always been that-a-way," commented Daniel, Darlene's husband, trying to explain the phenomenon. "The people in the towns always seem to get the idea that fruit pickers are dirty. Because they may work ten or fifteen miles off from where they live, and rather than to come home and clean up and then go to the store and buy something for the next day's lunch or supper that night, they just stop on the way home. It saves havin' to go back to town. I guess you could call it conservation of energy, but we seem to have gotten an unclean reputation from doin' this."

Fruit pickers must also use stores more frequently because of their limited storage space and refrigeration. Often there are no sanitary facilities in the field, so their hands as well as their clothes can be dirty from contact with fruit, trees, and ladders. Their hands are torn, covered with hundreds of scratches and cuts from the trees. They are tired, hungry, and dirty by the time they come to the store to buy their food and spend their hard-earned money. If the attitude of the grocery-store clerk is hostile, the experience is not soon forgotten.

"For some reason or other, seems like the communities have a poor outlook on migrants," said Daniel's older brother, Walter. With deep lines etched into his face, Walter looked much older than his forty years. Unlike Travis and Daniel, who wore crisply ironed western shirts with blue jeans, Walter's clothes were rumpled and old, as if he had no time for such frivolities as dress. His demeanor was serious and thoughtful as he continued. "I think local people figure we don't have roots or aren't a part of anything. When in reality, we do have roots, very strong roots, and we are a part of something. We're a part of feeding these people who have this contempt for us."

John Steinbeck noted this same contradiction in *Their Blood Is Strong* in 1938. "Thus, in California we find a curious attitude toward a group that makes our agriculture successful," he wrote. "The migrants are needed, and they are hated. . . . They are never received into a community nor into the life of a community. Wanderers in fact, they are never allowed to feel at home in the communities that demand their services."

Migrants feel that they contribute to the economics of the community not only by their work but by the money they spend locally. "You know, this thing about not spending any money in the community is an absolute lie," said Thelma. "Our cars break down and we get 'em worked on; we buy lots of food and gas and other things too when the job is good and pay for a place to stay lots of times."

The perception that they are taken advantage of by the communities they frequent extends to other services that fruit pickers rely on. "We put five hundred dollars into that truck of ours and you wouldn't believe it," Linda related acridly. "All in this little part that fell off, and this crook in Othello charged us an arm and a leg cuz he knew we couldn't get out of that nasty little town without it. I think I would've left and run away back home if I had a home to run to."

In addition to grocery stores, car-repair places, gas stations, and campgrounds, migrants use state or community services for health care. Because of a disinclination to use such services as well as the difficulty of obtaining regular health care on the migrant run, such services are usually used only for a health crisis, and preventative health care is rarely sought out by migrants. Cultural factors add to the Okies' reluctance to seek health care. A suspicion of medical practitioners; a belief that they can often cure themselves (or a more fatalistic belief that they were meant to be sick); and denial of all but the most major illness, combined with a strong work ethic, all contribute to this behavior.

At a Slaughterhouse

CHARLIE LEDUFF

This selection is by a New York Times *reporter who signed up for work in the slaughterhouse. While not poor himself he took a job at the slaughterhouse so he could describe the working conditions and how race structures the work environment there. What did he find in terms of the intersection of work and race? What is the situation of the illegal immigrants there? How do divisions by race actually benefit the employers of a slaughterhouse? What might a union do for these workers? Why do you think they voted down having a union?*

Tar Heel, N.C.—It must have been 1 o'clock. That's when the white man usually comes out of his glass office and stands on the scaffolding above the factory floor. He stood with his palms on the rails, his elbows out. He looked like a tower guard up there or a border patrol agent. He stood with his head cocked.

One o'clock means it is getting near the end of the workday. Quota has to be met and the workload doubles. The conveyor belt always overflows with meat around 1 o'clock. So the workers double their pace, hacking pork from shoulder bones with a driven single-mindedness. They stare blankly, like mules in wooden blinders, as the butchered slabs pass by.

It is called the picnic line: 18 workers lined up on both sides of a belt, carving meat from bone. Up to 16 million shoulders a year come down that line here at the Smithfield Packing Co., the largest pork production plant in the world. That works out to about 32,000 a shift, 63 a minute, one every 17 seconds for each worker for eight and a half hours a day. The first time you stare down at that belt you know your body is going to give in way before the machine ever will.

On this day the boss saw something he didn't like. He climbed down and approached the picnic line from behind. He leaned into the ear of a broad-shouldered black man. He had been riding him all day, and the day before. The boss bawled him out good this time, but no one heard what was said. The roar of the machinery was too ferocious for that. Still, everyone knew what was expected. They worked harder.

SOURCE: Charlie LeDuff, "At a Slaughterhouse, Some Things Never Die," *New York Times* (June 16, 2000). Copyright © 2000 by the New York Times Co. Reprinted with permission.

The white man stood and watched for the next two hours as the blacks worked in their groups and the Mexicans in theirs. He stood there with his head cocked.

At shift change the black man walked away, hosed himself down and turned in his knives. Then he let go. He threatened to murder the boss. He promised to quit. He said he was losing his mind, which made for good comedy since he was standing near a conveyor chain of severed hogs' heads, their mouths yoked open.

"Who that cracker think he is?" the black man wanted to know. There were enough hogs, he said, "not to worry about no fleck of meat being left on the bone. Keep treating me like a Mexican and I'll beat him."

The boss walked by just then and the black man lowered his head.

WHO GETS THE DIRTY JOBS

The first thing you learn in the hog plant is the value of a sharp knife. The second thing you learn is that you don't want to work with a knife. Finally you learn that not everyone has to work with a knife. Whites, blacks, American Indians and Mexicans, they all have their separate stations.

The few whites on the payroll tend to be mechanics or supervisors. As for the Indians, a handful are supervisors; others tend to get clean menial jobs like warehouse work. With few exceptions, that leaves the blacks and Mexicans with the dirty jobs at the factory, one of the only places within a 50-mile radius in this muddy corner of North Carolina where a person might make more than $8 an hour.

While Smithfield's profits nearly doubled in the past year, wages have remained flat. So a lot of Americans here have quit and a lot of Mexicans have been hired to take their places. But more than management, the workers see one another as the problem, and they see the competition in skin tones.

The locker rooms are self-segregated and so is the cafeteria. The enmity spills out into the towns. The races generally keep to themselves. Along Interstate 95 there are four tumbledown bars, one for each color: white, black, red and brown.

Language is also a divider. There are English and Spanish lines at the Social Security office and in the waiting rooms of the county health clinics. This means different groups don't really understand one another and tend to be suspicious of what they do know.

You begin to understand these things the minute you apply for the job.

BLOOD AND BURNOUT

"Treat the meat like you going to eat it yourself," the hiring manager told the 30 applicants, most of them down on their luck and hungry for work. The Smithfield plant will take just about any man or woman with a pulse and a sparkling urine sample, with few questions asked. This reporter was hired using his own name and acknowledged that he was currently employed, but was not asked where and did not say.

Slaughtering swine is repetitive, brutish work, so grueling that three weeks on the factory floor leave no doubt in your mind about why the turnover is 100 percent. Five thousand quit and five thousand are hired every year. You hear people say, They don't kill pigs in the plant, they kill people. So desperate is the company for workers, its recruiters comb the streets of New York's immigrant communities, personnel staff members say, and word of mouth has reached Mexico and beyond.

The company even procures criminals. Several at the morning orientation were inmates on work release in green uniforms, bused in from the county prison.

The new workers were given a safety speech and tax papers, shown a promotional video and informed that there was enough methane, ammonia and chlorine at the plant to kill every living thing here in Bladen County. Of the 30 new employees, the black women were assigned to the chitterlings room, where they would scrape feces and worms from intestines. The black men were sent to the butchering floor. Two free white men and the Indian were given jobs making boxes. This reporter declined a box job and ended up with most of the Mexicans, doing knife work, cutting sides of pork into smaller and smaller products.

Standing in the hiring hall that morning, two women chatted in Spanish about their pregnancies. A young black man had heard enough. His small town the next county over was crowded with Mexicans. They just started showing up three years ago—drawn to rural Robeson County by the plant—and never left. They stood in groups on the street corners, and the young black man never knew what they were saying. They took the jobs and did them for less. Some had houses in Mexico, while he lived in a trailer with his mother.

Now here he was, trying for the only job around, and he had to listen to Spanish, had to compete with peasants. The world was going to hell.

"This is America and I want to start hearing some English, now!" he screamed.

One of the women told him where to stick his head and listen for the echo. "Then you'll hear some English," she said.

An old white man with a face as pinched and lined as a pot roast complained, "The tacos are worse than the niggers," and the Indian leaned against the wall and laughed. In the doorway, the prisoners shifted from foot to foot, watching the spectacle unfold from behind a cloud of cigarette smoke.

The hiring manager came out of his office and broke it up just before things degenerated into a brawl. Then he handed out the employment stubs. "I don't want no problems," he warned. He told them to report to the plant on Monday morning to collect their carving knives.

$7.70 AN HOUR, PAIN ALL DAY

Monday. The mist rose from the swamps and by 4:45 A.M. thousands of headlamps snaked along the old country roads. Cars carried people from the backwoods, from the single and double-wide trailers, from the cinder-block houses and wooden shacks: whites from Lumberton and Elizabethtown; blacks from Fairmont and Fayetteville; Indians from Pembroke; the Mexicans from Red Springs and St. Pauls.

They converge at the Smithfield plant, a 973,000-square-foot leviathan of pipe and steel near the Cape Fear River. The factory towers over the tobacco and cotton fields, surrounded by pine trees and a few of the old whitewashed plantation houses. Built seven years ago, it is by far the biggest employer in this region, 75 miles west of the Atlantic and 90 miles south of the booming Research Triangle around Chapel Hill.

The workers filed in, their faces stiffened by sleep and the cold, like saucers of milk gone hard. They punched the clock at 5 A.M., waiting for the knives to be handed out, the chlorine freshly applied by the cleaning crew burning their eyes and throats. Nobody spoke.

The hallway was a river of brown-skinned Mexicans. The six prisoners who were starting that day looked confused.

"What the hell's going on?" the only white inmate, Billy Harwood, asked an older black worker named Wade Baker.

"Oh," Mr. Baker said, seeing that the prisoner was talking about the Mexicans. "I see you been away for a while."

Billy Harwood had been away—nearly seven years, for writing phony payroll checks from the family pizza business to buy crack. He was Rip Van Winkle standing there. Everywhere he looked there were Mexicans. What he didn't know was that one out of three newborns at the nearby Robeson County health clinic was a Latino; that the county's Roman Catholic church had a special Sunday Mass for Mexicans said by a Honduran priest; that the schools needed Spanish speakers to teach English.

With less than a month to go on his sentence, Mr. Harwood took the pork job to save a few dollars. The word in jail was that the job was a cakewalk for a white man.

But this wasn't looking like any cakewalk. He wasn't going to get a boxing job like a lot of other whites. Apparently inmates were on the bottom rung, just like Mexicans.

Billy Harwood and the other prisoners were put on the picnic line. Knife work pays $7.70 an hour to start. It is money unimaginable in Mexico, where the average wage is $4 a day. But the American money comes at a price. The work burns your muscles and dulls your mind. Staring down into the meat for hours strains your neck. After thousands of cuts a day your fingers no longer open freely. Standing in the damp 42-degree air causes your knees to lock, your nose to run, your teeth to throb.

The whistle blows at 3, you get home by 4, pour peroxide on your nicks by 5. You take pills for your pains and stand in a hot shower trying to wash it all away. You hurt. And by 8 o'clock you're in bed, exhausted, thinking of work.

The convict said he felt cheated. He wasn't supposed to be doing Mexican work. After his second day he was already talking of quitting. "Man, this can't be for real," he said, rubbing his wrists as if they'd been in handcuffs. "This job's for an ass. They treat you like an animal."

He just might have quit after the third day had it not been for Mercedes Fernández, a Mexican. He took a place next to her by the conveyor belt. She smiled at him, showed him how to make incisions. That was the extent of his on-the-job training. He was peep-eyed, missing a tooth and squat from the starchy prison food, but he acted as if this tiny woman had taken a fancy to him. In truth, she was more fascinated than infatuated, she later confided. In her year at the plant, he was the first white person she had ever worked with.

The other workers noticed her helping the white man, so unusual was it for a Mexican and a white to work shoulder to shoulder, to try to talk or even to make eye contact.

As for blacks, she avoided them. She was scared of them. "Blacks don't want to work," Mrs. Fernández said when the new batch of prisoners came to work on the line. "They're lazy."

Everything about the factory cuts people off from one another. If it's not the language barrier, it's the noise—the hammering of compressors, the screeching of pulleys, the grinding of the lines. You can hardly make your voice heard. To get another's attention on the cut line, you bang the butt of your knife on the steel railings, or you lob a chunk of meat. Mrs. Fernández would sometimes throw a piece of shoulder at a friend across the conveyor and wave good morning.

THE KILL FLOOR

The kill floor sets the pace of the work, and for those jobs they pick strong men and pay a top wage, as high as $12 an hour. If the men fail to make quota, plenty of others are willing to try. It is mostly the blacks who work the kill floor, the stone-hearted jobs that pay more and appear out of bounds for all but a few Mexicans.

Plant workers gave various reasons for this: The Mexicans are too small; they don't like blood; they don't like heavy lifting; or just plain "We built this country and we ain't going to hand them everything," as one black man put it.

Kill-floor work is hot, quick and bloody. The hog is herded in from the stockyard, then stunned with an electric gun. It is lifted onto a conveyor belt, dazed but not dead, and passed to a waiting group of men wearing blood-stained smocks and blank faces. They slit the neck, shackle the hind legs and watch a machine lift the carcass into the air, letting its life flow out in a purple gush, into a steaming collection trough.

The carcass is run through a scalding bath, trolleyed over the factory floor and then dumped onto a table with all the force of a quarter-ton water balloon. In the misty-red room, men slit along its hind tendons and skewer the beast with hooks. It is again lifted and shot across the room on a pulley and bar, where it hangs with hundreds of others as if in some kind of horrific dry-cleaning shop. It is then pulled through a wall of flames and met on the other side by more black men who, stripped to the waist beneath their smocks, scrape away any straggling bristles.

The place reeks of sweat and scared animal, steam and blood. Nothing is wasted from these beasts, not the plasma, not the glands, not the bones. Everything is used, and the kill men, repeating slaughterhouse lore, say that even the squeal is sold.

The carcasses sit in the freezer overnight and are then rolled out to the cut floor. The cut floor is opposite to the kill floor in nearly every way. The workers are mostly brown—Mexicans—not black; the lighting yellow, not red. The vapor comes from cold breath, not hot water. It is here that the hog is quartered. The pieces are parceled out and sent along the disassembly lines to be cut into ribs, hams, bellies, loins and chops.

People on the cut lines work with a mindless fury. There is tremendous pressure to keep the conveyor belts moving, to pack orders, to put bacon and ham and sausage on the public's breakfast table. There is no clock, no window, no fragment of the world outside. Everything is pork. If the line fails to keep pace, the kill men must slow down, backing up the slaughter. The boxing line will have little to do, costing the company payroll hours. The blacks who kill will become angry with the Mexicans who cut, who in turn will become angry with the white superintendents who push them.

10,000 UNWELCOME MEXICANS

The Mexicans never push back. They cannot. Some have legitimate work papers, but more, like Mercedes Fernández, do not.

Even worse, Mrs. Fernández was several thousand dollars in debt to the smugglers who had sneaked her and her family into the United States and owed a thousand more for the authentic-looking birth certificate and Social Security card that are needed to get hired. She and her husband, Armando, expected to be in debt for years. They had mouths to feed back home.

The Mexicans are so frightened about being singled out that they do not even tell one another their real names. They have their given names, their work-paper names and "Hey you," as their American supervisors call them. In the telling of their stories, Mercedes and Armando Fernández insisted that their real names be used, to protect their identities. It was their work names they did not want used, names bought in a back alley in Barstow, Tex.

Rarely are the newcomers welcomed with open arms. Long before the Mexicans arrived, Robeson County, one of the poorest in North Carolina, was an uneasy racial mix. In the 1990 census, of the 100,000 people living in Robeson, nearly 40 percent were Lumbee Indian, 35 percent white and 25 percent black. Until a dozen years ago the county schools were de facto segregated, and no person of color held any meaningful county job from sheriff to court clerk to judge.

At one point in 1988, two armed Indian men occupied the local newspaper office, taking hostages and demanding that the sheriff's department be investigated for corruption and its treatment of minorities. A prominent Indian lawyer, Julian Pierce, was killed that same year, and the suspect turned up dead in a broom closet before he could be charged. The hierarchy of power was summed up on a plaque that hangs in the courthouse commemorating the dead of World War I. It lists the veterans by color: "white" on top, "Indian" in the middle and "colored" on the bottom.

That hierarchy mirrors the pecking order at the hog plant. The Lumbees—who have fought their way up in the county apparatus and have built their own construction businesses—are fond of saying they are too smart to work in the factory. And the few who do work there seem to end up with the cleaner jobs.

But as reds and blacks began to make progress in the 1990's—for the first time an Indian sheriff was elected, and a black man is now the public defender—the Latinos began arriving. The United States Census Bureau estimated that 1,000 Latinos were living in Robeson County last year. People only laugh at that number.

"A thousand? Hell, there's more than that in the Wal-Mart on a Saturday afternoon," said Bill Smith, director of county health services. He and other officials guess that there are at least 10,000 Latinos in Robeson, most having arrived in the past three years.

"When they built that factory in Bladen, they promised a trickledown effect," Mr. Smith said. "But the money ain't trickling down this way. Bladen got the money and Robeson got the social problems."

In Robeson there is the strain on public resources. There is the substandard housing. There is the violence. Last year 27 killings were committed in Robeson, mostly in the countryside, giving it a higher murder rate than Detroit or Newark. Three Mexicans were robbed and killed last fall. Latinos have also been the victims of highway stickups.

In the yellow-walled break room at the plant, Mexicans talked among themselves about their three slain men, about the midnight visitors with obscured faces and guns, men who knew that the illegal workers used mattresses rather than banks. Mercedes Fernández, like many Mexicans, would not venture out at night. "Blacks have a problem," she said. "They live in the past. They are angry about slavery, so instead of working, they steal from us."

She and her husband never lingered in the parking lot at shift change. That is when the anger of a long day comes seeping out. Cars get kicked and faces slapped over parking spots or fender benders. The traffic is a serpent. Cars jockey for a spot in line to make the quarter-mile crawl along the plant's one-lane exit road to the highway. Usually no one will let you in. A lot of the scuffling is between black and Mexican.

BLACK AND BLEAK

The meat was backing up on the conveyor and spilling onto the floor. The supervisor climbed down off the scaffolding and chewed out a group of black women. Something about skin being left on the meat. There was a new skinner on the job, and the cutting line was expected to take up his slack. The whole line groaned. First looks flew, then people began hurling slurs at one another in Spanish and English, words only they could hardly hear over the factory's roar. The black women started waving their knives at the Mexicans. The Mexicans waved theirs back. Blades got close. One Mexican spit at the blacks and was fired.

After watching the knife scene, Wade Baker went home and sagged in his recliner. CNN played. Good news on Wall Street, the television said. Wages remained stable. "Since when is the fact that a man doesn't get paid good news?" he asked the TV. The TV told him that money was everywhere—everywhere but here.

Still lean at 51, Mr. Baker has seen life improve since his youth in the Jim Crow South. You can say things. You can ride in a car with a white woman. You can stay in the motels, eat in the restaurants. The black man got off the white man's field.

"Socially, things are much better," Mr. Baker said wearily over the droning television. "But we're going backwards as black people economically. For every one of us doing better, there's two of us doing worse."

His town, Chad Bourne, is a dreary strip of peeling paint and warped porches and houses as run-down as rotting teeth. Young men drift from the cinder-block pool hall to the empty streets and back. In the center of town is a bank, a gas station, a chicken shack and a motel. As you drive out, the lights get dimmer and the homes older until eventually you're in a flat void of tobacco fields.

Mr. Baker was standing on the main street with his grandson Monte watching the Christmas parade march by when a scruffy man approached. It was Mr. Baker's cousin, and he smelled of kerosene and had dust in his hair as if he lived in a vacant building and warmed himself with a portable heater. He asked for $2.

"It's ironic isn't it?" Mr. Baker said as his cousin walked away only eight bits richer. "He was asking me the same thing 10 years ago."

A group of Mexicans stood across the street hanging around the gas station watching them.

"People around here always want to blame the system," he said. "And it is true that the system is anti-black and anti-poor. It's true that things are run by the whites. But being angry only means you failed in life. Instead of complaining, you got to work twice as hard and make do."

He stood quietly with his hands in his pockets watching the parade go by. He watched the Mexicans across the street, laughing in their new clothes. Then he said, almost as an afterthought, "There's a day coming soon where the Mexicans are going to catch hell from the blacks, the way the blacks caught it from the whites."

Wade Baker used to work in the post office, until he lost his job over drugs. When he came out of his haze a few years ago, there wasn't much else for him but the plant. He took the job, he said, "because I don't have a 401K." He took it because he had learned from his mother that you don't stand around with your head down and your hand out waiting for another man to drop you a dime.

Evelyn Baker, bent and gray now, grew up a sharecropper, the granddaughter of slaves. She was raised up in a tar-paper shack, picked cotton and hoed tobacco for a white family. She supported her three boys alone by cleaning white people's homes.

In the late 60's something good started happening. There was a labor shortage, just as there is now. The managers at the textile plants started giving machine jobs to black people.

Mrs. Baker was 40 then. "I started at a dollar and 60 cents an hour, and honey, that was a lot of money then," she said.

The work was plentiful through the 70's and 80's, and she was able to save money and add on to her home. By the early 90's the textile factories started moving away, to Mexico. Robeson County has lost about a quarter of its jobs since that time.

Unemployment in Robeson hovers around 8 percent, twice the national average. In neighboring Columbus County it is 10.8 percent. In Bladen County it is 5 percent, and Bladen has the pork factory.

Still, Mr. Baker believes that people who want to work can find work. As far as he's concerned, there are too many shiftless young men who ought to be working, even if it's in the pork plant. His son-in-law once worked there, quit and now hangs around the gas station where other young men sell dope.

The son-in-law came over one day last fall and threatened to cause trouble if the Bakers didn't let him borrow the car. This could have turned messy; the 71-year-old Mrs. Baker keeps a .38 tucked in her bosom.

When Wade Baker got home from the plant and heard from his mother what had happened, he took up his pistol and went down to the corner, looking for his son-in-law. He chased a couple of the young men around the dark dusty lot, waving the gun. "Hold still so I can shoot one of you!" he recalled having bellowed. "That would make the world a better place!"

He scattered the men without firing. Later, sitting in his car with his pistol on the seat and his hands between his knees, he said, staring into the night: "There's got to be more than this. White people drive by and look at this and laugh."

LIVING IT, HATING IT

Billy Harwood had been working at the plant 10 days when he was released from the Robeson County Correctional Facility. He stood at the prison gates in his work clothes with his belongings in a plastic bag, waiting. A friend dropped him at the Salvation Army shelter, but he decided it was too much like prison. Full of black people. No leaving after 10 P.M. No smoking indoors. "What you doing here, white boy?" they asked him.

He fumbled with a cigarette outside the shelter. He wanted to quit the plant. The work stinks, he said, "but at least I ain't a nigger. I'll find other work soon. I'm a white man." He had hopes of landing a roofing job through a friend. The way he saw it, white society looks out for itself.

On the cut line he worked slowly and allowed Mercedes Fernández and the others to pick up his slack. He would cut only the left shoulders; it was easier on his hands. Sometimes it would be three minutes before a left shoulder came down the line. When he did cut, he didn't clean the bone; he left chunks of meat on it.

Mrs. Fernández was disappointed by her first experience with a white person. After a week she tried to avoid standing by Billy Harwood. She decided it wasn't just the blacks who were lazy, she said.

Even so, the supervisor came by one morning, took a look at one of Mr. Harwood's badly cut shoulders and threw it at Mrs. Fernández, blaming her.

He said obscene things about her family. She didn't understand exactly what he said, but it scared her. She couldn't wipe the tears from her eyes because her gloves were covered with greasy shreds of swine. The other cutters kept their heads down, embarrassed.

Her life was falling apart. She and her husband both worked the cut floor. They never saw their daughter. They were 26 but rarely made love anymore. All they wanted was to save enough money to put plumbing in their house in Mexico and start a business there. They come from the town of Tehuacán, in a rural area about 150 miles southeast of Mexico City. His mother owns a bar there and a home but gives nothing to them. Mother must look out for her old age.

"We came here to work so we have a chance to grow old in Mexico," Mrs. Fernández said one evening while cooking pork and potatoes. Now they were into a smuggler for thousands. Her hands swelled into claws in the evenings and stung while she worked. She felt trapped. But she kept at it for the money, for the $9.60 an hour. The smuggler still had to be paid.

They explained their story this way: The coyote drove her and her family from Barstow a year ago and left them in Robeson. They knew no one. They did not even know they were in the state of North Carolina. They found shelter in a trailer park that had once been exclusively black but was rapidly filling with Mexicans. There was a lot of drug dealing there and a lot of tension. One evening, Mr. Fernández said, he asked a black neighbor to move his business inside and the man pulled a pistol on him.

"I hate the blacks," Mr. Fernández said in Spanish, sitting in the break room not 10 feet from Mr. Baker and his black friends. Mr. Harwood was sitting two tables away with the whites and Indians.

After the gun incident, Mr. Fernández packed up his family and moved out into the country, to a prefabricated number sitting on a brick foundation off in the woods alone. Their only contact with people is through the satellite dish. Except for the coyote. The coyote knows where they live and comes for his money every other month.

Their 5-year-old daughter has no playmates in the back country and few at school. That is the way her parents want it. "We don't want her to be American," her mother said.

'WE NEED A UNION'

The steel bars holding a row of hogs gave way as a woman stood below them. Hog after hog fell around her with a sickening thud, knocking her senseless, the connecting bars barely missing her face. As co-workers rushed to help the woman, the supervisor spun his hands in the air, a signal to keep working. Wade Baker saw this and shook his head in disgust. Nothing stops the disassembly lines.

"We need a union," he said later in the break room. It was payday and he stared at his check: $288. He spoke softly to the black workers sitting near him. Everyone is convinced that talk of a union will get you fired. After two years at the factory, Mr. Baker makes slightly more than $9 an hour toting meat away from the cut line, slightly less than $20,000 a year, 45 cents an hour less than Mrs. Fernández.

"I don't want to get racial about the Mexicans," he whispered to the black workers. "But they're dragging down the pay. It's pure economics. They say Americans don't want to do the job. That ain't exactly true. We don't want to do it for $8. Pay $15 and we'll do it."

These men knew that in the late 70's, when the meatpacking industry was centered in northern cities like Chicago and Omaha, people had a union getting them $18 an hour. But by the mid-80's, to cut costs, many of the packing houses had moved to small towns where they could pay a lower, nonunion wage.

The black men sitting around the table also felt sure that the Mexicans pay almost nothing in income tax, claiming 8, 9, even 10 exemptions. The men believed that the illegal workers should be rooted out of the factory. "It's all about money," Mr. Baker said.

His co-workers shook their heads. "A plantation with a roof on it," one said.

For their part, many of the Mexicans in Tar Heel fear that union would place their illegal status under scrutiny and force them out. The United Food and Commercial Workers Union last tried organizing the plant in 1997, but the idea was voted down nearly two to one.

One reason Americans refused to vote for the union was because it refuses to take a stand on illegal laborers. Another reason was the intimidation. When workers arrived at the plant the morning of the vote, they were met by Bladen County deputy sheriffs in riot gear. "Nigger Lover" had been scrawled on the union trailer.

Five years ago the work force at the plant was 50 percent black, 20 percent white and Indian, and 30 percent Latino, according to union statistics. Company officials say those numbers are about the same today. But from inside the plant, the breakdown appears to be more like 60 percent Latino, 30 percent black, 10 percent white and red.

Sherri Buffkin, a white woman and the former director of purchasing who testified before the National Labor Relations Board in an unfair-labor-practice suit brought by the union in 1998, said in an interview that the company assigns workers by race. She also said that management had kept lists of union sympathizers during the '97 election, firing blacks and replacing them with Latinos. "I know because I fired at least 15 of them myself," she said.

The company denies those accusations. Michael H. Cole, a lawyer for Smithfield who would respond to questions about the company's labor practices only in writing, said that jobs at the Tar Heel plant were awarded through a bidding process and not assigned by race. The company also denies ever having kept lists of union sympathizers or singled out blacks to be fired.

The hog business is important to North Carolina. It is a multibillion-dollar-a-year industry in the state, with nearly two pigs for every one of its 7.5 million people. And Smithfield Foods, a publicly traded company in Smithfield, Va., has become the No. 1 producer and processor of pork in the world. It slaughters more than 20 percent of the nation's swine, more than 19 million animals a year.

The company, which has acquired a network of factory farms and slaughterhouses, worries federal agriculture officials and legislators, who see it siphoning business from smaller farmers. And environmentalists contend that Smithfield's operations contaminate local water supplies. (The Environmental Protection Agency fined the company $12.6 million in 1996 after its processing plants in Virginia discharged pollutants into the Pagan River.) The chairman and chief executive, Joseph W. Lutter III, declined to be interviewed.

Smithfield's employment practices have not been so closely scrutinized. And so every year, more Mexicans get hired. "An illegal alien isn't going to complain all that much," said Ed Tomlinson, acting supervisor of the Immigration and Naturalization Service Bureau in Charlotte.

But the company says it does not knowingly hire illegal aliens. Smithfield's lawyer, Mr. Cole, said all new employees must present papers showing that they can legally work in the United States. "If any employee's documentation appears to be genuine and to belong to the person presenting it," he said in his written response, "Smithfield is required by law to take it at face value."

The naturalization service—which has only 18 agents in North Carolina—has not investigated Smithfield because no one has filed a complaint, Mr. Tomlinson said. "There are more jobs than people," he said, "and a lot of Americans will do the dirty work for a while and then return to their couches and eat bonbons and watch Oprah."

NOT FIT FOR A CONVICT

When Billy Harwood was in solitary confinement, he liked a book to get him through. A guard would come around with a cartful. But when the prisoner asked for a new book, the guard, before handing it to him, liked to tear out the last 50 pages. The guard was a real funny guy.

"I got good at making up my own endings," Billy Harwood said during a break. "And *my* book don't end standing here. I ought to be on that roof any day now."

But a few days later, he found out that the white contractor he was counting on already had a full roofing crew. They were Mexicans who were working for less than he was making at the plant.

During his third week cutting hogs, he got a new supervisor—a black woman. Right away she didn't like his work ethic. He went too slow. He cut out to the bathroom too much.

"Got a bladder infection?" she asked, standing in his spot when he returned. She forbade him to use the toilet.

He boiled. Mercedes Fernández kept her head down. She was certain of it, she said: he was the laziest man she had ever met. She stood next to a black man now, a prisoner from the north. They called him K. T. and he was nice to her. He tried Spanish, and he worked hard.

When the paychecks were brought around at lunch time on Friday, Billy Harwood got paid for five hours less than everyone else, even though everyone punched out on the same clock. The supervisor had docked him.

The prisoners mocked him. "You might be white," K. T. said, "but you came in wearing prison greens and that makes you good as a nigger."

The ending wasn't turning out the way Billy Harwood had written it: no place to live and a job not fit for a donkey. He quit and took the Greyhound back to his parents' trailer in the hills.

When Mrs. Fernández came to work the next day, a Mexican guy going by the name of Alfredo was standing in Billy Harwood's spot.

Parenting in Poverty

Two out of three impoverished adults in the United States are women, a consequence of the prevailing institutional sexism in society. With few exceptions, U.S. society provides poor job and earnings opportunities for women. This fact, combined with the relatively high frequency of divorce (85 percent of children of divorced parents, live with their mother) and the large number of never-married women with children, has resulted in the high probability of women who head families being poor (28.7 percent of female-headed families with no husband present were below the poverty line in 2005, compared to 5.1 percent of married-couples living in poverty) (DeNavas-Walt, Proctor, and Lee, 2006). Women with children with no husband present, on average, were in 2005, $8,610 *below* the poverty threshold. In short, the highest risk of poverty results from being a woman and having children, a trend that economist Nancy Folbre has called the "pauperization of motherhood" (Folbre, 1985). This generalization is even stronger when race/ethnicity is considered with gender—single African American and Latina women with children fare worse than White women with children.

Mothers without partners are faced with the quadruple burden of earning a wage, paying the bills, doing the housework, and parenting.

> *These families are highly susceptible to poverty, because they typically rely on the earnings of a single adult and incur expenses for child care. Because child support enforcement is poor, few receive substantial transfers from absent parents. Because levels of public assistance are low, many live in poverty even if they are "on welfare."* (Heinz, Folbre, and the Center for Popular Economics, 2000:80).

Parenting by the poor, of course, is not limited to women. Poor fathers may also be single parents facing the often conflicting demands of work, survival, and parenting. Fathers in poor two-parent families often work at two jobs to make up for low wages and benefits.

NOTES AND SUGGESTIONS FOR FURTHER READING

Albelda, Randy, and Chris Tilly (1997). *Glass Ceilings and Bottomless Pits: Women's Work, Women's Poverty.* Boston: South End Press.

Andersen, Margaret L., and Patricia Hill Collins (Eds.) (2006). *Race, Class, and Gender: An Anthology.* Belmont, CA: Wadsworth.

Baca Zinn, Maxine, and Bonnie Thornton Dill (Eds.) (1994). *Women of Color in U.S. Society.* Philadelphia: Temple University Press

Berrick, Jill Duerr (1995). *Faces of Poverty: Portraits of Women and Children on Welfare.* New York: Oxford University Press.

Butler, Sandra S. (1994). *Middle-Aged, Female and Homeless: The Stories of a Forgotten Group.* New York: Garland.

Children's Defense Fund (2001). *The State of America's Children: 2001.* Washington, D. C.

Choi, Namkee G., and Lidia J. Snyder (1999). *Homeless Families with Children: A Subjective Experience of Homelessness.* New York: Springer.

Connolly, Deborah R. (2000). *Homeless Mothers: Face to Face with Women and Poverty.* Minneapolis, MN: University of Minnesota Press.

DeNavas-Walt, Carmen, Bernadette D. Proctor, and Cheryl Hill Lee (2006). *Income, Poverty, and Health Insurance Coverage in the United States: 2005.* Current Population Reports, P60–231. Washington, D.C.: U.S. Census Bureau (August).

Edin, Kathryn, and Laura Lein (1997). *Making Ends Meet: How Single Mothers Survive Welfare and Low Wage Work.* New York: Russell Sage Foundation.

Folbre, Nancy (1985). "The Pauperization of Motherhood: Patriarchy and Social Policy in the United States." *Review of Radical Political Economics* 16 (4).

Gallay, Leslie S., and Constance A. Flanagan (2000). "The Well Being of Children in a Changing Economy: Time for a New Social Contract in America," pp. 3–33 in *Resilience across Contexts: Family, Work, Culture, and Community,* Ronald D. Taylor and Margaret C. Wang (Eds.). Mahwah, NJ: Lawrence Erlbaum Associates.

Heintz, James, Nancy Folbre, and the Center for Popular Economics (2000). *The Ultimate Field Guide to the U.S. Economy: A Compact and Irreverent Guide to Economic Life in America.* New York: The New Press.

Kozol, Jonathan (1988). *Rachel and Her Children: Homeless Families in America.* New York: Crown.

Schein, Virginia E. (1995). *Working from the Margins: Voices of Mothers in Poverty.* Ithaca, NY: Cornell University Press.

Sherman, Arloc (1997). *Poverty Matters: The Cost of Child Poverty in America.* Washington, D.C.: Children's Defense Fund.

Sidel, Ruth (1996). *Keeping Women and Children Last: America's War on the Poor.* Baltimore, MD: Penguin.

The Empty Christmas

TAMICIA RUSH

This essay was written as a class assignment by an African American single mother at Olive-Harvey College in South Chicago. In her essay, she remembers a painful Christmas when she was just seven years old. As you read this selection, use your sociological imagination to analyze her situation. How would the different theoretical perspectives view the mother's and father's behavior? Think about the line between private family life and public institutions. At what point, if any, should society intervene in private family life?

The night before Christmas, the air was full of anticipation. My seven-year-old face was shining like the sun, awaiting the return of Santa Claus or, as I knew him, my parents to bring any kind of gift.

I sat in front of the tree that I had put up days before. It was not the best tree. It stood about six feet tall, but leaned against the window like a wreath because there was no stand. The tree had many branches missing, so it was very hard to make it look nice. The lights on that tree were very big and bulky because they were outdoor lights, but they were the only lights in the house. In all, there were about ten ornaments on the tree, which were shedding their thread like a snake shedding its skin. The tree was bare of tinsel and garland because my mother was not there to buy any.

My mother was not there most of the time. She would go off on little adventures and when she came back she acted like she had not been anywhere. When she was gone, there would be no food to eat and no parental supervision in the nasty house. This particular time she went to a friend's house where she said my gifts were. I waited from December 22 to Christmas day for her to return.

SOURCE: Unpublished essay by Tamicia Rush. It is reprinted here with her permission.

When I woke up Christmas morning and looked under the tree, to my surprise there was nothing there. I really believed that I was going to get something this time because she had told me that this Christmas was going to be different. My mother was not even in her room. I went and sat on the sofa and looked at the empty space under the tree and felt the emptiness in my heart. I cried for about an hour. My eyes were blood-shot red and my nose was running like faucet water on a winter day. I felt like no one cared.

As I reached over and got a piece of tissue, the door-bell rang. I went to the door and opened it, thinking that it was my mother ringing because she had lost her keys. But it wasn't, it was my father. He came in, said "Merry Christmas," and gave me a kiss. He asked me if I had been crying, I told him yes, and then he asked "why?" I said because I hadn't eaten anything for three days and I didn't get anything for Christmas. He told me not to worry. I didn't even have to tell him that my mother wasn't there, he just knew. A blank look came over him, as if he was planning something. He turned and left out the door and, when he came back, he had a bag in his hand. He gave me the bag and in it was a pair of boots and a glove set. It wasn't what I was looking for, but it would do.

My dad and I sat and talked for a minute and then my mother walked through the door. I immediately looked down at her hands and they were as empty as a night sky without stars. She did not speak, she just went straight into her bedroom. She was not alone. My father got up, gave me a couple of dollars, and left. If he hadn't left, he would have been fighting.

After her friend left, she didn't say why she was gone for three days or why there weren't any gifts. She went on pretending like nothing happened and so did I. But, in my heart, I will never forget that Christmas.

Karla

STEVEN VANDERSTAAY

Introduction by Steven VanderStaay:

"We'll start with what happened," Karla begins. Young, bright, a mother of two children, she is part of a growing phenomenon: single-parent mothers on assistance who cannot afford a place to live. Cities handle such families differently. New York City houses many women like Karla in so-called welfare hotels, while other cities place them in barrack-style emergency shelters or housing projects. Karla could find nowhere to go. Karla is an African American in her twenties. We met at a Salvation Army shelter for homeless families.

Think about this selection from the two theoretical perspectives. What options does this young mother have? What are the life chances of her children? What role should society take in helping this struggling family? Compare/contrast this selection with the previous essay by Tamicia Rush.

I was working up until the time I had my second baby. I lived with my mom but we weren't getting along. She took care of the first child but the second, that was too much. Then she felt that once I had the children . . . well, her words were, "Two grown ladies can never manage in the same house." So I got on AFDC and went to stay with my littlest girl's aunt.

Well, three weeks ago now, her landlord called and said the building didn't pass inspection. See, the building was infested with bugs and mice.

I didn't have any money saved 'cause I was spending all the AFDC and food stamps on us. I do have qualifications for a lot of jobs, but they're all $3.35. And it's not worth getting a job where you have no medical or dental insurance, not if you have kids. It's not worth giving up welfare. I would work at $3.35 if they let me keep Medicaid and the food stamps, but they don't. They'll cut you off.

SOURCE: Steven Vanderstaay, *Street Lives: An Oral History of Homeless Americans* (Philadelphia: New Society Publishers, 1992), pp. 170–171. Used by permission of the author.

But AFDC's not enough to live on either. I started looking for another place but all the apartments I could afford were just like the one we were living in. It wasn't worth leaving one condemnation to go to another.

Then my daughter's aunt, she moved in with her sister. There was no way I could afford an apartment on my own, not and eat too—and like I said, they were all as bad as the first place. So me and the kids—I have a 3-year-old and a 9-month-old—we just stayed in the building. They boarded it up but we got in through the back window.

There was this older lady that lived next door. We were friends and if she could have helped me she would have. But she already had her four grown kids, plus their kids, livin' with her in a two-bedroom apartment. There's a lot of that these days.

She gave us blankets, though, and I wrapped us up in them. We'd stay outside all day, do something—go to the library or I'd take 'em to the museum. Something. Nights we'd go back into the apartment, light candles, and sleep.

Then it rained real bad. And it was cold. The electrical was off, the gas was off, we were going by candlelight. Mice and rats came out really bad. I woke up one morning and there was a mouse on my 9-month-old's head . . . we couldn't stay in there.

So we went outside, walked around all day. Night came and we slept in a car I found. We were wet and both my kids caught a cold real bad. I took 'em to the emergency room and we slept at the hospital.

The next night we were in this laundromat . . . it was so awful. I was crying, the kids were still sick. And my oldest, Robert, he asked a lot of questions: "Momma, why did we sleep in the car? Why are we outside? It's raining, Momma, I'm cold. I don't feel good."

I couldn't explain. And we had been out for the last three days, never being able to rest. He hadn't eaten anything that night 'cause I didn't have any more money.

Then a man at the laundromat, he gave me $4 to get Robert something to eat. And I stole my baby a can of milk.

Vinela Tejeda

GREG HALPERN

Since 1998, Greg Halpern has been photographing and interviewing Harvard University's lowest paid service workers. In this selection, Vinela Tejeda explains what it is like to raise three daughters and work as a custodian at Harvard Medical School. As an immigrant, she has come to the United States hoping for a better life for her children. Given her life situation, what do you see for her children's future? What structural barriers will they face?

Those are my daughters. And that's in our apartment, in the Jamaica Plain projects. Diani is the oldest, Vanessa is in the middle, and Aurora is the youngest. My schedule is to get up very early, prepare breakfast, get Diani ready to get on the school bus, bring my other daughter to school, then drop Aurora off at my sister's. I get home tired. Tired from work. So I am happy to be home. I take off all my clothes and I bathe. Then I start cleaning, washing clothes, and I don't even feel like eating, because work, it gives me—well, seeing such things—I don't even feel like eating. But I have to prepare supper. Then Diani gets home. Then Vanessa gets home. And I always have appointments, things to do with the girls. If I have something to do with one of the girls I go with that girl and the others watch television. And that's it. That's how my time passes, and that's how all my days go.

I tell my daughters to study so that they will never work like I do. I have done this work for twelve years. My mom and dad, when I got to the U.S., they said for me not to do this kind of work. They said that I'd have a rough life and that it would be scary. But I told them I had to do it, and that I wouldn't do it so much for myself as for the girls.

My hope is in my children. I want for them to study and to learn the language well and prepare themselves—for another class of work. There will always be people cleaning the toilets at Harvard. But I want the best jobs for them. For myself, I cannot ask for anything very high up, realistically speaking. But I would love to work at least in a store. I worked as a cashier in my country. But in the very least I'd

SOURCE: Halpern, Greg. 2003. *Harvard Works Because We Do*. New York: Quantuck Lane Press, pp. 125–127.

want a job less heavy. Maybe in a supermarket. The only thing I'm afraid of is my English, because the customer could ask something and I would not know what it is. But when you get the chance to come to this country, you go, and you may not have had the chance to learn English yet. And so here I am.

After high school, you see, I didn't want to go to college; only to come to the United States, to find a better future for me and my children. And so I came to the U.S. like everybody does—the unofficial way. And I came without my kids. I wanted to work in a bank because I liked accounting. But as I came here, I had to start work as soon as I came here because I had to save money to bring Diani here. And things here started getting more complicated because I didn't have papers, and I could not go to school and I had to work, and I had to keep cleaning. I couldn't get out of it.

I clean Vanderbilt Hall, where the medical students live. For the most part I clean rest rooms and kitchens. The hardest are the bathtubs, the showers, the stoves, everything in the kitchens. Sometimes the students leave pots and pans out in the kitchens for days, which can be difficult. But there are others that are really good people. With the students, I am as they wish. If they greet me, I greet them. And if they don't greet me, well I don't greet them either.

There are about seven of us, all women, who work here cleaning all six floors. I am not particularly proud of myself, but at least I always finish my work. I feel good about the fact that I complete my work. And thank God the supervisors have never had to call me in.

Mondays are the hardest days to clean because one finds everything strewn all over the place. The bathrooms are all wet with toilet paper, paper towels all over the place. The bathtub full of hairs, but one has to clean it. I put on my gloves and I protect myself. Where hundreds of students live, using the kitchen, using the bathroom, imagine how things get. There is also a ton of work to be done before the students come back from the summer. Every corner needs to be cleaned.

We have to protect ourselves when cleaning the rest rooms. We use gloves, and they give us good chemicals. I don't like that part but I do it. I do it because I need to. I don't know English well and I can't really apply at another job. So I have to do it. But it's okay, especially because I have a good supervisor, who is really great with us. He helps us and he doesn't pressure us too much.

I work seven days a week. I work eight hours on Saturdays and Sundays, doing the same job, in the same building, but it is for a different company. The problem with that is that I work two part-time jobs for two different companies, and so I do not qualify for health benefits with either one. I'd love to work one full-time job during the week, and to have benefits and weekends free to be with my daughters. But they say full time is not available right now. I don't like leaving the little ones home alone on the weekend. Because now when I leave, Diani, my oldest, stays there with the younger ones, or sometimes my sister will come stay with them. She doesn't have much of a home, my sister, so sometimes she'll spend the night too. We make room. Vanessa and Diani sleep together. I sleep with the little one. I like to be here at night to help them with homework and just to keep an eye on them.

I would like health benefits very much. Very much. I was absent two weeks once, because I was having an operation on a vein in my leg, and that week I didn't make any money because I couldn't work. When you take a leave to have a baby it's the same thing. Because I have no benefits. They give you two months to be at home but you aren't making any money.

When I had my daughters, I worked until I couldn't anymore. Past eight months. But I needed to, to save the money. They try to be considerate when you are pregnant, though. They give you lighter work and they try to get someone else to clean the bathtubs for you, because if you slip that can be dangerous. Now after the Living Wage Campaign, at least they've given us a raise to eleven dollars and thirty-five cents. It's better, but I'm still only at a hundred and sixty-two dollars a week, after taxes—six hundred and forty-eight dollars a month.

When I am working, I think at times about how I feel uncomfortable with this life here. "Always the same," I think, "always the same." But then I calm down because I realize I just have to work. I have three daughters, I have to support them. At other times I think of taking off for my country. And again I tell myself, "I'd better not. Now my girls are studying here. Now they speak English. I am obliged to stay." I feel trapped sometimes. Or I feel it's an embarrassment to be working in bathrooms and all. Or it makes me feel embarrassment or shame around the students, because at times they're not considerate when they make a mess in the bathrooms. And I will have to clean that up. Sometimes I think I made a bad decision in wanting to come to the United States. But at the same time, I think I have also acquired many things. I had two of my daughters here. And I am now legal here in this country; I have acquired my citizenship. And at least I work, although it's not a great job. At least I have my apartment. At least I have a roof. I don't have money but at least I live tranquilly. Having children has held me back, but I do not feel bad about that because they will move on. I would like us to move on together, maybe move back to Santo Domingo. Build a nice house there, for me and my daughters to live in comfortably and peacefully.

REFLECTION QUESTIONS

FOR PART IV

After reading the selections on living on the economic margins, reflect on the following questions:

1. Compare and contrast the readings in this section. Are the different individuals and families living on the economic margins affected in the same way?
2. How do stigma and shame fit into each selection? What survival strategies do the individuals use to cope with their situations?
3. How do gender/race/ethnicity/age/location structure their experiences?
4. Analyze each article carefully and group them by individual/cultural and structural theories of poverty. What theory is best reflected in each reading? Explain.
5. Select one particular essay, such as Susan Sheehan's "Ain't No Middle Class," and analyze it first *without* using a sociological imagination and then analyze it again *with* a sociological imagination.

PART V

The Impact of Societal Institutions on Individual Lives

"Focusing on the poor and ignoring the system of power, privilege, and profit which makes them poor, is a little like blaming the corpse for murder."

Michael Parenti (1978)

As we have seen, one view of the poor is that they are to blame for their economic deprivation. From this perspective the system is good, but flawed people fail. This emphasis ignores the social organization that oppresses them. Michael Parenti has criticized those who ignore the system as victim blamers. "Focusing on the poor and ignoring the system of power, privilege, and profit which makes them poor, is a little like blaming the corpse for the murder" (Parenti, 1978:24).

The alternative view is that poverty is not fundamentally a matter of individual behavior but rather a matter of public institutions and accepted practices that create or perpetuate poverty. Sociologists focus on society's institutions and their role in producing and perpetuating poverty, which are the subjects of the section. We examine, in turn, housing/neighborhoods, the welfare system, the health care system, schools and schooling, and work and working.

CHAPTER 6

Housing/Homeless Shelters/ Neighborhoods

According to the U.S. Interagency Council on Homelessness, more than 2 million Americans experience homelessness at least sometime during the course of a year (Jones, 2007). About 10 percent (200,000) are "chronically homeless." The rest are homeless for a time (typically 4 months) because of a temporary situation such as job loss, illness or accident, or domestic crisis (Ward, 2007).

What puts many people in jeopardy of homelessness is the high cost of rent. Affordable housing for the poor is in ever shorter supply. **Gentrification** (the redevelopment of poor and working-class urban neighborhoods into upscale enclaves) and other forms of urban development (building highways, stadiums, parks, parking garages) have reduced the number of affordable rental units, previously found in cheap residential hotels and single residence occupancy (SRO) housing, and affordable public housing. (The government, by the way, reduced its number of public housing units in New Orleans by 5,000 after Hurricane Katrina.) In June 2005 the official government estimate was that the United States lacked 1.6 million units of low-income housing. This squeeze on relatively cheap rentals, boosts the rents faster than inflation and wage increases. The National Low Income Housing Coalition notes that 2005 was the first year on record, that a full-time worker at minimum wage could not afford a one-bedroom apartment anywhere in the United States at average market rates (Urbina, 2006).

The government assumes that the poor should not pay more than 30 percent of their income for housing, yet according to the American Housing Survey, 7.5 million households were "severely burdened" by their housing costs, meaning that more than half their income went for rent or mortgage payments (Broder, 2005). Department of Housing and Urban Development (HUD) estimates more than 6 million poor families spend more than half their income on housing. In 2007 the national median rent was $943 a month. Even at the minimum wage of $7.25 an hour set for 2008, a full-time worker would spend 81 percent of their income on this median rental.

Less than 30 percent of low-income renters receive any housing subsidy, leaving only about 1.3 million poor families receiving vouchers—a government rent subsidy that pays the difference between 30 percent of their income and market rents anywhere they choose to live. Federal money for housing has declined every year since 2000 (El Nassar, 2006). The government's housing policies to aid the poor, by the way, cost about $30 billion a year, while at the same time another government housing policy allows homeowners to save $115 billion a year by allowing interest and taxes on houses to be tax deductible.

The shortage of affordable housing leaves the poor with three unappealing options—paying excessively high rents, living in substandard housing, or homelessness. Sometimes the choice is forced, since the poor are only an economic disaster brought on by theft, fire, illness, or job loss away from being evicted and the resulting homelessness. When homeless is the only option, there will be a continual struggle with finding food, warmth, and a place to clean up.

In 29 major cities, the homeless outnumber the number of beds in temporary shelters forcing many to literally spend the night in cars, in doorways, under bridges, or in the streets. More than one-third of the homeless are families with children. Most U.S. cities are unfriendly to the homeless with official policies banning loitering, trespassing, panhandling, and carrying open containers of alcohol. A number of cities conduct nightly "police sweeps" of their streets to harass the homeless. New York City requires the homeless to work 20 hours a week in exchange for shelter. Sacramento, California pays for one-way bus tickets out of state for homeless with family or jobs to go to. Chicago has privatized sidewalks in front of businesses, which means that anyone who loiters there is trespassing. Thus, the homeless are twice cursed—they are not only without shelter, they are punished for not having a shelter.

LIVING IN POOR NEIGHBORHOODS

The poor cluster in neighborhoods where the housing is cheap. These places are cheap because of their undesirability. Often these areas are exposed to environmental hazards such as toxic wastes, high concentrations of lead, and other pollutants (Bullard, 2000). They may be cheap because they are in the flood plain. Poor urban neighborhoods, typically, are not provided the same services found in more affluent neighborhoods such as banks, retail outlets, and adequate public transportation. Neighborhood schools often are in disrepair and are not equipped with adequate libraries, computers, and special equipment for children who are disabled.

The city neighborhoods where poverty is concentrated have relatively high rates of street crime, making the neighborhoods relatively unsafe. When good job opportunities are scarce, young people in the inner city become more susceptible to and attracted by the opportunities in the criminal economy. Street crimes such as drug trafficking, burglary, prostitution, and car theft become their work (Hagedorn, 1998). The gangs that organize around these activities, while sources of meaningful social relationships, status, and protection for their members, make life in these bleak and isolated inner city neighborhoods dangerous and problematic.

NOTES AND SUGGESTED READINGS

Belkin, Lisa (1999). *Show Me A Hero: A Tale of Murder, Suicide, Race, and Redemption.* New York: Little, Brown.

Bennett, Larry, Janet L. Smith, and Patricia A. Wright (Eds.) (2006). *Where Are Poor People to Live? Transforming Public Housing Communities.* Armonk, NY: M. E. Sharpe.

Broder, David (2005). "Nation's Affordable Housing Shortage Critical." *Denver Post* (June 2):7B.

Bullard, Robert D. (2000). *Dumping in Dixie: Race, Class, and Environmental Quality,* 3rd ed. Boulder, CO: Westview Press.

Burt, Martha R., and Laudan Y. Aron (2001). *Helping America's Homeless.* Washington, D.C.: The Urban Institute.

DeOllos, Ione Y. (1997). *On Becoming Homeless: The Shelterization Process for Homeless Families.* Lanham, NY: University Press of America.

Duneier, Mitchell (1999). *Sidewalk.* New York: Farrar, Strauss and Giroux.

Eighner, Lars (1993). *Travels with Lizbeth.* New York: St. Martin's Press.

El Nasser, Haya (2006). "Survey: Fewer Affordable Homes Available." *USA Today* (December 7):7A.

Guzewicz, Tony D. (1994). *Down and Out in New York City: Homelessness, a Dishonorable Poverty.* New York: Nova Science Publishers.

Hagedorn, John (1998). *People and Folks: Gangs, Crime and the Underclass in a Rustbelt City,* 2nd ed. Chicago: Lake View Press.

Homeless, Joe (1992). *My Life on the Street: Memoirs of a Faceless Man.* Far Hills, NJ: New Horizon Press.

Jones, Charisse (2007). "Cities Go Further to Help Homeless." *USA Today* (January 24):3A.

Liebow, Elliot (1993). *Tell Them Who I Am: The Lives of Homeless Women.* New York: Free Press.

MacLeod, Jay (1995). *Ain't No Makin' It: Aspirations and Attainment in a Low-Income Neighborhood.* Boulder, CO: Westview Press.

Maggi, Laura (2000). "The Squeeze." *The American Prospect* (December 4):28–29.

Massey, Douglas, and Nancy Denton (1993). *American Apartheid: Segregation and the Making of the Underclass.* Cambridge, MA: Harvard University Press.

Neal, Ruth, and April Allen (1996). *Environmental Justice: An Annotated Bibliography,* Report Series EJRC/CAU-1-96 (Updated June 1998). Atlanta, GA: Environmental Justice Resource Center.

Parenti, Michael (1978). *Power and the Powerless,* 2nd ed. New York: St. Martin's Press.

Passaro, Joanne (1996). *The Unequal Homeless: Men on the Streets, Women in Their Place.* New York: Routledge.

Popkin, Susan J., Victoria E. Gwiasda, Lynn M. Olson, Dennis P. Rosenbaum, and Larry Buron (2000). *The Hidden War: Crime and the Tragedy of Public Housing in Chicago.* New Brunswick, NJ: Rutgers University Press.

The Progressive (2000). "The Housing Crunch." Volume 64 (May):8–10.

Ralston, Meredith L. (1996). *"Nobody Wants to Hear Our Truth": Homeless Women and Theories of the Welfare State.* Westport, CT: Greenwood Press.

Snow, David A., and Leon Anderson (2003). "Street People." *Contexts* 2 (Winter):12–17.

Timmer, Doug A. (1988). "Homeless as Deviance: The Ideology of the Shelter." *Free Inquiry in Creative Sociology* 16 (2):163–170.

Timmer, Doug A., D. Stanley Eitzen, and Kathryn D. Talley (1994). *Paths to Homelessness: Extreme Poverty and the Urban Housing Crisis.* Boulder, CO: Westview Press.

Urbina, Ian (2006). "Keeping It Secret As the Family Car Becomes a Home." *New York Times* (April 2). Online: http://select.nytimes.com/search/restricted/article?res=F70C14FF 38540C718CDDAD0894

Vale, Lawrence J. (2001). *From the Puritans to the Projects: Public Housing and Public Neighbors.* Cambridge, MA: Harvard University Press.

Venkatesh, Sudhir Alladi (2001). *American Project: The Rise and Fall of a Modern Ghetto.* Cambridge, MA: Harvard University Press.

Ward, Chip (2007). "America Gone Wrong: A Slashed Safety Net Turns Libraries into Homeless Shelters." *Alternet* (April 2). Online: www.alternet.org/story/50023

Shelter

BOBBY BURNS

This selection consists of excerpts from Bobby Burns' diary, his personal account of being homeless on the streets of Tucson, Arizona. He is a college graduate and substitute teacher. Due to a series of events, medical problems, and a drug/alcohol problem, he finds himself without a home, without a job, and in a homeless shelter. Thinking sociologically, what do you learn about shelter life through this author's experience? How would you structure a job program designed to help homeless individuals get back on their feet?

Today I will apply for food stamps for the first time in my life. I arrive at the office at 7:00 A.M., and once the office opens I complete the long application and wait to be called. I feel like I am begging, like a bum off a street corner. The individuals working in this agency treat everyone the same—coldly and impersonally. I sense they see all homeless persons as lazy. I feel angry, humiliated, and ashamed. But as with any agency like this, they have what we need, and we must endure the situation. Long waits are typical in a food stamp office. I wonder if food stamps will bring me a sense of empowerment at the grocery store, being able to buy the things I like in the way of snacks.

Finally, after two hours, my name is called. A young clerk interviews me as she intently reviews my application. She asks me several questions with a bit of a holier-than-thou attitude, then tells me I qualify for $118 in food stamps each month. In two days, I will receive emergency food stamps worth $65. Being homeless has a few perks.

My next stop for the day is the city's Special Services/Transportation offices for a reduced-rate bus card. Getting around any city requires transportation, and I must rely on city buses. Again I sense a cold and insensitive attitude. Many social service agency personnel show little respect or compassion for people who happen to be without an address. Homelessness to me means that I have no home at

SOURCE: From *Shelter: One Man's Journey from Homelessness to Hope* by Bobby Burns, © 1998 by Bobby Burns. Reprinted by permission of the University of Arizona Press.

the moment. It's not a disease a person can catch by simply coming into contact with me.

Before I became homeless, I never took the time to think about or understand who became homeless. I looked through them. What I did know about the homeless I learned from the rhetoric put out by the media or from what I saw with my own eyes. My impression was that their predicament had to be their own fault. Homelessness was their problem, it wasn't mine—until I became part of that population. Now I realize people become homeless for countless reasons. They're not all thugs and bums; some are people who've just fallen on bad times. It seems people get concerned about helping the homeless around the holidays in November and December; they tend to forget the rest of the year. I've learned that homelessness is the same year-round, with some individuals remaining homeless for many years.

My perception of Ivan [shelter worker] is that he is condescending, rude, and arrogant. He talks down to me and another man, and I get the impression he's only half present and his heart isn't in his work. However, he deals with guys like me every day. And who am I? Just another homeless man passing through his doors who says he is trying to find a job. The types of individuals he encounters range from highly employable to those with few or no skills.

Job Connection provides two options to homeless men. A two-week program is for people just passing through town who want to earn enough money to move on. Most jobs pay daily—better known as day labor. One day you might be shoveling up someone's sewer pipes, another day you might be hauling trash to a garbage dump for eight hours for minimum wage. This Job Connection program places no restrictions on clients except that their stay in the shelter is up after two weeks.

The other program, for four to eight weeks, has strings attached. The sooner one finds work, the better. The program offers a résumé service, job skills training, and a message phone. Ivan makes it clear that if I'm not working a full-time job in four weeks, I'm out of the program. If I find work, I can have an additional four weeks in the program.

Each pay day, every client in the program must place 75 percent of his wages in savings, and he can use the remainder any way he wants. Each person is responsible for getting a money order in his name and handing it over to Ivan. Earnings are returned at the end of the program. A person can get ahead and land back on his feet if he sticks to the plan. I believe I can if I don't drink. I have no excuse not to succeed. My meals and rent are free. Finding a job seems a minor concern. I agree to the terms of the contract and sign on the dotted line.

My next priority is to go back to the county Health Department for my TB results. A nurse looks at my left arm and says my test is negative. She hands me a card showing that I am TB-free, which I will have to show the shelter. It's 11:30 A.M. and I decide to eat lunch at a downtown greasy spoon. I order a bowl of soup, a half-sandwich of tuna, and a cold glass of iced tea. I sit on the café patio as the lunch crowd comes and goes. The weather is sunny and breezy.

I later return to the R & R office to see if my food stamps have arrived. A volunteer hands me my mail. A letter from the Arizona Department of Economic

Security informs me that I will receive my food stamps within five days. Leaving the office, I see a man trying to sell his food stamps to another man for cash. This sort of thing happens all the time. With cash you have more latitude. With food stamps you face certain restrictions. I walk downtown pondering what I should be doing with myself. Idle time is what gets me in trouble with booze and drugs, this I know.

Time has gone by fast today. I walk a few blocks from downtown to catch the shelter bus. As I approach the pickup point, I notice about twenty men waiting for the bus, some men I have never seen before. A few are talking, and the rest stand in silence as if they have nothing in common with one another. The bus ride is mellow as the big white bus passes through the downtown.

Uncertainty enters my mind as I size up the other men, who look as unsure and wary as I. As the bus arrives at the shelter, a manager waits at the front door with a clipboard in his hand. "Report to the second door on your right if it's your first time in the shelter," he yells.

Those of us who already have beds give our names and bunk numbers by rote. All of my possessions are shuffled onto and under my bed. I feel discouraged as I look around the cluttered barracks. Homelessness is undeniable. Still, I have problems in accepting that I have fallen this low. The oppressive environment on a daily basis, the day-to-day grind, gets to me. Every day I face the constant noise, the bothersome loudspeaker, the rules, the schedule, strange people in and out. But if I can put up with navy boot camp, then I can put up with the shelter.

The Residents of Rockwell Gardens

SUSAN J. POPKIN, VICTORIA E. GWIASDA, LYNN M. OLSON,
DENNIS P. ROSENBAUM, AND LARRY BURON

In The Hidden War: Crime and the Tragedy of Public Housing in
Chicago *the authors surveyed residents and observed life in three Chicago
housing projects over a period of four years. The result is a portrait of life
in some of the poorest neighborhoods in the United States. This selection
is the perspective of one of the residents of Rockwell Gardens. Analyze
Dawn's housing situation/neighborhood from the individual/cultural and
structural perspectives. What are some possible solutions to the problems
of Rockwell Gardens?*

DAWN'S STORY

Dawn is a long-time resident of Rockwell Gardens—the development widely
considered the most dangerous of the Chicago Housing Authority's (CHA) high-
rise projects. She is a thoughtful, articulate woman in her early thirties and has
lived in Rockwell since she was fourteen. Dawn became pregnant as the result of a
rape when she was sixteen; after the birth of her second child two years later, she
dropped out of school to care for her children. Dawn's mother could not help her
with child care because she had young children of her own, and Dawn could not
find another sitter she felt she could trust.

Her children are now teenagers, and she spends most of her time and energy
protecting them from what she calls "the pressure" of the surrounding environment: young men pressure her daughter for sex, and gang members try to recruit
her son. For years, she has monitored her children closely by taking them to parks
outside the development to play and keeping them indoors as much as possible.
"They mostly sit on the porch in the building. . . . [They go out] with me. . . . Sometime they go to the store and back, but I don't really let them hang in front of the
buildings and stuff. If they go to a playground, they go in the Maplewood Courts

SOURCE: Susan J. Popkin, Victoria E. Gwiasda, Lynn M. Olson, Dennis P. Rosenbaum, and Larry
Buron. *The Hidden War: Crime and Tragedy of Public Housing in Chicago* (Piscataway, NJ: Rutgers University Press, 2000), pp. 39–43. Used by permission of the publisher.

playground [an adjacent, low-rise development] because they don't shoot over there. Or across the [freeway] bridge to the big park." Although her son sometimes goes to the store or participates in after-school programs, Dawn says her daughter no longer goes outside alone.

Dawn has been on welfare since the birth of her first child. She says she always wanted to be a nurse when she was growing up, but "her children held her back." Although she did eventually get her GED, her only work experience has been an "off-the-books" job as a housekeeper for a few years. She desperately wants a better life for herself and her children, but she lacks practical ideas about how to improve her situation.

Living in CHA housing has taken a toll on Dawn and her family. Everyone she knows lives in public housing: her entire extended family lives in CHA developments all around the city. She says that no one in her family has "made it," that all the developments are "just the same." Three members of her extended family have died because of gang violence, one as a result of a domestic dispute. Several, addicted to drugs, have lost custody of their children. In April 1996, she told us that, since January, she had already been to three funerals for people from Rockwell, which she said was "typical." Dawn is often depressed, but says she had no one to talk to about her feelings because "people in the projects, they don't want to hear your problems. They tell you 'I have problems of my own.'"

Throughout the two years we interviewed her, Dawn offered many insights into the challenges of life in Rockwell. Although her greatest concerns were drug trafficking and violence, the daily problems that she found most frustrating were poor maintenance and unresponsive housing authority management. For example, in 1994, Dawn said she had been coping with severe plumbing problems for two years:

My tub water don't shut off—the hot water . . . and the kitchen won't shut off. . . . Well, they just fixed my sink not too long ago because they had to take the whole pipe out of the wall because it was full of that greasy, gunky stuff and the water wouldn't flow through and it kept running out, running out. That took them two years to get up and fix that. I had to wash my dishes in my tub every day. . . . [In the bathroom] my walls were white, [now] they yellowish-brownish from the hot water. I have to close the door at night to keep from going crazy hearing that water! . . . . I been waiting six months for them to fix that.

Vandalism compounded the maintenance problems and, Dawn felt, made her building an even more frightening place to live.

Some people may set their garbage . . . in front of the incinerator, which they not supposed to do that, they supposed to take it downstairs to the main floor [because the incinerators don't work], but they don't. Either the kids will set it on fire, or the big boys will come and just throw it down the steps, and it's really dark, we can't see! You know . . . I bust my head, bumped into the light room door, it being dark. . . . And then when they do put bulbs in every day, the guys will like take sticks and break the bulbs or take 'em out and make it dark. Seem like they like it dark.

In Dawn's view, drugs, particularly cocaine, have completely devastated the Rockwell community. She spoke poignantly of seeing friends who were once "strong women" wasting away because of their crack addictions. She said she could no longer let some people she knows into her apartment because they would try to steal whatever they could to support their habit.

> *Man, the rock's [crack] been here seem like forever. Because when I used to come from the grocery store and I be bringing my groceries in, the elevators be broke, and we used to have to carry our stuff up the stairs . . . and there's people in the hallway smoking crack with . . . they was actually using t.v. antennas. . . . People come to your door and—they say, "Can I use your bathroom," I always tell them no, and I know them, but I tell them no because they wanna go in there and break off a piece of your t.v. antenna.*

Dawn said she had never used drugs herself, and she stayed away from "project men," whom she described as pressuring their girlfriends to become users so they could use their welfare money to buy drugs.

Dawn was particularly concerned about how the disintegration of the community affected the children of Rockwell. She agonized over the children she saw being abused or neglected by mothers addicted to cocaine, crack, and heroin. She told the following story to illustrate the extremes to which addicts went to feed their addiction: "Their women just go crazy for that stuff, they do anything. . . . Anything. They don't care. One lady sold her baby for some rock. . . . To the man, it was a guy who sold cocaine over there, she . . . gave him her baby, she told him to hold my baby until I come back, I'm gonna go get the money, give me the rocks."

Dawn used to try to intervene when she saw hungry or abandoned children in her building. When she could afford to, she fed them herself. But when she found children who were unsupervised—for example, a five-year-old taking care of a four-month-old—she would sometimes call the Department of Children and Family Services to report the situation. When the social workers came, she would help getting the children dressed and ready to be taken away. She also used to call the police to report shootings or other crimes. Eventually, her family convinced her that it was too dangerous to get involved, a position that causes her much pain. She spoke of her torment over having kept silent after she witnessed a young neighbor using a gun:

> *When you in the projects, you do a lot of things, you see a lot of things, but you know you don't wanna say nothing because it can get you hurt . . . but it be on your conscience, and it drives me crazy when I can't say nothing. . . . I see this little boy, he's about twelve years old. He's shooting, I see him shooting at the other [kids]. And I'm looking at this, and I know his mother and everything. Everybody telling me, "No, don't say nothing, don't tell his mother." And now he's dead, the little boy is dead now, and it made me feel if I had a told his mother, maybe he'd still be here.*

Dawn said she had high hopes when the CHA first started the sweeps in Rockwell in 1988; she believed they would help to control the gangs and drug trafficking. For a time, she felt that conditions did improve a little, but, by the time we met her in 1994, she told us that all the good effects had disappeared. However, she was hopeful that the CHA's latest effort—hiring a company owned by the Nation of Islam to provide security and manage the development—would help. Also, she reported that things were getting calmer following a gang truce in Rockwell.

But from 1994 to 1996, Dawn became increasingly disillusioned and unhappy. In her view, the "Muslims" proved no better than any other security guards who had patrolled Rockwell over the years. The new management cleaned up the buildings, but she still had serious maintenance problems in her apartment. Drug abuse was still rampant, and the gangs still dominated the development. Sometimes she felt that things had improved for a little while because of a gang truce or the arrest of a particularly powerful gang leader, but the gang war between the Disciples and the Vice Lords always "flared up" again after a month or two.

In spring 1996, Dawn finally moved out of Rockwell Gardens to another, smaller CHA development. A friend of hers had moved there and told that it was "nice." Dawn was dismayed to find that, although the complex was cleaner than Rockwell and the apartments were better, she still faced many of the same problems: "I only been there not long at all and they been shooting, I been hearing gun shots, one boy done got killed, right out by the building in the back."

The Welfare System

From the time of the Great Depression to 1996 the United States provided a minimal safety net for those in need. The New Deal under President Roosevelt and the Great Society under President Johnson created the minimum wage; federal aid to education; health and nutrition programs; food stamps; energy assistance; subsidized housing; and Aid to Families with Dependent Children (Moen and Forest, 1999:644–647). These minimal but helpful programs have gradually been dismantled, beginning with President Nixon and accelerating under President Reagan. This dismemberment quickened appreciably in 1996, when the federal government made welfare assistance to families temporary and withdrew $55 billion of federal aid to the poor.

THE PERSONAL RESPONSIBILITY AND WORK OPPORTUNITY RECONCILIATION ACT OF 1996

In 1996 the Republican-dominated Congress and a middle-of-the-road Democratic president passed a sweeping welfare law that ended the 61-year-old safety net for the poor. The major provisions of this law (as later amended) included the following:

- Through federal block grants states were given a fixed amount of money for welfare and considerable flexibility in how to spend it.
- The law insisted on work. The states were required to demand that parents work within two years of receiving cash assistance, although states were free to shorten the period before welfare recipients must work.
- The law mandated a five-year lifetime limit on the receipt of assistance, which states can reduce if they wish.
- The law required that unmarried teen parents must live at home or in another adult-supervised setting and attend school to receive welfare assistance.
- Various federal assistance programs targeted for the poor were cut by $54.5 billion over six years. Included in these budget cuts were $27 billion from the food stamp program, $7 billion from the children's portion of the Supplemental Security Income program, $3 billion for child nutrition, and $2.5 billion for social services. Cuts were also made by tightening the qualifying criteria for being defined as a disabled child.
- The welfare law denied a broad range of public benefits to legal immigrants.

- The federal money given to the states was capped at $16.4 billion annually. This is significant because it means that there is no adjustment for inflation, business downturns, and population growth.

In sum, this new welfare legislation ended the entitlement which guaranteed that states must give help to all needy families with children. Now assistance for poor families was temporary—Aid to Families with Dependent Children (AFDC) was replaced with Temporary Assistance for Needy Families (TANF)—with parents required to work.

A question arising from the requirement that all former AFDC mothers work is whether a single mother is "able" to work. Traditionally, she was not considered so. AFDC was created in 1935 with the goal of keeping women at home with their children. The 1996 legislation changed that, forcing poor women with children to work—without the training, without the jobs, and without the childcare. Through twisted logic, the same conservative politicians who want poor mothers to work want middle-class mothers to give up their jobs because a stay-at-home mother is positive for children.

Two additional problems arise with forcing single mothers to work. First, most of the available work for women with little education and few skills pays at or slightly above the minimum wage, a wage that gives a full-time worker an annual income that is several thousand dollars *below* the poverty line. Work also entails the additional costs of child care, transportation, and clothing. Second, when economic times are good, there may be enough jobs available for those no longer eligible for welfare but what happens to these women and their children when there is an economic downturn and the last hired are the first fired?

Social policy is about design, involving the setting of societal goals and determining the means to achieve them. Should we create and invest in policies and programs that protect citizens from poverty, unemployment, inferior educations, and inadequate medical care, or should the market economy sort people into winners, players, and losers based on their abilities and efforts? Decision makers in the United States have opted to eliminate most of the safety net for those on the economic margins, especially single women with children. Are these policy makers on the right track? Is this design the solution to poverty or should the United States change its design?

NOTES AND SUGGESTIONS FOR FURTHER READINGS

Blumenberg, Evelyn (2000). "Moving Welfare Participants to Work: Women, Transportation, and Welfare Reform." *Affilia* 15 (Summer):259–276.

Edelman, Peter (1997). "The Worst Thing Bill Clinton Has Done." *Atlantic Monthly* (March):43–58.

Eitzen, D. Stanley, and Maxine Baca Zinn (In Press). *Social Problems,* 11th edition. Boston: Allyn and Bacon.

Ellwood, David T. (2000). "Anti-Poverty Policy for Families in the Next Century: From Welfare to Work—and Worries." *Journal of Economic Perspectives* 14:187–198.

Funiciello, Theresa (1993). *Tyranny of Kindness: Dismantling the Welfare System to End Poverty in America.* New York: Atlantic Monthly Press.

Gans, Herbert J. (1995). *The War against the Poor: The Underclass and Antipoverty Policy.* New York: Basic Books

Handler, Joel F. (1995). *The Poverty of Welfare Reform.* New Haven, CT: Yale University Press.

Harris, Kathleen Mullan (1996). "The Reforms Will Hurt, Not Help Poor Women and Children." *The Chronicle of Higher Education* (October 4):37.

Moen, Phyllis, and Kay B. Forest (1999). "Strengthening Families: Policy Issues for the Twenty-First Century," pp. 633–663 in *Handbook of Marriage and the Family,* 2nd ed., Marvin B. Sussman, Suzanne K. Steinmetz, and Gary W. Peterson (Eds.). New York: Plenum Press.

O'Connor, Alice (2001). *Poverty Knowledge: Social Science, Social Policy, and the Poor in Twentieth-Century U.S. History.* Princeton, NJ: Princeton University Press.

Peck, Jamie (2001). *Workfare States.* New York: The Guilford Press.

Polakow, Valerie (1999). "Savage Distributions: Welfare Myths and Daily Lives," pp. 241–262 in *A New Introduction to Poverty: The Role of Race, Power, and Politics,* Louis Kushnick and James Jennings (Eds.). New York: New York University Press.

Seccombe, Karen (1999). *"So You Think I Drive a Cadillac?"* Boston: Allyn and Bacon.

Welfare As They Know It

PLAINTIFFS IN CAPERS V. GIULIANI

The following selection consists of testimony in a class-action suit brought on behalf of New York City workfare participants. Workfare participants are individuals who are required to work in order to receive welfare benefits. This particular class-action suit involved those individuals who were assigned to the Departments of Sanitation and Transportation in New York City, and their testimonies document the hazardous working conditions they encounter. As a result of their testimonies, a State Supreme Court Justice ruled that the city was obligated to improve the working conditions of its 5,000 workfare participants. Think about welfare reform that requires recipients to work to receive their benefits. What problems with this system are brought to light by the following testimonies? Are any working conditions better than none at all? Think about workfare and women with small children at home. What potential problems do you foresee for these women?

TAMIKA CAPERS, AGE TWENTY-ONE

Since February 26, 1997, I have been cleaning highways and the areas next to highways in the Work Experience Program (WEP) for the New York City Department of Transportation. The work consists of raking, sweeping, picking up garbage, cutting tall grass by hand with a long-handled Weedwacker, and clipping tree branches overhead.

While we clean the highways, cars, trucks, and tractor-trailers whiz by only a few feet away. Cones are put up to protect us, but they are spaced so far apart that the cars ignore them and swerve inside when the traffic is heavy. Last month, a car went out of control and ran up on the grass, heading right for two of my co-workers, who had to dash out of the way to avoid being hit. When the car returned to the highway, it stopped, causing a three-car pileup.

We have no access to a toilet either in the parking lot where we are picked up each morning or out on the highway. If we need to urinate or move our bowels,

Source: Plaintiffs in *Capers v. Giuliani*, "Welfare As They Know It," *Harper's Magazine* 295 (November 1997), pp. 24–26.

we have to squat behind a tree or bush or ask one of our co-workers to hold up a plastic bag to shield us from the passing cars. We have not been given insect repellent, and I am afraid to relieve myself outdoors, because I will be exposed to the many biting insects flying and crawling around us. My stomach cramps from holding my urine. During my menstrual period, there is no place to go to change my pad. I have to wait until the end of our shift, and by then my clothes are soaked with blood.

ANASTACIO SERRANO, AGE FORTY-FOUR

On March 10, 1997, I began my WEP assignment on a cleaning crew of four people. We sweep twenty to thirty blocks of street per day in the Williamsburg section of Brooklyn. Sometimes our group travels in a van behind a garbage truck. When we see trash, the van stops and the four of us get out of the van, sweep up the mess, and put it into the garbage truck. The supervisor sits in the van the entire time.

I keep a log of my daily activities in WEP. On June 18, while riding in the van, we came across two dead cats and two dead dogs. They had been dumped by the side of the road. Because I have no gloves, I had to pick them up with my bare hands. The animals had been run over by automobiles and were oozing blood and entrails. When I picked up the animals with my bare hands to throw them into the garbage truck, the guts splattered on my shoes and pants. My coworker vomited. My supervisor, sitting in the van, said nothing. I have seen other people who were terminated by my supervisor for refusing to pick up things, and I was afraid that if I refused to leave the van or left the carcasses in the gutter I would be terminated also.

Because I have no dust mask or eye protection, I suffer from the dust that blows up in my face while I am sweeping. I have glaucoma, which requires me to use pilocarpine hydrochloride drops four times a day. The dust gets in my eyes and dries up the solutions. I can hardly see by lunchtime. I have only one eye that I can see from now, and I am worried that I may eventually lose my sight completely.

I have trouble sleeping for the first time in my life. I toss and turn at night because of the pain in my eyes and back and from the stress of having to endure the daily humiliation of this program.

MERY MEJIA, AGE THIRTY-SEVEN

Since February 1997 I have been working on a crew that cleans the ramps and service roads near the highways. I cut weeds and grass all morning by swinging a long wooden stick with a flat metal blade. The tool is heavy and hurts my shoulders after a few minutes. I'm about five feet tall, and some of the grass is taller than I am.

While working, I see rats everywhere along the roads. They don't bite us, because we scream and run away. They are about eight inches long, with long, stringy tails. They are sometimes right next to us. There are also all sorts of plants, maybe poison ivy, that give me rashes. But the supervisors give us no work clothes, either in the winter or the summer. The only things we get for protection are an orange vest, a pair of cotton gloves, and a hard hat. The gloves and the hard hat are filthy, but I am not allowed to take anything home to wash it. They gave out boots for one week in February, but they were all size 12 and did not fit me.

Because there is no place to go to the bathroom, I do not drink water. This makes me feel like I am suffocating. When I work I feel nauseated and light-headed, and I get terrible headaches. When I finally do go to the bathroom my urine is very dark brown, which makes me concerned about my kidneys. One of the other women in my crew fainted from the heat, but we caught her before her head hit the ground.

When I work, the dust gets on my clothes, in my eyes, and in my nose. When I blow my nose during work the mucus is dark brown because I don't have a dust mask. I change my clothes when I get home, but I have to wash then with all the other family clothes, because I cannot afford to wash them separately. Sometimes my clothes are black with dirt.

My health and my spirits have been worn down by this program.

OMAR TORRES, AGE THIRTY-EIGHT

I never received an orientation or any type of preparation before beginning my WEP assignment in June of 1995. Not once on the job have I been advised what type of clothing to wear. Once I was assigned to clean graffiti off of a fleet of fifty garbage trucks. I was never provided with goggles, though I used heavy equipment to spray graffiti cleaner onto the garbage trucks. I have scars on my legs where I was burned by splashing graffiti-cleaning fluid.

Before beginning any particular job for the day, the supervisors distribute the orange safety vests that WEP workers are required to wear. The vests at the garage where I am based are kept in a cat-litter box on the floor. I am not allowed to take the vest home to clean it, nor am I allowed to keep one for my individual use.

I cannot take my lunch to work, because there is nowhere to store it. I am not allowed to keep any belongings, including food, at the garage. I cannot carry it with me while I am cleaning the streets, because there is no clean place to keep it. Some people tie their lunch to their garbage barrel handle.

My supervisor refuses to listen to my problems. When I verbally challenge his opinions about working conditions, he threatens to terminate me. I am very frustrated by the unjust way I am treated. The supervisors are like overseers on a plantation. They constantly threaten the WEP workers with sanctions and termination. They try to brainwash you into thinking that no lawyer can help you, and tell us not to talk to them. Daily I have to think about whether a store will let me use the bathroom. It is constant stress. I feel like we are treated as if we were not human beings. I should not have to go through this just to work.

SYLVIA RUFF, AGE FIFTY-SEVEN

Since March 1997 I have worked for the New York City Department of Sanitation, sweeping up streets and picking up garbage. The garbage includes broken glass, nails, syringes, needles, used diapers, used condoms, used tampons, and dead rats. We also encounter a lot of half-empty containers with strange-smelling liquids in them and a lot of dirty, discarded clothing, which may be infested with germs.

There is nowhere to wash your hands before lunch, and my hands are often dirty from picking up garbage. I always worry about germs and often I do not eat. And now that the weather is hot, I get terribly thirsty on the job, but there is no bathroom to use and I am afraid of having to urinate with nowhere to go. Even if I dared to drink, there is nowhere at the work site to get water. The supervisors threaten to sanction us when we leave our route to go to a restaurant and get water.

One day in early June when it rained, I was given a lightweight orange poncho to wear, which left my forearms and my legs exposed. The hood was designed so that I could not see to my right or left. Since I need to see oncoming traffic, I could not use the hood. It was pouring rain, and we were out for hours, standing in puddles as we tried to sweep. I got soaked through. I had to wring out the sleeves on my own jacket, and when I got home my feet looked like prunes.

The fear of humiliation I face because I have nowhere to relieve myself is degrading. The exposure to chemicals and waste products is unhealthy for me. I am worried about bringing my polluted clothing into the house and endangering my son's health as well as my own. Not knowing what I am being exposed to makes me constantly anxious, and it is a daily struggle to overcome this. The constant threats by the supervisors to sanction us for leaving our route and the inhumane working conditions make it seem like we're on a chain gang instead of in a work-experience program. I have been told—and I believe—that this work will not lead to a job. As long as we are forced to do this dead-end work, we at least need access to bathrooms and clean water, adequate personal protective clothing and equipment, and meaningful training about the hazards we face.

Money: Milwaukee, Summer 1999

JASON DEPARLE

Since the sweeping welfare reform of 1996, politicians often note the "success" of that reform largely in these terms: 1) welfare rolls cut by half; and 2) the number of women now working in the labor force. In this selection, author Jason DeParle closely examines the lives and finances of two women who have left welfare, and asks the question: Are they really better off financially? Are their children better off? What do you think?

"Who the hell is FICA?" Angie fumed. "They be eatin' my ass *up*." if Opal and Marcus were one source of frustration, her pay stub was another and closer to her heart. Leaving welfare, juggling multiple jobs, Angie had done all a welfare reformer could ask. And she had done it with a kind of willed faith that work would eventually pay. "I want my own house," she said, after some Brown Street kids tossed a rock through her window. "With a fence!"

On the surface, she was making good progress. Had she stayed on welfare, her cash and food stamps would have come to about $14,400 a year. In her first three years off welfare, her annual income (in constant dollars) averaged more than $24,900. On paper, she was up more than $10,000—a gain of nearly 75 percent.

Yet it didn't feel that way. Usually she said she has "a little more money, but it ain't that much." On a bleak day, she said, "No, I'm not better off economically—not yet."

While that may just sound like Angie grousing, it's a pretty fair read of the evidence. Like almost all recipients, Angie never lived on welfare alone; she had boyfriends of varying means and a series of (mostly) covert jobs. Quantifying the help from her boyfriends is hard. But through the tax returns lying in the bottom of her closet and her old welfare records, it's possible to see how Angie's part of the finances really worked. A comparison of her last four years on welfare with her first three years off produces a box score that looks like this:

SOURCE: "Money, Milwaukee, Summer 1999" from *American Dream: Three Women, Ten Kids, and a Nation's Drive to End Welfare* by Jason DeParle. Used by permission of Viking Penguin, a division of Penguin Group (USA) Inc.

	On Welfare	**Off Welfare**
Earnings:	$ 6,500	$16,100
Tax Credits:	$ 2,300	$ 5,600
Payroll Taxes:	$ −500	$−1,200
Cash Welfare:	$ 8,400	$ 0
Food Stamps:	$ 4,800	$ 4,400
Total Income:	$21,500	$24,900

As a strategy for promoting work, the law did its job: Angie's annual earnings more than doubled. Adding in tax credits (and subtracting FICA), the amount she brought home from the workplace rose by $12,200 a year. Yet the drop in welfare and food stamps cost her $8,800. On balance, she was up $3,400, a gain of 16 percent.

Or was she, really? The more she worked, the more her work expenses increased. There was bus fare, babysitting, work uniforms, and snacks from the vending machine. In Angie's case, the child-care costs were minimal, since the kids mostly minded themselves. But figure just $30 week for bus rides and the stolen car, a conservative estimate, and you wipe out nearly half the gain. In leaving welfare, Angie also lost her health insurance. The kids remained on Medicaid, which was crucial with Kesha's asthma attacks. But for twenty of her first thirty-six months off the rolls, Angie earned just enough to get disqualified. On welfare, she could call a cab and get driven to a doctor for free. But, with pains shooting down her back from lifting patients, Angie walked around uninsured.

Other than her back, Angie was healthy. Jewell was not. After she left welfare, her earnings rose *sixfold*, to nearly $13,000 a year. But her public aid fell 93 percent—she lost all of her welfare and most of her food stamps after she failed to file the monthly earnings reports required of people who work. While her overall income rose from about $14,700 to $16,600 (a gain of 13 percent), she also lost her health insurance for two years, and Jewell had bleeding ulcers. "I just dealt with that pain," she said. "I just got a lot of Tums, Rolaids, stuff like that." In the end, she was hospitalized and her wages were garnished to pay the bill, a circumstance that struck her as nothing unusual. "Anybody that works is gonna get their check garnished," she said. "Everybody in Milwaukee owes a hospital bill."

In going to work, Angie and Jewell didn't just face new expenses. They also faced new uncertainty. Angie's income soared for a year, when she bought a car and worked two jobs. Then it crashed for three months after the car was stolen. So the experience registered less like a stable advance than a roller coaster ride. In Jewell's case, the ride was particularly steep. Her income leaped to $25,000 when she worked in the Alzheimer's ward, then fell to $8,000 the next year when she lost her job and focused on Ken. On welfare, they had a senile landlady who forgot to collect the rent. Off welfare, Jewell had rent to pay and her nephew Quinten to feed. Angie had Opal and Brierra.

So did they come out ahead in economic terms? Probably, a bit. And their earnings may grow with time, which wouldn't happen on welfare. Still, three years after they left the rolls, their material lives didn't *feel* much different. Their economic progress, such as it was, vanished in the noise of living.

Trapped in the Double-Bind
of Welfare

ALEJANDRA MARCHEVSKY AND JEANNE THEOHARIS

In this selection, the authors examine the lives of women enrolled in the federal welfare-to-work program (called GAIN in this article). Their stories demonstrate the difficulties of administering such a program, especially when women are trying to combine low-wage work with caring for children. Compare this selection with the previous selection by DeParle. Given the problems with the program, is it a surprise that women choose to leave welfare altogether? Keep in mind that these women who voluntarily leave welfare are then counted in the success stories of welfare reform. What are some positive and negative aspects of the welfare-to-work program?

At the same time that Latina immigrants alternately appropriated the language of choice and critiqued the ways that their choices were constrained and forced upon them by the welfare state, they also protested the impossibility of choice inside this system. They found themselves faced with daily impossible decisions, most of which led to harmful consequences for their families. Seeing few opportunities for effective resistance or empowerment inside the contradictory web of welfare rules, many Latinas chose to resist by leaving the system altogether. Ultimately, however, leaving welfare was itself an impossible choice because the loss of supplemental income, food stamps, and medical coverage pushed these women and their families into a more precarious existence.

Numerous critics of the AFDC and TANF programs have talked about welfare as a series of impossible choices, specifically noting that benefit levels have been

SOURCE: Alejandra Marchevsky and Jeanne Theoharis. 2006. *Not Working: Latina Immigrants, Low-Wage Jobs, and the Failure of Welfare Reform*. New York: New York University Press. pp. 187–197.

set so low and rules so stringent that the only way to continue existing inside the system is by breaking the rules.[1] Cruikshank, for example, notes:

> *The worst double-bind followed from the fact that AFDC grants were made at levels well below the established poverty line. Everyone knew that welfare grants were not enough to live on and this fact more than any other created an atmosphere of fear and suspicion. Welfare recipients knew, probation officers knew, therapists and ex-boyfriends knew, fraud investigators knew: if you lived in one place and had well-fed and well-cared for children, you were in all likelihood committing welfare fraud; if you were homeless or living in substandard housing, if your kids were poorly dressed and truant, then you were a likely candidate for child-protective services.[2]*

The welfare recipient is always assumed guilty of fraud or parental neglect until proven innocent. Because most disciplinary actions take place at the hands of individual caseworkers and welfare review boards (not in civil or criminal court), the recipient is constituted as a unique political subject at the mercy of bureaucratic practices rather than the civil liberties that most Americans enjoy. Indeed, a number of Latinas in this study had been investigated for welfare fraud without the opportunity to confront their accusers. Myrna's home was twice raided by welfare officials following unsubstantiated, anonymous accusations that she had a live-in boyfriend and that she was physically abusing her children. As Myrna herself explained, she had no choice but to allow the fraud investigators to search her home and to answer their questions; refusal to cooperate would not only have been understood by the state as an admission of guilt, but it also would have been a violation of the rules of the welfare system and grounds for the termination of her benefits. Myrna was faced with an impossible choice: to forfeit her constitutional rights to due process and privacy or to forfeit the social entitlements that enable her to shelter and feed her family.

Even in cases where women were not directly investigated by the state, they nevertheless characterized life on welfare as a constant struggle to satisfy an ever-changing and contradictory body of rules and expectations. Over and over this group of Latina mothers explained that they were being judged according to a set of standards that always set them up for failure. This theme permeated their descriptions of the most mundane experiences, from dressing their children for school, to shopping for food, to interacting with teachers, doctors, and social workers. Herminia, for example, recounted a home visit from the Child Protective Services Department, when she was reprimanded by a social worker for buying clothing for her granddaughter that was "too nice." As she recalled:

> *When I showed her my granddaughter's dresses, the social worker told me, "Don't be buying her clothes like that all the time." . . . But I tell her that I have to have my granddaughter dressed*

---

[1]Gilliom notes that because welfare benefit levels are set so low, the system itself produces an inevitable struggle between recipients (who break the rules by working under the table, taking in boarders, etc.) and welfare administrators constantly trying to catch them. Mundane acts of resistance give welfare recipients a sense of autonomy and agency as women carve out private spaces outside the view and reach of the welfare state.

[2]Cruikshank, 116.

nicely. . . . They give me money to take care of my grandchildren and I invest it in them. I don't want them to tell me [how to spend my money].

For Herminia Hernandez, this confrontation with the social worker exemplified the double-bind of welfare. She had proudly shown off her granddaughter's new clothing as proof that she was fulfilling her obligations as a guardian to the children in her custody—in fact, had the social worker determined that the child was not adequately dressed, Herminia could have lost custody rights. However, Herminia's attempt to satisfy society's standards of middle-class motherhood became an opportunity for the welfare state to police her private life and question the soundness of her choices. Just as Norma was scolded by her GAIN counselor for buying an expensive work outfit, Herminia was reprimanded for allowing her granddaughter to enjoy material comforts that, in the social worker's estimation, Herminia would not be able to provide in the future. Thus, despite the new TANF program's celebration of hard work and self-determination, it ultimately treats Herminia's class position as fixed and pre-determined. Yet when women like Herminia protest the structural obstacles that stand in the way of their mobility, they are chastised and disciplined for their lack of motivation and self-esteem.

Other Latinas highlighted this double-bind by recounting the ways that they were being forced to "choose" between complying with the GAIN rules (which often conflicted with the best interests of their family) or privileging their family's well-being above the rules (which would ultimately result in the loss of their welfare benefits). Maria Sanchez, for example, described an incident in which she needed to take her sick son to the doctor, yet was threatened with sanctions if she missed a session of GAIN:

They don't care if you eat, if you sleep, if you're clothed, if you're shoeless, nothing. They don't care if you get sick. They don't. . . . I had to take one of my kids to the doctor. I called [the GAIN worker] and I told her, "You know, my son is very sick." "I don't care," she said, "I want you here at such and such hour." She said, "You can do it." I didn't say anything. I was quiet. So she said, "Obligations are obligations." I told her, "My son comes first."

Maria's GAIN worker demanded that she prioritize her "obligation" to the program above her son's health. Maria not only defied these orders, but she also justified her resistance to GAIN's inflexible regime of rules by appropriating the program's discourse of personal responsibility—"my son comes first." Our research documented countless stories like Maria's. Norma, for example, recounted a very similar confrontation that took place in her Job Club:

Like this lady had a sick son, and she went in and told them, "You know, my son is sick. He is vomiting a lot and he has a high fever. So, I just came to sign in and to tell you that I can't stay in class today." The caseworker said, "Is your son dying? . . . Unless your son is dying and he has a life-threatening condition, then you can't leave or you'll be cut off." So then I told her, "Oh, if my son is sick and I leave, I don't care if I get cut off, because my son comes first."

Challenging a racist society that puts Latino children on the bottom, women like Maria Sanchez and Norma Gonzalez reasserted their fundamental right and responsibility to righteous motherhood by putting their children first.

However, while these Latina mothers critiqued these impossible choices, they did not entirely escape the self-blame and sense of failure that often accompanies being forced to make an impossible choice. Despite her condemnation of the inflexibility and heartlessness of the new welfare rules, Maria blamed herself for her family's disqualification from TANF and the eventual removal of her five children from her custody and into the foster care system. Similarly, Norma collapsed into self-blame when recounting how she and her mother carried her sick son three miles to the nearest hospital in the middle of the night because they could not afford a taxi:

> There was a time when my mom didn't have no money and I didn't have no money, so she walked with me and we took turns carrying Marvin to the emergency room. So you know, I feel really bad telling you about this. I feel . . . I don't know. It made me feel really, really bad that I was not doing my job as a parent.

Norma originally began telling this story to Alejandra in order to illustrate how "welfare is not enough." However, through the course of the interview session, Norma's critique of the system quickly turned inward into a critique of herself. When pressed by Alejandra to provide a specific explanation for her culpability (What exactly could she have done differently in this situation? What would a "better" mother have done?), Norma's response was tautological: She was a bad mother because welfare did not provide her with enough to be a good mother to her son. Rather than blame the system for placing her family in an impossible situation, she blamed herself for that situation.

Yet, even when Norma blames herself, she is claiming a certain degree of agency—eschewing a class defeatism ("this is just the way the world works") and nihilism ("nothing will ever change"). For many of the women, then, self-blame was closely aligned to a claim for power; if they could be responsible for the negative circumstances of their lives in the present, then they had sufficient power and self-possession to shape their destinies in the future. This is, however, a deceptive bind: Their claim to agency becomes articulated through a language of self-blame—potentially personally harmful—within a system predicated on their lack of agency. The discourses of choice and personal responsibility are effective tools of discipline in the welfare system precisely because they resonate with poor women's own desires for recognition, dignity, and agency.

DOUBLE-CONSCIOUSNESS AND THE CHOICE BETWEEN WELFARE AND WORK

Norma's self-narrative, like those of most of the Mexican immigrant women in this study, dances on the hyphen between moralizing individualism, self-blame, and social critique. From the same space that these Latinas challenged the racism of the welfare state, they launched an attack on African Americans who they claim are the "real welfare problem." In the same breath that these women asserted that work does not pay for those at the bottom of the economic structure, they affirmed their own work ethic and their willingness to accept any job, no matter the pay or conditions. They critiqued the impossible standards of motherhood that society imposes on women of color, and at the same time contrasted themselves to other black and Latina women in their neighborhood who "don't care about their children like I do." Although some engaged in small, daily acts of defiance (from not reporting cash income to refusing job placements), most continued to comply with the rules and to echo the ideologies of welfare reform—even as they voiced a broader critique of the welfare system and the low-wage labor market.

From W E. B. Du Bois, we hear about how people objectified as "problems" exist on the margin between seeing themselves through the eyes of society and constructing their own identities:

> Between me and the other world there is ever an unasked question: unasked by some through feelings of delicacy; by others through the difficulty of rightly framing it. All nevertheless, flutter round it. . . . How does it feel to be a problem? It is a peculiar sensation, this double consciousness, this sense of always looking at one's self through the eyes of others, of measuring one's soul by the tape of the world that looks on in amused contempt and pity.[3]

Legal scholar Patricia Williams elaborates on this recurring self-regard when she writes, "What complicates this structure of thought insofar as racism is concerned, however is that the distancing does not stop with the separation of the white self from the black other . . . the black self is placed at a distance even from itself, as in my example of blacks being asked to put themselves in the position of the white shopkeepers [and DPSS workers] who scrutinized them."[4]

From the Latinas in this study, we learn about the multiple contradictions of negotiating this double vision inside the welfare state. In a system that tracks welfare recipients' movements through national data systems and launches surprise inspections of their homes, one's survival rests on avoiding being noticed. Yet, being seen as an individual still holds the elusive promise of humanization and empowerment. This individual self, however, is necessarily crafted in opposition to the "problem" other—to the bad mother who trades her food stamps for drugs, to the illegal immigrant cheating the system. Within a system where following and defying the rules produces harmful effects on one's family, these women understand that their choices will always be judged and limited by a society that constructs them as a problem. Composing a sense of self—even a self in opposition to the welfare queen—then, still requires seeing oneself through the eyes of a world that "looks on with pity and contempt."

It is only in the context of this double vision inside the welfare state, and the growing intimidation and insecurity brought on by welfare reform, that we can understand why most Latina mothers in this study said that work is better than welfare. Most of the Latinas did not see welfare and work as mutually defining alternatives. But in the course of the interviews, women were asked, "How does working compare to welfare?"

[3]W. E. B. Dubois, *The Souls of Black Folk*, 1–3.

[4]Patricia Williams, *The Alchemy of Race and Rights* (Cambridge, MA. 1991), 62.

ANGELA: Well, with work, you are receiving a paycheck every 15 days or every week, and with welfare it's every month. And what they send you. . . . For example, if I didn't get any help from him [her fiancé] with $496 I would only be able to pay the rent. What about the bills, the children's clothing? And what they send us in food stamps is not enough for the whole month. It's only enough for 15 days of food. After the 15 days, what do we do?

MARGARITA: Sometimes I think that [my life] will improve because if I work, I can have credit anywhere. But right now I can't have credit because I'm on welfare. And if I work, the [creditor] is going to say, "Oh, she is working. She has someone to vouch for her." But if I'm on welfare, who is going to vouch for me?

MYRNA: What's good is to make the people work. They should really try to work. . . . But I also understand that there're lots of people who have lots of kids, and to work just to pay the babysitter, that's real hard. . . . Also, like at the day care centers, you know, it's full. You have to sign up, wait your turn. You can't just get childcare right away. They have waiting lists. And for me, that I work the graveyard shift, it's hard because not just anybody can watch my kids.

CARMEN: Working? I love it. I love it 'cause you feel better. Whether you get your paycheck every week or every two weeks, you do feel better because you know you are going to get that check . . . and not be waiting for a month. 'Cause can I say my [welfare] check is going to be there when I go pick it up? I've been through that. Like when I started working, there was some problem, and I didn't get my check and food stamps.

NORMA: I think that working is always better because, you know, you don't have to sit around and wait, depend on them to send you something. Because you know that if you're working, you're going to get it [paid]. But, if you're depending on them to send it to you, and they *know* you're depending on them, they just send it when they want to?

LUPE: I would say [that], in a way, it's better, you know, for them to send people to work 'cause, there's just some people that just, you know, stay at home because they know, "Hey, my money's gonna come."

These Latina mothers asserted that working is better than being on welfare; they wanted to work and not be dependent on the government; their children would be "better off" if they were working; and although they themselves were honest and responsible, there were too many other people out there abusing the system.

Similar responses have been echoed by welfare recipients across the country, appearing in recent media coverage, social science reports and policy briefs, and promotional videos and brochures used by government programs like GAIN to sell the message of welfare reform to recipients. There are two predominant ways of reading welfare recipients' affirmation of the messages behind welfare reform. In most journalistic and applied policy accounts, they are framed as the transparent reporting of authentic experience. If welfare recipients say welfare reform is a good idea, then it must be true.[5] Other scholars reduce welfare recipients' dislike of welfare to the power of dominant ideology—welfare recipients as duped and further oppressed—rather than analyzing more closely what women are saying.[6]

Yet, what would it mean to read the above statements in another light? First, it would require hearing the variety of other things that Latina immigrants are saying alongside this. Although there was a continual allusion to bad women on welfare in the interview transcripts, there was also a notion of collectivity and solidarity. For these women, the humiliation of welfare was not just individual but collective. They built alliances in welfare offices and job clubs, shared rides, stuck up for each other, and protected each other's privacy. Myrna often gave part of her welfare money to her neighbor, who was undocumented and could not receive aid. Margarita counted on Angela to watch her children when she had a job interview or needed to run a quick errand. Norma helped other Latina immigrants in her Job Club fill out job applications in English and protested when one of her classmates, who suffered from epilepsy, was punished for leaving class early.

Moreover, through the course of the interviews, it became increasingly clear that these women were not talking about any literal person they knew; there was no actual welfare queen living next door or down the block and when pressed to name a woman they knew who "sold her food stamps for drugs," "who was lazy and had too many babies," they could not. This is because they were not, in fact, constructing an oppositional identity to other real women but to the welfare queen as a symbol—and in the process carving out a place for self-definition. Their discursive strategy illustrates the power of this anti-welfare ideology; women did not always attempt, and perhaps could not imagine, how to discredit the image wholesale. Rather what they were able to do was take the symbol as a counterpoint for who they were, who their mothers were, who their sisters and neighbors were. The symbol of the welfare queen opened up a space for talking about their motherhood, their morals regarding family, work, and responsibility, and their fears that other people—including the state—did not share this morality.

Similarly, when these Latinas praised work and its benefits, they were operating from the category of the ideal of work—set apart from their actual experiences as workers and their knowledge and expectations of the labor market. Even though they said they would feel better about themselves if they were working, their accounts of work provided substantive evidence to the contrary. They relayed stories of harassment and humiliation on the job, of jobs that left them physically exhausted, of mind-numbing boredom and continual stress. Many women said

[5]Ironically, this is one of the rare times that poor women get to be the experts on their own lives; in most articles, the many other things that women say do not get taken up in policy formulations.

[6]More recently, we have seen attempts by scholars to balance a discussion of the repressive, effects of the welfare state with more empowering images of collective political resistance. Grace Chang's *Disposable Domestics*, for example, intermixes ethnographic interviews with Latina and Asian immigrants with case studies of contemporary labor and welfare rights activism. Chang's narrative flattens immigrant women into illustrative "stories" of Third World women's subjugation in the global economy, which are then used to offset or frame local organizing drives and political campaigns.

that work was better because they could count on getting a paycheck, whereas they could not count on getting a welfare check. But often, their actual work experiences did not bear out this belief. Their work hours were constantly changing (and usually never enough) and included jobs where they did not even get paid for the work they had done. And even though they held out the promise of a good job, their understanding of how the labor market functioned revealed that they did not believe any good jobs were available to them. Finally, although they emphasized the idea of respect on the job, most of their accounts of work highlighted the absence of dignity in low-wage jobs.

Conversely, these Latinas were not critiquing the concept of welfare but rather their lived experiences within the welfare system. All but one of the immigrant women in this study shared stories of harassment, discrimination, or unfairness from their caseworkers. Caseworkers regularly yelled at them, threatened to cut off part or all of their benefits, and told them that because they were not real Americans they didn't deserve any help from the government. All said that they wanted to get off of welfare because benefits were shrinking every day while humiliation and punishment were growing. Indeed, if we look at these women's comments above on the advantages of working relative to receiving welfare, nearly all framed this comparison in terms of the unpredictability and lack of accountability on the part of the welfare system.

Still, even though these women critiqued the discriminatory nature of the welfare system, they maintained a language of rights regarding the need for public assistance, and they asserted that welfare provided families with an important protection against hunger and homelessness. In the midst of saying that they wanted to be off welfare, women still asserted that welfare had been crucial to their family's survival. Margarita wanted to get off welfare so that "they will leave me alone. I will be tranquil and everything. They are not going to be sending me anywhere. . . . But if it wasn't for welfare can you imagine how I could have done it? Now that they take it away, how many children are going to go hungry?" Similarly, asked where she would be in five years, Carmen said she would be working and off of welfare. But then she interrupted herself saying, "I mean [welfare] does help. It helps families."

These Latinas could cast leaving welfare as a personal goal and claim its absolute necessity as social policy. They worried about the fate of other families in the wake of welfare reform and critiqued the hypocrisy and shortsightedness in cuts in social spending. For instance, Norma Gonzalez observed:

> Now, it's awful because all they think about is saving money. But they don't think about the kids. . . . I mean it's awful. They are going to have the biggest homeless state in all of the United States, because, you know, they're not really thinking about anything else except saving money. They're not thinking about the people that are going to be homeless. You know, kids are going to be homeless. And they're not thinking about the people that are going to go hungry.

Similarly, Angela Perez commented that her benefits had been reduced every year but that she had never received an explanation from the welfare office about these reductions:

No, just that they were cutting because there was no money from the government. I would say, well why do they have money for . . . what is it that they are doing in Saudi Arabia, or sending airplanes to war and all of that? What are they doing that for? Instead of the government spending money on weapons and to kill people, what about the people over here?

The Mexican immigrant women interviewed for this study were initially attracted to welfare reform programs that promised job training, education, and English instruction, and they believed in the promise of equal opportunity trumpeted under welfare reform. Yet their experiences in these programs taught them that this was, in fact, a cheapened form of citizenship reserved for those groups who continue to be posited as racial outsiders to the national community.[7] Indeed, Zoraida Torres's fear at the outset of welfare reform implementation in L.A. County seems all too prescient: "Some days I get discouraged and think that as soon as they see that so many Latinos are becoming citizens, then they'll put another law in our way so that our citizenship doesn't mean anything anymore."

[7]Writing about public efforts to Americanize Los Angeles' Mexican immigrants in the 1920s, historian George Sanchez concludes that "Rather than provide Mexican immigrants with an attainable picture of assimilation, Americanization programs could offer these immigrants only idealized versions of American values. In reality what was presented turned out to be little more than second-class citizenship." George Sanchez, *Becoming Mexican-American* (Oxford, 1993), 105–106. Sanchez tells us that while Mexican immigrant women earlier in the century were originally attracted to Americanization's promises of inclusion and equality, it did not take them long to realize that they and their families were being assimilated into the bottom of a racially stratified society.

CHAPTER 8

Schools and Schooling

When inadequate health care and inadequate diet are added to the exposure to toxic chemicals, they reduce the odds of poor children succeeding in school. "At age 5, poor children are often less alert, less curious, and less effective at interacting with their peers than are more privileged youngsters" (Hewlett, 1991:56). Moreover, more privileged youngsters are more likely to attend enriched preschool programs than the children of the poor, again increasing the readiness gap between the privileged and the economically disadvantaged. When attending school, poor children are much more likely than privileged children to find their classrooms inadequately staffed, overcrowded, and ill equipped. Schools in U.S. society are financed primarily locally through property taxes. This results in affluent districts having significantly greater resources for educating their children that economically marginal districts have for their children (Kozol, 1991). As a result, poor children are more likely than affluent children to attend schools that need repair, they have fewer books and supplies, and their teachers are more likely to have less training.

Children from poor families would have a better chance to succeed if they were exposed to enriched preschool experiences. Head Start is a program with positive results for children, but the program is underfunded, resulting in only 60 percent of those eligible receiving that advantage. Meanwhile, more affluent children attend a variety of early development programs, have tutors to help them succeed, as well as receiving educational advantages such as home computers, travel experiences, and visits to zoos, libraries, and various cultural activities. As a result, children of the impoverished tend to underachieve.

NOTES AND SUGGESTIONS FOR FURTHER READING

Ayers, William, and Patricia Ford (Eds.) (1996). *City Kids, City Teachers: Reports from the Front Row.* New York: The New Press.

Books, Sue (Ed.) (1998). *Invisible Children in the Society and Its Schools.* Mahwah, NJ: Lawrence Erlbaum Associates.

Children's Defense Fund (2005). *The State of America's Children.* Washington, D.C.

Hewlett, Sylvia Ann (1991). *When the Bough Breaks: The Cost of Neglecting Our Children.* New York: Basic Books.

Kozol, Jonathan (1991). *Savage Inequalities: Children in America's Schools.* New York: Crown.

Levin, Murray (1998). *Teach Me! Kids Will Learn When Oppression Is the Lesson.* New York: Monthly Review Press.

McNeil, Linda M. (2000). "Creating New Inequalities: Contradictions of Reform." *Phi Delta Kappan* 81 (June):729–734.

Symonds, William C. (2001). "How to Fix America's Schools." *Business Week* (March 19): 67–80, and the editorial on page 118.

Traub, James (2000). "What No School Can Do." *New York Times Magazine* (January 15). Online: http://nytimes.com/library/magazine/home/20000116mag-traub8.html

Seventh Grade Disaster

DELPHIA BOYKIN

This essay was written by an African American woman about her experience as a volunteer in a Southside Chicago inner-city middle school. Analyze this reading using the sociological perspective regarding the impact of institutions on individual lives. From this selection, what do you predict about the future of these seventh grade students? How would you analyze the environment and life chances of these students from each theoretical perspective? What are some possible solutions to the high turnover rate of teachers in inner-city schools?

During a conversation with a friend, she mentioned that her daughter brought home a note from school asking for volunteers to help with the students. I thought about applying, and it appealed to me because child development is a field that interests me for a career.

From September of 1998 through September, 1999, I volunteered to work in the Goldsmith Middle School. When I got there, the principal decided it would be best if I helped out a little in the seventh grade classroom. I was not prepared with any degrees, I had never worked with children before, and I had been out of school for ten years.

My first day there I thought, "This will be fun." I walked into the classroom and a nice elderly man named Mr. Nelson greeted me. I thought that we would be together for the rest of the year. Then he informed me that he was a substitute teacher. Mr. Nelson and I did well for a week, but then he left.

Within that school year, Mr. Jones, the superintendent, changed teachers five times. These frequent adjustments really affected the students. The children were so confused at this period that we had only four or five kids passing. The atmosphere was very chaotic.

Each teacher demonstrated a unique personality and method of teaching. The main subject in the seventh grade was math. One teacher named Mrs. Moody taught straight from the book. On the other hand, Mrs. Wright composed her les-

SOURCE: Delphia Boykin, "Seventh Grade Disaster," unpublished essay. Reprinted with permission of the author.

son plans. She followed Mrs. Moody by only one month, so anyone can understand the confusion in the students.

The enrollment in the seventh grade was thirty-seven students crowded into a closet-size room approximately 8½ by 11 feet. This made it difficult to learn. The children were so close together that they could not bend their elbows. Under these circumstances, they were encouraged to play and talk. They would engage in conversations about their interests, with no regard for the teacher.

I can remember one day in the middle of winter, the snow was about six inches deep. I walked into the school and was told the teacher would not be in so I had to teach the class alone. The teacher had abruptly resigned. During that time I learned how difficult it is to work with many children at one time. There I was in a class with thirty-seven kids and no idea about how to manage them.

The next week another teacher came; this made me very happy, not for my sake, but for the sake of the students. I thought, "A new teacher—we can get down to business." Everything was going fine for three months and then he left.

The students had an equivalency test the week that he left, which made this the most challenging week of my tour of duty. I knew nothing about giving a test. I could barely follow the instructions for taking one myself. Naturally they told me the time limit for each test, but it was hard to monitor the kids and the clock. I could not wait for it to be over. I said to myself, "I made it through again."

One day in January I started gathering my papers to take them home to grade. Mr. Hobbs, the vice principal, came in and asked if I would mind doing the report cards. I said yes, even though I had to grade sixth, seventh, and eighth grade math papers. When the parents came to get the grades, they were very frustrated with the whole school system and there was nothing I could do about the situation.

I really felt alone because Mr. Ivy, the sixth grade teacher, and Mrs. Woodard, the eighth grade teacher, had fewer problems because of their past years of experience. Mrs. Woodard helped me a great deal, but it was impossible for her to teach my class and hers also.

When I started volunteering in the school, I thought it would be a great learning experience. Of course, we had training classes weekly for a month, but it was not adequate to prepare me for this horrid experience.

Mrs. Gray, the principal, had her hands full. Three schools were combined and she was the principal of all three schools. The years prior to my arrival had run much smoother because the previous seventh grade teacher had stayed for eight years before retiring. When the new teachers were hired, they wanted more money and better benefits. Mrs. Gray disagreed with this change so she continued to get substitutes.

Due to the circumstances, most of the children were failing. This was not their fault; they could not learn under these conditions. One student, Michael, wanted to excel but was failing because, as soon as he learned one method of teaching, another teacher arrived with a different method of teaching.

When I reflect upon this time, I realize there are many problems in the school system. The classrooms are crowded, the students are under taught, and the turnover of teachers is rapid.

Always Running

LUIS RODRIGUEZ

Luis Rodriguez immigrated from Mexico at a young age. This excerpt from his life story demonstrates the difficulties faced by children who are non-English speakers. Many states have adopted English-only laws that affect the school system. Would Luis' experiences have been different if he had been taught in his own language, or is total immersion in English the best method of teaching? What faults of the school system are highlighted in this excerpt? How do you think the different theoretical perspectives would approach the teaching of poor/minority students whose first language is not English?

Our first exposure in America stays with me like a foul odor. It seemed a strange world, most of it spiteful to us, spitting and stepping on us, coughing us up, us immigrants, as if we were phlegm stuck in the collective throat of this country. My father was mostly out of work. When he did have a job it was in construction, in factories such as Sinclair Paints or Standard Brands Dog Food, or pushing door-bells selling insurance, Bibles, or pots and pans. My mother found work cleaning homes or in the garment industry. She knew the corner markets were ripping her off but she could only speak with her hands and in choppy English.

Once my mother gathered up the children and we walked to Will Rogers Park. There were people everywhere. Mama looked around for a place we could rest. She spotted an empty spot on a park bench. But as soon as she sat down an American woman, with three kids of her own, came by.

"Hey, get out of there—that's our seat."

My mother understood but didn't know how to answer back in English. So she tried in Spanish.

"Look spic, you can't sit there!" the American woman yelled. "You don't belong here! Understand? This is not your country!"

Mama quietly got our things and walked away, but I knew frustration and anger bristled within her because she was unable to talk, and when she did, no one would listen.

SOURCE: *Always Running—La Vida Loca, Gang Days in L.A.* by Luis J. Rodriguez. (Curbstone Press, 1993). Reprinted with permission of Curbstone Press. Distributed by Consortium.

We never stopped crossing borders. The Rio Grande (or *Rio Bravo*, which is what the Mexicans call it, giving the name a power "Rio Grande" just doesn't have) was only the first of countless barriers set in our path.

We kept jumping hurdles, kept breaking from the constraints, kept evading the border guards of every new trek. It was a metaphor to fill our lives—that river, that first crossing, the mother of all crossings. The Los Angeles River, for example, became a new barrier, keeping the Mexicans in their neighborhoods over on the vast east side of the city for years, except for forays downtown. Schools provided other restrictions: don't speak Spanish, don't be Mexican—you don't belong. Railroad tracks divided us from communities where white people lived, such as South Gate and Lynwood across from Watts. We were invisible people in a city which thrived on glitter, big screens, and big names, but this glamour contained none of our names, none of our faces.

The refrain "this is not your country" echoed for a lifetime.

First day of school.

I was six years old, never having gone to kindergarten because Mama wanted me to wait until La Pata became old enough to enter school. Mama filled out some papers. A school monitor directed us to a classroom where Mama dropped me off and left to join some parents who gathered in the main hall.

The first day of school said a lot about my scholastic life to come. I was taken to a teacher who didn't know what to do with me. She complained about not having any room, about kids who didn't even speak the language. And how was she supposed to teach anything under these conditions! Although I didn't speak English, I understood a large part of what she was saying. I knew I wasn't wanted. She put me in an old creaky chair near the door. As soon as I could, I sneaked out to find my mother.

I found Rano's class with the mentally disabled children instead and decided to stay there for a while. Actually it was fun; they treated me like I was everyone's little brother. But the teacher finally told a student to take me to the main hall.

After some more paperwork, I was taken to another class. This time the teacher appeared nicer, but distracted. She got the word about my language problem.

"Okay, why don't you sit here in the back of the class," she said. "Play with some blocks until we figure out how to get you more involved."

It took her most of that year to figure this out. I just stayed in the back of the class, building blocks. It got so every morning I would put my lunch and coat away, and walk to my corner where I stayed the whole day long. It forced me to be more withdrawn. It got so bad, I didn't even tell anybody when I had to go to the bathroom. I did it in my pants. Soon I stunk back there in the corner and the rest of the kids screamed out a chorus of "P.U.!" resulting in my being sent to the office or back home.

In those days there was no way to integrate the non-English-speaking children. So they just made it a crime to speak anything but English. If a Spanish word sneaked out in the playground, kids were often sent to the office to get swatted or to get detention. Teachers complained that maybe the children were saying bad things about them. An assumption of guilt was enough to get one punished.

A day came when I finally built up the courage to tell the teacher I had to go to the bathroom. I didn't quite say all the words, but she got the message and promptly excused me so I didn't do it while I was trying to explain. I ran to the bathroom and peed and felt good about not having that wetness trickle down my pants leg. But suddenly several bells went on and off. I hesitantly stepped out of the bathroom and saw throngs of children leave their class. I had no idea what was happening. I went to my classroom and it stood empty. I looked into other classrooms and found nothing. Nobody. I didn't know what to do. I really thought everyone had gone home. I didn't bother to look at the playground where the whole school had been assembled for the fire drill. I just went home. It got to be a regular thing there for a while, me coming home early until I learned the ins and outs of school life.

Not speaking well makes for such embarrassing moments. I hardly asked questions. I just didn't want to be misunderstood. Many Spanish-speaking kids mangled things up; they would say things like "where the beer and cantaloupe roam" instead of "where the deer and antelope roam."

That's the way it was with me. I mixed up all the words. Screwed up all the songs.

"You can't be in a fire and not get burned."

This was my father's response when he heard of the trouble I was getting into at school. He was a philosopher. He didn't get angry or hit me. That he left to my mother. He had these lines, these cuts of wisdom, phrases and syllables, which swept through me, sometimes even making sense. I had to deal with him at that level, with my brains. I had to justify in words, with ideas, all my actions—no matter how insane. Most of the time I couldn't.

Mama was heat. Mama was turned-around leather belts and wailing choruses of Mary-Mother-of-Jesus. She was the penetrating emotion that came at you through her eyes, the mother-guilt, the one who birthed me, who suffered through the contractions and diaper changes and all my small hurts and fears. For her, dealing with school trouble or risking my life was nothing for discourse, nothing to debate. She went through all this hell and more to have me—I'd better do what she said!

Mama hated the *cholos*. They reminded her of the rowdies on the border who fought all the time, talked that *calo* slang, drank mescal, smoked marijuana, and left scores of women with babies bursting out of their bodies.

To see me become like them made her sick, made her cringe and cry and curse. Mama reminded us how she'd seen so much alcoholism, so much weed-madness, and she prohibited anything with alcohol in the house, even beer. I later learned this rage came from how Mama's father treated her siblings and her mother, how in drunken rages he'd hit her mom and drag her through the house by the hair.

The school informed my parents I had been wreaking havoc with a number of other young boys. I was to be part of a special class of troublemakers. We would be isolated from the rest of the school population and forced to pick up trash and clean graffiti during the rest of the school year.

"Mrs. Rodriguez, your son is too smart for this," the vice principal told Mama. "We think he's got a lot of potential. But his behavior is atrocious. There's no excuse. We're sad to inform you of our decision."

They also told her the next time I cut class or even made a feint toward trouble, I'd be expelled. After the phone call, my mom lay on her bed, shaking her head while sobbing in between bursts of how God had cursed her for some sin, how I was the devil incarnate, a plague, testing her in this brief tenure on earth.

My dad's solution was to keep me home after school. Grounded. Yeah, sure. I was thirteen years old already. Already tattooed. Already sexually involved. Already into drugs. In the middle of the night I snuck out through the window and worked my way to the Hills.

At sixteen years old, Rano turned out much better than me, much better than anyone could have envisioned during the time he was a foul-faced boy in Watts.

When we moved to South San Gabriel, a Mrs. Snelling took a liking to Rano. The teacher helped him skip grades to make up for the times he was pushed back in those classes with the retarded children.

Mrs. Snelling saw talent in Rano, a spark of actor during the school's thespian activities. She even had him play the lead in a class play. He also showed some facility with music. And he was good in sports.

He picked up the bass guitar and played for a number of garage bands. He was getting trophies in track-and-field events, in gymnastic meets, and later in karate tournaments.

So when I was at Garvey, he was in high school being the good kid, the Mexican exception, the barrio success story—my supposed model. Soon he stopped being Rano or even José. One day he became Joe.

My brother and I were moving away from each other. Our tastes, our friends, our interests were miles apart. Yet there were a few outstanding incidents I fondly remember in relationship to my brother, incidents which despite their displays of closeness failed to breach the distance which would later lie between us.

When I was nine, for example, my brother was my protector. He took on all the big dudes, the bullies on corners, the ones who believed themselves better than us. Being a good fighter transformed him overnight. He was somebody who some feared, some looked up to. Then he developed skills for racing and high-jumping. This led to running track and he did well, dusting all the competition.

I didn't own any talents. I was lousy in sports. I couldn't catch baseballs or footballs. And I constantly tripped when I ran or jumped. When kids picked players for basketball games, I was the last one they chose. The one time I inadvertently hit a home run during a game at school—I didn't mean to do it—I ended up crying while running around the bases because I didn't know how else to react to the cheers, the excitement, directed at something I did. It just couldn't be me.

But Rano had enemies too. There were two Mexican kids who were jealous of him. They were his age, three years older than me. One was named Eddie Gambits, the other Rick Corral. One time they cornered me outside the school.

"You José's brother," Eddie said.

I didn't say anything.

"Wha's the matter? Can't talk?"

"Oh, he can talk all right," Ricky chimed in. "He acting the *pendejo* because his brother thinks he so bad. Well, he ain't shit. He can't even run."

"Yeah, José's just a *lambiche,* a kiss ass," Eddie responded. "They give him those ribbons and stuff because he cheats."

"That's not true," I finally answered. "My brother can beat anybody."

"Oh, you saying he can beat me," Eddie countered.

"Sure sounds like he said that," Ricky added.

"I'm only saying that when he wins those ribbons, *esta derecho,*" I said.

"It sounds to me like you saying he better than me," Eddie said.

"Is that what you saying, man?" Ricky demanded. "Com' on—is that what you saying?"

I turned around, and beneath my breath, mumbled something about how I didn't have time to argue with them. I shouldn't have done that.

"What'd you say?" Eddie said.

"I think he called you a punk," Ricky agitated.

"You call me a punk, man?" Eddie turned me around. I denied it.

"I heard him, dude. He say you are a punk-ass *puto,*" Ricky continued to exhort.

The fist came at me so fast, I don't even recall how Eddie looked when he threw it. I found myself on the ground. Others in the school had gathered around by then. When a few saw it was me, they knew it was going to be a slaughter.

I rose to my feet—my cheek had turned swollen and blue. I tried to hit Eddie, but he backed up real smooth and hit me again. Ricky egged him on; I could hear the excitement in his voice.

I lay on the ground, defeated. Teachers came and chased the boys out. But before Eddie and Ricky left they yelled back: "José ain't nothing, man. You ain't nothing."

Anger flowed through me, but also humiliation. It hurt so deep I didn't even feel the fracture in my jaw, the displacement which would later give me a disjointed, lopsided, and protruding chin. It became my mark.

Later when I told Rano what happened, he looked at me and shook his head.

"You didn't have to defend me to those dudes," he said. "They're assholes. They ain't worth it."

I looked at him and told him something I never, ever told him again.

"I did it because I love you."

I began high school a *loco,* with a heavy Pendleton shirt, sagging khaki pants, ironed to perfection, and shoes shined and heated like at boot camp.

Mark Keppel High School was a Depression-era structure with a brick and art-deco facade and small, army-type bungalows in back. Friction filled its hallways. The Anglo and Asian upper-class students from Monterey Park and Alhambra attended the school. They were tracked into the "A" classes; they were in the school clubs, they were the varsity team members and lettermen. They were the pep squads and cheerleaders.

But the school also took in the people from the Hills and surrounding community who somehow made it past junior high. They were mostly Mexican, in the "C" track (what were called the "stupid" classes), and who made up the rosters of the wood, print, and auto shops. Only a few of these students participated in school government, in sports, or in the various clubs.

The school had two principal languages. Two skin tones and two cultures. It revolved around class differences. The white and Asian kids (except for "barrio" whites and the handful of Hawaiians, Filipinos, and Samoans who ended up with the Mexicans) were from professional, two-car households with watered lawns and trimmed trees. The laboring class, the sons and daughters of service workers, janitors, and factory hands, lived in and around the Hills (or a section of Monterey Park called "Poor Side").

The school separated these two groups by levels of education: The professional-class kids were provided with college-preparatory classes; the blue-collar students were pushed into "industrial arts."

Work and Working

The jobs held by those in poverty or near poverty involve doing society's "dirty work." Some of these jobs are migrant farm workers who follow the harvests, picking fruit and vegetables, workers in slaughter houses who process meat, poultry, and fish, dishwashers in restaurants, and maids who clean rooms in hotels. These and other low-end jobs involve low pay (some pay below the minimum wage), little or no benefits, and some involve a high risk of injury from the activity or from exposure to toxic chemicals.

WAGES

About 20 percent of the nation's poor families have at least one family member holding a full-time job yet they remain poor. There are at least two related reasons for this anomaly. First, the federal minimum wage, despite occasional raises, has not kept up with inflation, seeing a loss of more than 30 percent in purchasing power from 1968 to the present. Second, a minimum wage of $7.25 (which goes into effect in 2008) means that someone working full-time for 50 weeks would earn only $14,500 a year, which is much below the poverty threshold for a family of three.

ALIENATION

Alienation refers to the separation of human beings from each other, from themselves, and from the products they create. Worker alienation occurs when they are controlled in the work setting, when they receive no satisfaction and personal fulfillment from the work they do, when their work is not appreciated by others, when their work is repetitious, and when they are not paid a fair wage for their efforts. Clearly, those at the bottom of the job hierarchy are subject to these manifestations of alienation. Many, therefore, feel a profound dissatisfaction and resentment against their employers and society. At a personal level, this may lead workers to join together in a union or other collective group to improve working conditions (**agency**), or it may manifest itself in absenteeism, work slow down, and alcohol or other drug abuse. Studs Terkel, in introducing his book *Working*, summarized the personal impact of alienating work:

> *This book, being about work, is, by its very nature, about violence—to the spirit as well as the body. It is about ulcers as well as accidents, about shouting matches as well as fistfights, about*

nervous breakdowns, as well as kicking the dog around. It is, above all (or beneath all), about daily humiliations. To survive the day is triumph for the walking wounded among the great many of us. (Terkel, 1975:xiii).

RISK

Those who work at low wages often do dangerous work. Migrant farm workers, for example, are exposed to herbicides and pesticides sprayed on the fields where they work. The water they drink may be contaminated, and their living conditions are often unsanitary. As a result these workers have a life expectancy 30 years below the national average. Those workers in packing plants and chicken and fish processing plants, use sharp knives for gutting the carcasses, which leads to a high probability of being cut and they are highly susceptible to repetitive motion syndrome. In other low wage jobs, workers may be exposed to nuclear radiation, chemical compounds, coal tars, dust, and asbestos fibers.

SWEATSHOPS

A **sweatshop** is a substandard work environment where workers are paid less than the minimum wage and are not paid overtime premiums, and where other laws are violated. Although sweatshops occur in various types of manufacturing, they occur most frequently in the garment industry. The workers in these establishments are mostly Latina and Asian immigrant women who are paid much below the minimum wage, receive no benefits, and work in crowded, unsafe, and stifling conditions.

NOTES AND SUGGESTIONS FOR FURTHER READING_____

Bernhardt, Annette (2000). "The Wal-Mart Trap." *Dollars and Sense*, Number 231 (September/October):23–25.

Chang, Grace (2000). *Disposable Domestics: Immigrant Women Workers in the Global Economy.* Cambridge, MA: South End Press.

Chatterley, Cedric N, and Alicia J. Rouverol with Stephen A. Cole (2000). *"I Was Content and Not Content": Story of Linda Lord and the Closing of Penobscot Poultry.* Carbondale: Southern Illinois University Press.

Duncan, Cynthia M. (1999). *World's Apart: Why Poverty Persists in Rural America.* New Haven, CT: Yale University Press.

Ehrenreich, Barbara (2000). "Maid to Order: The Politics of Other Women's Work." *Harper's* 300 (April):59–70.

Ehrenreich, Barbara (2001). *Nickel and Dimed: On (Not) Getting by in America.* New York: Metropolitan Books.

Heinz, James, Nancy Folbre, and the Center for Popular Economics (2000). *The Ultimate Field Guide to the U.S. Economy.* New York: The New Press.

Levy, Frank (1998). *The New Dollars and Dreams: American Incomes and Economic Change.* New York: The Russell Sage Foundation.

Mishel, Lawrence, Jared Bernstein, and John Schmitt (2007). *The State of Working America 2006–2007.* Ithaca, NY: Cornell University Press.

Newman, Katherine S. (1999). *No Shame in My Game: The Working Poor in the Inner City*. New York: Alfred A. Knopf and the Russell Sage Foundation.

Rubin, Lillian B. (1994). *Families on the Faultline: America's Working Class Speaks About the Family, the Economy, Race, and Ethnicity*. New York: HarperCollins.

Shulman, Beth (2003). *The Betrayal of Work: How Low Wage Jobs Fail 30 Million Americans*. New York: The New Press.

Sonneman, Toby R., and Rick Steigmeyer (1992). *Fruit Fields in My Blood: Okie Migrants in the West*. Moscow: University of Idaho Press.

Terkel, Studs (1975). *Working: People Talk about What They Do All Day and How They Feel about What They Do*. New York: Avon Books.

Looking for Work, Waiting for Work

TOBY F. SONNEMAN

*This selection is an in-depth look at the life of migrant fruit pickers. These
workers provide a valuable service to our economy, and yet they receive
little in return. Explain their working conditions from individual/cultural
and structural perspectives. What are the disadvantages and advantages
of migrant work? What steps could migrant workers take to improve their
lives and working conditions?*

In late April, the early variety of cherries in the orchards around Stockton, California, begins to turn from pale green to reddish-pink, and the roads are full of pickers looking for work. Often migrant fruit pickers return, like migratory birds, to the orchards where they have worked every spring for years. For those pickers who find themselves without a job to return to, there are days ahead of driving back roads looking for work, talking to growers, contractors, and other pickers for leads or connections to a job.

Even for those lucky enough to have an annual job to come to, there may be a long period of waiting before the work actually begins. In a journal I kept years ago, I described the situation of waiting for work in a migrant camp:

27 MAY

Arriving in Lodi yesterday to a full camp. Everything seems much the same as last year—the old crew with a few new additions. Some of the people have new rigs—usually larger or newer trailers and trucks. The kids have grown bigger. The ground is still that dusty burnt ash. The smoky dust blows into the trailers, turns the children coal gray, and covers everything with a film of dirt.

It's hot here, in the nineties, but the evening breeze and the shade of a few tall trees make it more tolerable.

We expected the mood of the camp to be dismal. Almost everyone has been camping here for a month or a month and a half, yet there's been only half a day of

SOURCE: Toby F. Sonneman, *Fruit Fields in My Blood: Okie Migrants in the West* (Moscow, ID: University of Idaho Press, 1993), pp. 53–61. Reprinted by permission of the University of Idaho Press.

work. The early cherries were rained out. Now we're waiting for the late cherries to start—a rather hopeless prospect also. Most of the blossoms came off in the rain, leaving hardly any cherries on the trees. As if that weren't bad enough, we have a bigger-than-average crew. Soft-hearted Otis has let on a lot of extra people—friends and relatives of the crew. He planned on needing them in the early cherries but since that fell through they've all waited for the late cherries.

A combination of desperation and excitement pervades the camp full of pickers waiting for the job to begin. Each day of waiting is filled with anxiety and anticipation but little activity. There's not much to do in the surrounding community that doesn't involve spending money, and money is in short supply for migrants this time of year. They've spent what they have in travel, and they may have gone for months without work. Consequently this time of waiting becomes a time to socialize with other pickers in the camp, and the focus of the conversation is often speculation about the crop.

Among Okie migrants, it's the men who seem to have more time to socialize, while the women—in traditional roles—cook, clean, shop, and watch the children. Men especially tend to define the limbo time of waiting with a particular ritual each morning.

After early breakfasts, men drift out of their trailers, coffee cups or cigarettes in hand. The trailers are parked close together on a cleared patch of land surrounded by orchard. The dirt road through the orchard borders the migrant camp on one side. The men walk casually across the road to the orchard, greeting each other with a nod of the head. "Mornin', Otis. Ya think we're ever goin' to get to pick this fruit?"

The men form a small circle on the edge of the orchard. There are six or seven of them, their ages ranging from twenty-five to sixty. Rick and I hang back along the edge of the circle, listening and occasionally participating. Although I am conspicuously the only woman in the group, the men take little notice of me. They examine the unripe fruit carefully, placing clusters of the small pale cherries in their hands, discussing their condition minutely, as if they could will them to ripen sooner. "They still look pretty green to me. I reckon it's ten days away," Otis comments. "Well, now I wisht I'd stayed in Arizona. There ain't much goin' on there, but at least I could make enough to buy groceries."

One of the younger men leans against the trunk of a tree. He has the look of another time: his face is pale and narrow, with a long forehead and deep-set hazel eyes, topped by a shock of blond curls. Striped overalls and a worn work shirt cover his thin body. "Well, you know a fruit tramp," he grins, hooking his thumbs in his overall pockets. "When he decides to go, he's gone! We'd be pickin' oranges down there in Porterville, and someone'd say, 'Cherries are a good four weeks off, no use in goin' up north.' Next mornin' they'd change their mind and they'd be gone. Sometimes they'd go up there for a day and turn right around and come back, and then go up there again. Yeah, about six weeks before the cherries start, there's no tellin' what will happen!"

"It's funny," agrees another, addressing his explanation to Rick. "We only pick cherries about forty days a year, but we call ourselves cherry pickers."

"The cherries is all there is now." A stocky man squats near the ground, drawing lines in the dust with a twig. "If you don't' make it in the cherries, you ain't gonna make it. Though there's some that make it in the apples too. But you can't hit it in the cherries and then try to make the same kind of money in the prunes and peaches and apples and oranges all through the year. If you did, you'd be dead by the time you were twenty-five!"

"Well, we make pretty good in the cherries," another man says. "But by the time you figure there's eight people working, and the whole rest of the year when we can't make that much, I doubt if I make more 'n twenty dollars a day."

"I ain't too sure we're going to make it at all this year," the young man in overalls says wryly. "We might just be standin' around the welfare office if they don't ripen up here real quick. You know, they say there's only a dime's difference between the man that works and the man that don't work—and the one that don't work is the one with the dime!"

As everyone chuckles at that last line, a truck pulls up beside the group and the grower, a young man with a tanned face, leans his head out of the window. One of the older pickers takes a few steps out of the group to talk with him. "They're still awful green. Just not ripening up in this cool weather," the picker says, shaking his head.

"Yeah, I'm hoping we don't get any more rain now," comments the grower. "I reckon they're ten days off. Well, the field man will be out Wednesday to let us know." The grower waves goodbye and the truck ambles down the orchard road.

The men stand around a little awkwardly, their ostensible purpose of evaluating the cherries now gone. Then they start to disperse, making excuses as they move away. "Well, I guess I should see if Marge is ready to go into town," says one. "Yeah, I got to look at that truck of mine. That starter's been actin' up," says another. They seem disheartened as they walk back across the road. They know there won't be any work for at least ten days, and there's nothing to do but wait. The cherries won't be ripe up north for weeks to come. But often there are other jobs in the area if one has the patience and persistence to pursue them.

Going to search for a job can be a time-consuming and discouraging task. "Come back around five A.M. on Thursday and I'll see if I can put you on," a grower is apt to say. "If some of my pickers don't show up, I'll have a ladder for you." Pickers who really want the job must rise early, get ready for the day's work and drive—often ten miles or more. More often than not they will be told, "Sorry, I'm full up."

Before most pickers will even ask about a job they will spend many hours and gallons of gas driving around checking out the orchards. They're looking for large cherries, trees loaded with fruit, and trees spaced apart so their limbs aren't tangled together. Preferably, the trees are well pruned and a picker can reach all the cherries with a ten- or twelve-foot ladder.

Often a group of relatives or friends camped out together at a pickers' camp will go look for another job together. Since they may come to an orchard camp weeks before the work there is scheduled to begin, they need other work to fill in the time.

One time when we were staying in a migrant camp with about a week before our next job was to start we set out with several other pickers to look for another job. Like them, we couldn't miss days of possible work during the short-lived cherry season. Ruby, an older woman, had said she could use her "connection" to a grower to get us all jobs. But before we committed ourselves to asking for a job, we wanted to check out the orchard surreptitiously to be sure that we could all do well there. Crammed into a car with six other people, we drove several miles down back roads lined with orchards, until Ruby directed us to turn down a dirt driveway. We stopped in the middle of the orchard. The orchard was quiet—the cherries weren't quite ripe enough for picking so no one else was there. We swung open the four car doors and got out to congregate for a few minutes under the closest tree.

"Man, these trees are really loaded!" exclaimed Walter. His brother Daniel chewed thoughtfully on a cherry. "They sure are roped on there alright." The men drifted off to another tree, picking up branches to feel how heavily they were set with cherries and eating an occasional cherry to assess its size and ripeness.

Meanwhile the women remained near the car. Darlene scrutinized the first tree with the observant eye of experience. "They're loaded alright, but look at the size of 'em. I bet a lot of these cherries won't even make twelve-row!" she said critically.

Ruby agreed. "There ain't nothin' worse than pickin' those little cherries. You pick and pick and your bucket never does seem to get full!"

The men returned, meandering through the orchard investigating a clump of cherries carefully. "There's some pretty loaded trees out there," Daniel concluded. "It looks like a good job to me."

The women disagreed. "You know how those little cherries just pack down in your bucket," Darlene reminded us.

Walter interrupted, saying "Let's just go on up there after awhile and ask about it. We can't be no worse off than we are now, with no job." Despite the pickers' attempt to be selective and discerning when looking for a job, the bottom line was often what was available when they badly needed a job. Because the best money is in the cherries and then in the apples, there is intense pressure to work every available day during these harvests. There is plenty of dead time in between harvests and in the winters—pickers want to insure that they have a minimum of days off during the harvests.

Besides driving around to look for work, pickers usually call ahead to a farmer they have worked for to confirm their next job. They also rely on the grapevine— word-of-mouth reports of crop conditions and jobs, which are often completely without truth. One year a rumor circulated that our next job up north—a job that many people were counting on to make the bulk of their money in the cherries— would not be hiring any of us. The rumor was that the farmer had fired the con-tractor and had hired a whole crew of "wetbacks." Everyone was upset about the possibility and the rumor persisted for several days until phone calls were made to the grower, who denied the rumor.

The spread of false rumors about crop conditions is also commonplace. "I hear that hailstorm in the Tri-Cities wiped out the whole crop." "They say the trees are so loaded up in Brewster that one person can make eighty dollars by noon." These are examples of both negative and positive rumors we've heard about crops. Often such reports have a grain of truth in them but are very exaggerated. If a picker tells you about a bumper crop, it's likely that it's a good crop although it may not be as good as you were led to believe. Similarly, impressive stories about how much money a picker made a day picking cherries are usually misleading. Although such stories can be true, they usually represent one long day of incredibly hard effort by an experienced picker in the best fruit. Pickers realize the distortions such stories can lead to, but they take pride in their picking skills and want to tell about their abilities. Unfortunately, farmers often use these unrepresentative high figures to try to prove that pickers are making plenty of money—in their view, too much.

Exaggerations or distortions also occur about the length of a job and when it will begin. If a picker says it's a ten-day job, it usually lasts a week; a week-long job is usually finished in five days. If picking is supposed to start Tuesday, more often than not it will be Wednesday or Thursday before it actually begins.

Pickers can also be misled by farmers and contractors, who rely on field men for the go-ahead to begin picking. They may be told that a job will begin on a certain date and even leave one job early to travel to the next one, only to have to wait for days before the work begins.

Even under the best circumstances, when a picker has secured and begun a good job, there are irritating delays, lay-offs because of rain or unripeness of a variety of fruit (for example, in the same cherry orchard, Bings, Lamberts, Vans, and other varieties will ripen at staggered times). A typical work record I kept during a ten-day period at a cherry orchard in Kennewick, Washington, illustrates this frustrating fact of agricultural work:

June 8—Worked 5 A.M. to 2:30 P.M., averaged 4 boxes a tree.
June 9—Got laid off at 1:00.
June 10—Rained out at 10:00.
June 11—Laid off.
June 12—Laid off.
June 13—Got a good set after half a day, 5 a.m.–2:30 P.M.
June 14—Doing pretty good but he called us out at 1:00 P.M.!
June 15—Finally made our $100! 5 A.M.–3 P.M.
June 16—Again! Started in Vans about noon.
June 17—Took until 1:30 to finish. Windy and dusty!

The record shows that within the ten days we spent on the job, we had only four full days of work. Of course, even on the three days that we had to quit at one o'clock, we had already put in eight hours of work, but we didn't consider that a full day of work in the cherries. Because of the long days during the cherry harvest and the pressure to make most of our money then, we needed to work nine or ten hours to "make our quota." That quota, which may differ from picker to picker and job to job, is a personal expectation of how many boxes will be picked each day. Countless factors can erode such expectations. Because rain causes picked cherries to rot in the box, pickers are called out of the orchard in anything more than a light drizzle. Moving to other sections of the orchard, finishing one variety of cherries and starting another takes large chunks of the pickers' time, for which they are not compensated. Finally, bad trees—ones with too few cherries or cherries that don't come off easily; or ones with unpruned or tangled limbs—can cause pickers to not meet their quotas.

But in spite of all the frustrations, delays, and disappointments, there is nothing so satisfying to a picker as a good day of fruit picking. It's a rare day when the weather is perfect, not too cool or too hot, and a promising row of loaded trees stretches out ahead. The camaraderie of the crew is pleasant and the boxes of cherries seem to fill almost effortlessly with plump fruit. These days are rare even in the best harvest, but they are always what a picker hopes for at the beginning of the fruit run and remembers long after the last fruit of the season is picked.

Chicken Run

AN INTERVIEW WITH LINDA LORD

This interview takes place in Belfast, Maine with a worker in a poultry-processing plant. As you read this selection, think about the phrase "society's dirty work." What kind of job conditions did Linda Lord face? After closing the factory, what does Linda Lord take away from her experience? In other words, what do you think are her life chances? What role can unions play in factory work such as this? Take this selection and first analyze it from a non-sociological perspective; then analyze it again using your sociological imagination.

Linda Lord began gutting chicken at Penobscot Poultry, a small processing plant in Belfast, Maine, shortly after she finished high school in the late 1960s. "The machine got, oh, maybe 65 to 70 percent of the birds," Lord says, "and the rest I had to do." Her saga, told by herself in the course of six interviews, is at the heart of "I Was Content . . . And Not Content," a story of low-tech work in the new high-tech economy. Belfast, the authors say, did little to attract new industry or retrain workers, instead setting up tax shelters for financial service companies like MBNA America. "Under what conditions does our economic system undermine our efforts to create healthy and stable communities?" they ask.

(The following abbreviations have been used: AR for Alicia J. Rouverol; CC for Cedric N. Chatterley; SC for Stephen A. Cole; and LL for Linda J. Lord.)

MARCH 1, 1988; GALLAGHER'S GALLEY, BROOKS, MAINE

SC: Linda, were you born in Brooks?

LL: No, I was born up in Waterville at the old sisters' hospital. But I've always lived here in Brooks. . . . I went to my freshman year at Moss Memorial High School, and then they were building the area school up on Knox Ridge, and I started my

SOURCE: Cedric N. Chatterley and Alicia J. Rouverol, with Stephen A. Cole. *"I Was Content and Not Content": The Story of Linda Lord and the Closing of Penobscot Poultry.* © 2000 by Cedric N. Chatterley and Alicia J. Rouverol, reprinted with permission of the Southern Illinois University Press.

sophomore year up there and graduated from Mount View [in 1967]. After high school I went right into the hospital for an operation, and I wasn't supposed to work for a year; and come September, I got edgy and I started working a short time over at the [Unity] hatchery before I went down to the plant.

SC: What did you do?

LL: I de-beaked chickens, sexed them, injected them, de-toed them, de-beaked them, you name it I did it. [laughs]

SC: What is de-beaking?

LL: De-beaking is burning part of the bill off so they don't peck each other as they get bigger. . . .

SC: And then you learned to sex chickens, too. We hear that's rather a specific and actually sort of hard-to-learn task. Did you like working out there?

LL: It was all right. It was a job. At that time I was young, and I wanted to stay close to home on account of my mom being ill. And I wasn't there very long before they transferred me down at the plant because things were getting slow. It was either they were going to be laying off, or I had a chance to go up to the plant. I had looked around for other jobs, and I figured, well, I had been working with the company, I'd stay with them. So I went down to Penobscot.

SC: Let me back up a little bit. Did you go to the hatchery to work initially because your dad had also worked in the poultry industry?

LL: My father had been a pullorum [poultry blood] tester for a good number of years with the University of Maine. He did work for Penobscot and at the time for Maplewood [closed 1980]. Of course, during the summers, I worked for him testing birds. So I got to know quite a lot. Of course, we raised birds, too; we had laying hens for Maplewood so I'd grown right up. But no, that wasn't why I went over to the hatchery. It was, at that time, that was just about the only place that was hiring, you know. And I wanted a job. I was getting edgy not doing anything, even though I was supposed to stay out a year and not even work.

SC: Did other people you know from Mount View also hook up with Penobscot for a job?

LL: Not too many, no. As a matter of fact, a lot of the guys in my class were wiped out in Vietnam. I think we lost four or five. And the ones that did come back were disabled or not with it or either freaked right out on dope, you know.

SC: That's a large number of people from one high school. Well, probably your graduating class wasn't all that large in the end.

LL: I think it was a little over—maybe like a hundred and twenty in our class. I can't remember now, but I've got it on the back of my diploma. . . .

SC: So they transferred you down to Penobscot. What did you start doing there?

LL: Transferring. That's hanging [poultry] from the "New York" room after the feathers have been taken off and they've gone through the foot cutter—they drop down to the belt. I was working on Line Two, which did big birds and small birds. . . . But I kept breaking the skin away from my nails and getting blood poisoning streamers going right up my arm, so that's when I signed up for the sticking job. And the pay was a lot better. At that time I was going through a divorce, so I was out to get as much money as I could to support myself.

SC: What specifically was your job then?

LL: Just putting the bird into the shackle going out on the eviscerating line, after the feet have been cut off. They drop down on a belt which came to you, and you just would put them in a shackle so they could go out to be opened up and their intestines drawn out, and get your heart and liver and so forth out of the bird.

SC: So it's rough on your hands. How do you think that caused blood poisoning?

LL: Well, you take that infection that would set in, even though you'd try washing your hands good. And eventually it would get into your blood system and pretty soon, if you didn't take antibiotics or something, you'd have red streamers going right up your arm. And you'd take what helped to cut the feathers so they would pick better—the solution they added with the water [to remove the feathers]—and you'd take it with the grease and stuff, and that would cause you more trouble and make your skin peel right off your hands, too. My hands now are even sensitive to hot and cold where I was transferring, and it's been a number of years.

SC: So how long did you do that?

LL: About four or five years, then I signed right up for the rest of the time to go right on sticking.

SC: Were there a fair number of other people who work on the lines who have had these kinds of problems?

LL: Everybody's had problems that's been there. A lot of people have had warts come out on their hands because of handling chicken. A lot of people have had tendonitis, you know. That work is hard work down there. And they've had blood poisoning, you name it. Or you get, well—what do they call it? You have like a rash break out all over you from the chickens, too, which eventually will blister right up with little pus sacks, and the skin will peel right off your hand, and they call it "chicken poisoning" is what they call it. And I've seen people get it from wearing rubber gloves.

SC: Wow. Were you ever able to get any satisfaction from the company in terms of better conditions so that wouldn't happen? You had health benefits, right?

LL: Yeah, and if you had blood poisoning or anything, they'd send you right down to the hospital to try to get it cleared up. At that time they would put you on easy jobs until you either got over tendonitis or the rash on your hands and so forth. But as workmen's comp passed a few laws and stuff, then they had people just stay right out of work. They didn't want you even in there doing light work.

SC: Did that mean that if people had a problem, they were less likely to tell the company if that meant they now had to go home?

LL: A lot of people would stick it out and not say much. Because you had to be out over three days in order to draw on workmen's comp. If you were out maybe one or two days, you just couldn't get anything—you lost a couple days work. So a lot of people just kept going.

SC: So that job you had four or five years, and that's a total of how many years that you were at Penobscot?

LL: Twenty years in all with the company.

SC: Twenty years. So after that [transferring] it was into the sticking room or the "blood tunnel"?

LL: The sticking room, the "blood tunnel," or what I called the "hell hole," where they had so much blood. [laughter] No one wanted to come in there when you were in there. You were just by yourself until you got done work.
        When I first started out sticking, we didn't have any machinery in there then, except for just the stunners. And that first stunner that made the bird's head hang down is where we usually sat—two of us. There were two stickers in there and we had to do every other bird running right in a full line. And then about '79 . . . they were thinking about increasing the production down there. So they went into the sticking machines, which at first didn't pan out very good. But after a while, about a half a year, they got it straightened out so it would do a pretty good job. And then you had to back up the machine.

SC: So initially the stunner stunned the bird, but you had to stick them.

LL: Right. Grab it, take a knife and cut the vein right in by the jaw bone.

SC: So, by stunning, essentially that means that the bird was in shock? Were the birds all pretty much dead by the time they got to you?

LL: No, they were still, you know, flopping their last flop before they died. That's why I was more or less, as you could see—with the rain kerchief, I was more or less covered right up so I wouldn't get too bloody. . . . The machine got, oh, maybe sixty-five to seventy percent of the birds, and the rest I had to do. . . .

SC: Did you make more money working in that job?

LL: Yeah, because that was top pay. I mean I got the same as the trailer truck drivers did. The last of it then was $5.69 an hour, which was more than what the people were getting on the line. Maybe five, ten, fifteen, or twenty cents more—because each job through that plant you had different wages. . . . The trailer truck drivers, or straight job drivers, and stickers and weighers got the same wages—$5.69 an hour.

The Story of a Garment Worker

LISA LIU

Lisa Liu is a garment worker in Oakland, California. She came to the United States from China more than a decade ago but found that while the United States has fewer restrictions on workers, in some ways life as a worker was much less secure than she had expected. She became active in efforts to tell other San Francisco-area garment workers about their rights through an Oakland-based community organization, Asian Immigrant Women Advocates. Compare this essay with the prior essays in this work section. How does the garment industry compare with food processing? What can the public do to help stop the kinds of exploitation found in this selection?

I'm a seamstress in a factory with twelve other people. We sew children's clothes—shirts and dresses. I've worked in the garment industry here for twelve years, and at the factory where I am now for over a year.

In our factory we have to work ten hours a day, six to seven days a week. The contractor doesn't pay us any benefits—no health insurance or vacations. While we get a half-hour for lunch, there are no other paid breaks in our shift.

We get paid by the piece, and count up the pieces to see what we make. If we work faster we get paid more. But if the work is difficult and the manufacturer gives the contractor a low price, then what we get drops so low that maybe we'll get forty dollars a day. The government says the minimum wage is $5.75, but I don't think that by the piece we can reach $5.75 an hour a lot of the time.

When we hurt from the work we often just feel it's because of our age. People don't know that over the years their working posture can cause lots of pain. We just take it for granted, and in any case there's no insurance to pay for anything different. We just wait for the pain to go away.

That's why we organize the women together and have them speak out their problems at each of the garment shops. If we stop being silent about these things,

SOURCE: David Bacon, "The Story of a Garment Worker," *Dollars and Sense*, Number 231 (September/ October 2000), pp. 11–12. Used by permission of the author.

we can demand justice. We can get paid hourly and bring better working conditions to the workers.

Our idea is to tell them how to fight for their rights and explain what rights they have. Everyone should know more about the laws. We let them know about the minimum wage and that there should be breaks after four hours of work. We organize classes to teach women that we can be hurt from work. And we've opened up a worker's clinic to provide medical treatment and diagnosis. We do this work with the help of Asian Immigrant Women Advocates here in Chinatown.

We can't actually speak to the manufacturers whose clothes we're sewing because they don't come down to the shops to listen to the workers. So when we have a problem it's difficult to bring it to them. Still, we've had campaigns where we got the manufacturer to pay back-wages to the workers after the contractor closed without paying them. We got a hotline then, for workers to complain directly to the manufacturers. That solved some problems. The fire doors in those shops aren't blocked anymore, and the hygiene is better.

But it's not easy for women in our situation, and many are scared. Because they only work in the Chinese community, they're afraid their names will become known to the community and the bosses will not hire them. That's why we try to do things together. There's really no other place for us to go. Most of us don't have the training or the skills to work in other industries. We mostly speak just one language, usually Cantonese, and often just the dialect Toishanese.

When I first came to the United States I needed a lot of time to work to stabilize myself. So after seven years that's why I'm only now having my first baby. We don't have any health insurance and we have to pay the bill out of our own pockets. Health insurance is very expensive in the United States. We can't afford it. In the garment industry here they do not have health insurance for the workers.

Before I came here, my experience in China was that life was very strict. I heard that in America you have a lot of freedom, and I wanted to breathe the air of that freedom. But when I came here I realized the reality was very different from what I had been dreaming, because my idea of freedom was very abstract. I thought that freedom was being able to choose the place where you work. If you don't like one place, you can go work in another. In China you cannot do this. When you get assigned to a post, you have to work at that post.

Since I've come to the United States, I feel like I cannot get into the mainstream. There's a gap, like I don't know the background of American history and the laws. And I don't speak English. So I can only live within Chinatown and the Chinese community and feel scared. I cannot find a good job, so I have to work the low-income work. So I learned to compare life here and in China in a different way.

Many people say life here is very free. But for us, it's a lot of pressure. You have to pay rent, living costs so much money, you have all kinds of insurance—car insurance, health insurance, life insurance—that you can't afford. With all that kind of pressure, sometimes I feel I cannot breathe.

Everywhere you go you just find low pay. All the shops pay by the piece, and they have very strict rules. You cannot go to the bathroom unless it's lunch time.

Some places they put up a sign that says, "Don't talk while you work." You're not allowed to listen to the radio.

Wherever you go, in all the garment factories, the conditions and the prices are almost the same. The boss says, "I cannot raise the price for you and if you complain any more, then just take a break tomorrow—don't come to work." So even though I can go from one job to another, where's the freedom?

Frank Morley

Custodian, Littauer Center
for Public Administration

GREG HALPERN

In 2001, fifty Harvard students staged a sit-in at the office of the university's president to demand a living wage for Harvard employees. Eventually, 300 dining hall workers voted unanimously for authorization to strike if Harvard did not give in to demands, custodians began organizing their own demonstrations, other workers began to speak out publicly, and hundreds of supporters rallied outside the building. As a result of the protest, Harvard increased the minimum wage to $11.35 per hour for all of the lowest paid workers on campus, an estimated $3,738,000 that is now redistributed annually to more than a thousand low-wage workers. This selection by Greg Halpern is his interview with Frank Morley, a custodian at Harvard. As you read this selection, think about why low wage workers often do not engage in unified collective action to fight for their rights.

I recently had to go into an office and the professor was in there, and he's got the problem written on the board, and he's sitting there studying that thing, and I'm standing there fixing the file cabinet. The drawers were jamming, and the man didn't even flinch. I swear, the man didn't even know I was there. About twenty minutes later, he asked me if I fixed his cabinet yet. I told him I finished it twenty minutes ago. You might initially think it's a class thing, but it's not that at all. It's just they're so busy, and in a way, I've always admired a person who can sit down and be totally riveted right on whatever they're doing.

I'm the only one who cleans this building during the day and I got ninety-four rooms here. Once, between my two jobs I worked thirty-five days straight without a day off. I can usually pull that off, but this week, for example, I'm starting to catch a cold. A lot of us are tired. Tired of watching every dime, too. But it's

SOURCE: Halpern, Greg. 2003. *Harvard Works because We Do*. New York: The Quantuck Lane Press. pp. 138–139.

like everyone's afraid to speak up. Most of the people who work for UNICCO come from other countries, primarily Spanish-speaking countries, because they're here on a green card there's intimidation going on. You hear stories that managers threaten to call the immigration office if they ask for a raise or if they ask for their vacation time. And if you lose your job with a green card, you have thirty days to get a new job or you're out of the country. One guy didn't get paid time and a half for his overtime, but the guy was so scared he wouldn't say anything. Once I requested a vacation and forty-five minutes later two supervisors came over and said, "What do you mean, you're taking a vacation?" See, UNICCO advertises that you get vacation, but in reality it's a little different. All that, and we have a union, Local Two-fifty-four of SEIU—the Service Employees' International Union.

My alarm goes off at four in the morning. That morning time is the only real time I have to myself. I shower, l shave, I listen to the news. Out the door by five-thirty. Get to the station by five-fifty. Catch the train at five fifty-five. Get to work at seven fifteen. All told it's an hour and forty-five minutes from Mansfield. I finish working for Harvard at four P.M., get on the train, grab a cup of coffee, throw down a doughnut, get off the train, and walk—twenty minutes from the station to the supermarket. I bag and stock until ten-thirty P.M., walk back to the train, take it home, get in the door around eleven-thirty. In bed around midnight—usually I hit the pillow and I'm out. Up again by four A.M. I've been on that schedule for a little over two years now.

There are a lot of days when you're walking around in a fog. But you don't think on it too much—you just go. There was a time when I was working Monday to Friday and four hours Saturday and four hours Sunday. I stopped that, but for a while after that I was still waking up early Saturday mornings, thinking I was going to work, getting dressed, until halfway through it I realized I didn't have to. Now, Saturdays I'll clean up at home, grocery-shop, do laundry. Sundays I sit down and watch football. Time is precious—at least at age sixty-one it is.

Right now I'm using the retirement money to pay back the money I borrowed from the bank. So I still got some money in the retirement fund, but that'll be gone soon. Still, I'd like to go out and indulge a little, you know? Sit down at a place and eat. I do that now when I get the tax refund. Nowadays, I tend to eat at work when I can. After the luncheons, we get a shot at the leftovers. So you save money where you can.

You've got to remember with a cleaning company that their primary purpose is to make a profit. Managers always try to cut expenses, and they see wages as expenses. They forget that it's people—it's a person they're talking about who's trying to live on that. For example, they'll keep your hours down below seventeen a week so they don't have to pay you benefits. That's part of their cost control. It's just that I'm tired up here, in the head, and I'm tired physically. Things bug me that normally don't. Sometimes I just need to back off and cool down a little.

I've been wearing a custodial uniform now going on twenty years. And I think by now they figure they own me like a piece of equipment, like a barrel or a buffing machine. Plus, people figure if I had any brains, I'd be doing something else. But it's really got nothing to do with being lazy or not having the smarts. I work hard, and I did a few years for a while at Roxbury College. I got an associate's degree in management, and I was going for the bachelor's. I was going to start my own business. That's when my father was diagnosed with cancer. My mother too, eight months later, so I hung up the school.

We recently got a raise, though, after three years of the Living Wage Campaign, the sit-in, and then finally after nine of us went so far as to get arrested at a rally. That was big news. It was pretty soon after that that we won our contract. So now I'll go from ten dollars to about eleven-fifty. That buck-fifty adds up to twelve dollars a day, sixty dollars a week, which may not sound like a lot to some people, but in my case you don't sneeze at it. Ever since the sixties, we always looked to the college students to get the action going. They'd get out there and do the work and get people to get out on the streets. The students have the knowledge to do the organizing. And they don't have jobs to lose and families to feed, so they can take the risks, they can get out there when we can't.

REFLECTION QUESTIONS

FOR PART V

The readings in this section focus on the effects that institutions have on individual lives. Reflect on the following general questions from Part V:

1. What effect does housing (affordability, availability, quality, neighborhood) have on a person's life experience?
2. How does the welfare system affect those people receiving welfare? How have changes in the system affected individuals? How do people outside the system view people on welfare?
3. How does the healthcare system affect an individual's life chances and quality of life? How can this system be improved?
4. If work is central to a person's identity, what does this mean for those who do society's "dirty work"? What types of exploitation are evident in the selections on work?
5. Compare/contrast the readings in Chapters 6–9. What common threads do you see in their experiences? How do race, class, gender, age, and location affect people's experiences with society's institutions?
6. Analyze each article carefully and group them by individual/cultural and structural theories of poverty. Why do you think one theory or another is best reflected in each reading? Explain your reasons.
7. Select one particular essay, such as Luis Rodriguez's "Always Running," and analyze it first *without* using a sociological imagination, and then analyze it again *with* a sociological imagination.

PART VI

Individual and Collective Agency and Empowerment

"The curse of poverty has no justification in our age. It is socially as cruel and blind as the practice of cannibalism at the dawn of civilization . . . the time has come for us to civilize ourselves by the total, direct, and immediate abolition of poverty."

Martin Luther King, Jr. (1967)

CHAPTER 10

Changes from the Bottom Up

The discipline of sociology focuses on the social context and the social forces that so strongly affect human behavior. But while society and its structures are powerful, the members of society are not totally controlled. We are not passive actors. People can take control of the conditions of their lives. Human beings cope with, adapt to, and change social structures to meet their needs. Individuals acting alone or with others, can shape, resist, challenge, and sometimes change the social institutions that impinge upon them. These actions constitute **human agency.** The essence of agency is that individuals through collective action are capable of changing the structure of society and even the course of history. But while agency is important, we should minimize the power of the structures that subordinate people, making change difficult or, at times, impossible (Eitzen and Baca Zinn, 2007:521–527).

At the individual level, the poor and the near poor can use various strategies to supplement their meager resources. Single mothers, for example, can do income-producing work such as house cleaning, laundry, repairing clothing, childcare, and selling items they have made (Harris, 1996; Schein, 1995), as well as giving and receiving help from family, friends, neighbors, boyfriends, and absent fathers. Those strategies are ways to cope with and adapt to the existing structural limitations. The focus here, however, is on joining with others to change social structures, to make them more equitable.

Individual actors seeking change will have little affect as individuals. If, however, they join with others who share their convictions and goals, and if they organize and map out a plan of action, they can make a difference (Kammeyer, Ritzer, and Yetman, 1997:632–633). In doing so they have created a social movement. A **social movement** is an issue-oriented group specifically organized to promote or resist change. These movements arise when people are sufficiently discontented that they will work for a better system.

At various times and places the poor and the near poor have organized to change oppressive situations. Janitors, hotel maids, garbage collectors, welfare mothers, farm workers, and others have sometimes succeeded in making the powerful meet their demands. Historically, the most successful social movements by the poor and powerless were the Montgomery bus boycott led by Martin Luther King, Jr. in the 1950s and the organization of farm workers by Cesar Chavez in the early 1960s. King and his organization of African Americans broke down segregated busing in the South with a Supreme Court decision and led to many more civil rights victories (Branch, 1988). The campaigns by Chavez and his farm workers, through grape boycotts and other tactics, led to an agreement in 1966 with the farm owners requiring that the owners provide clean drinking water, rest periods, and other benefits to the workers, and to the 1975 passage of the California Agricultural Labor Relations Act—the first law in the nation to guarantee farm workers the right to form unions and to bargain collectively (Griswold del Castillo, 1995).

Campaigns by the poor and the nonpoor have resulted in over 60 cities (including Baltimore, New York City, Boston, and Los Angeles) instituting living-wage ordinances to help lift low-paid workers out of poverty. These efforts continue as well as collective efforts such as the removal of pesticide exposure to farm workers and the elimination of sweatshops.

NOTES AND SUGGESTIONS FOR FURTHER READING

Branch, Taylor (1988). *Parting the Waters: America in the King Years 1954–63.* New York: Simon and Schuster Touchstone Books.

Clark, Christine, and James O'Donnell (1999). *Becoming and Unbecoming White: Owning and Disowning a Racial Identity.* Westport, CT: Bergin and Garvey.

Eitzen, D. Stanley, and Maxine Baca Zinn (2007). *In Conflict and Order: Understanding Society,* 11th ed. Boston: Allyn and Bacon.

Griswold del Castillo, Richard (1995). *Cesar Chavez: A Triumph of Spirit.* Norman: University of Oklahoma Press.

Jennings, James (1994). *Blacks, Latinos, and Asians in Urban America: Status and Prospects for Politics and Activism.* Westport, CT: Praeger.

Jennings, James (Ed.) (1997). *Race and Politics: New Challenges and Responses to Black Activism.* London: Verso.

Kammeyer, Kenneth C. W., George Ritzer, and Norman R. Yetman (1997). *Sociology,* 7th ed. Boston: Allyn and Bacon.

Kern, Jen (2001). "Working for a Living Wage." *Multinational Monitor* 22 (January/February):14–16.

Lofland, John (1996). *Social Movement Organizations: Guide to Research on Insurgent Realities.* New York: Aldine de Gruyter.

Piven, Frances Fox, and Richard A. Cloward (1977). *Poor People's Movements: Why They Succeed, How They Fail.* New York: Pantheon.

Pope, Jackie (1999). "Women in the Welfare Rights Struggle," pp. 287–304 in *A New Introduction to Poverty: The Role of Race, Power, and Politics,* Louis Kushnick and James Jennings (Eds.). New York: New York University Press.

Schein, Virginia E. (1995). *Working from the Margins: Voices of Mothers in Poverty.* Ithaca, NY: Cornell University Press.

Wright, Carter (2001). "A Clean Sweep: Justice for Janitors." *Multinational Monitor* 22 (January/February):12–14.

Wright, Talmadge (1997). *Out of Place: Homeless Mobilizations, Subcities, and Contested Landscapes.* Albany: State University of New York Press.

Surviving Chicago's Toxic Doughnut

HAZEL JOHNSON

Hazel Johnson, a 64-year-old African American woman, talks here about her fight against the toxic environment surrounding public housing in Chicago. This selection is an example of environmental racism/classism (the concentration of poor and racial minorities near hazardous and toxic environments). Can you think of other examples of environmental racism in different areas of the country? What does her organization (PCR) do to promote social change, and how does this demonstrate collective empowerment?

I am a mother of seven children and nine grandchildren. I have been a resident of the Altgeld Gardens community for 37 years. Altgeld Gardens is a public housing development located on the Southeast side of Chicago. I became a community representative, taking children on field trips to the amusement park and other places, during the summer months. I volunteered at the local parent school council and was elected to the Altgeld Local Advisory Council.

I started People for Community Recovery (PCR) in 1979. It was started as a group of women organizing on environmentally-related health problems in this community. PCR was incorporated October 25, 1982. Our organization is one of the first African American grassroots community-based environmental organizations in the Midwest. Our mission is to address multiple exposures to harmful toxins and pollutants surrounding public housing. For the past 20 years, I have been active in environmental issues in my community and other communities of color around the country. I got involved in environmental issues while watching the news and learned that the Southeast side of Chicago had the highest incidence of cancer of any community in the city.

Later, I connected with the city and state health departments. These agencies mailed me many reports on environmental problems in Southeast Chicago. PCR conducted its own land use survey of the neighborhood. We began knocking on my

SOURCE: Hazel Johnson, "Surviving Chicago's 'Toxic Doughnut,'" Environment Justice Resource Center (March 24, 2001), www.ejrc.cau.edu/voicesfromthegrassroots.htm. Reprinted by permission of Robert Bullard.

neighbors' doors asking them to fill out the health survey. We learned that people were suffering with severe health problems, including asthma, cancer, skin rashes, kidney and liver problems. To no one's surprise, we found alarming patterns. The Southside neighborhood, Altgeld Gardens in particular, was surrounded by all kinds of polluting industries, landfills, incinerators, smelters, steel mills, chemical companies, paint manufacturing plants, and a municipal sewage treatment facility. My neighborhood is also surrounded by more than 50 abandoned toxic waste dumps. We live in a "toxic doughnut."

Despite poor environmental conditions in our community, this did not discourage our group from wanting to learn more about the environmental conditions and the possible impact on residents' health. PCR began organizing residents to get the neighborhood cleaned up and treated fairly. For the past decade, we pressured corporate polluters, the city, and state officials to make them aware of their negligence and make them accountable. It has not been easy going up against the giant corporations, but we are fighting a life-and-death struggle. Through perseverance and dedication, we have successfully brought the needed attention to the environmental issues in Southeast Chicago. We have to fight for our children. We have educated ourselves on environmental issues and the health threats from nearby polluting industry. We have not waited for government to come in and determine the "cause" of our illnesses. We may not have Ph.D. degrees, but we are the 147 "experts" on our community.

In 1992, PCR undertook its own health survey of 825 Altgeld Gardens' residents. We were joined by volunteers from the University of Illinois School of Public Health (designed the survey instrument), Clareitian Medical Clinic (conducted training of interviewers), and St. James Hospital (designed the graphs). Their goal was to follow up on the long-standing anecdotal evidence of health problems. The results of the survey were no surprise. In addition to heightened risks of troubled pregnancies, the survey revealed a high incidence of chronic pulmonary disease, which includes emphysema and chronic bronchitis. Thirty-two percent of men and 20 percent of the women surveyed had asthma. Sixty-eight percent of those surveyed indicated that they experienced health problems that disappeared when they left Altgeld Gardens. More than 37 percent of the respondents cited noxious odor when asked to comment generally on their most common complaint.

The environmental justice work that we started in Chicago has allowed me to testify before Congress and meet two presidents of the United States. Our group has sponsored "toxic tours" of the community with dignitaries from around the world. We have hosted two environmental conferences. We are often asked to speak at universities and colleges, at workshops and training programs about urban environmental pollution and racism. Our environmental justice work has kept us busy. More importantly, it has paid off.

PCR's organizing efforts persuaded the Chicago Housing Authority and Chicago Board of Education to remove asbestos from the homes and schools in Altgeld Gardens. We assisted elderly tax-paying residents of Maryland Manor, another Chicago housing development, in getting water and sewage services. Our group also shut down a nearby hazardous waste incinerator and fought to get a comprehensive health clinic in the southside neighborhood.

PCR along with other people of color grassroots groups took their struggle to the Rio Earth Summit where they were joined in solidarity with other brothers and sisters around the world who are experiencing similar environmental and economic injustices. It did not take me long to realize that the environmental, economic, and health problems in the favelas of Rio de Janeiro looked a lot like the problems in my Southside Chicago neighborhood.

Our organization is growing and maturing, and we are still learning. In 1992, PCP, was a recipient of the President's Environmental and Conservation Challenge medal, the nation's highest environmental award. That was a great honor. However, the biggest award and honor I could get from government officials right now is for them to "do the right thing," by making the polluters clean up their act on the Southside.

PCR has formed alliances and coalitions with national environmental and civil rights organizations as well as other local grassroots environmental groups. We see ourselves as an integral part of the environmental and economic justice movement. Poor people and people of color must empower themselves to become politically active. Everything is political. We must learn how to fight for environmental justice at home and abroad. No one will save our communities but us.

Welfare Rights Organizing Saved My Life

DOTTIE STEVENS

Dottie Stevens, former welfare recipient and battered mother, talks about becoming involved in welfare rights and what that did for her life. What words or phrases that are used throughout this essay can be associated with empowerment? How would individual/cultural and structural theorists analyze her situation and actions? What can be learned from her experiences?

I grew up in east Boston, Massachusetts, a neighborhood with a large Italian population (mostly immigrants). For me, they represented large families, strange accents, and wonderful smells from delicious mysterious foods. Wine was on the table for all meals, and even the young children were encouraged to sip it from fancy glasses. My street was a mixture of nationalities. We were also Irish, French, English, Native American, and Chinese, as well as many other mixtures we couldn't figure out. My own background was Irish and German.

On the other side of my street was a housing project that went on for four blocks. It became my playground and community. My own home was a two-family house. Nana lived on the first floor and my mother, two brothers, two sisters and I occupied the second floor. Mom was divorced and had to apply for welfare to keep us together. I don't remember seeing Mom much after she began to work under the table, because the welfare's cash benefits wouldn't cover all the bills.

I found that if I wanted attention or something to eat, I could go to any of my friends' homes on the street or in the projects and blend in with their families, and feel I belonged. I liked to stay at my friend Angela's house the best. She had a mother *and* a father at home and they always had fresh, hot Italian bread to share with me. Angela had one brother, and many aunts and cousins, but what I was most impressed with were her four handsome uncles! They all communicated loudly, bellowing passionately to everyone in their space, arms and hands slicing

SOURCE: Dottie Stevens, "Welfare Rights Organizing Saved My Life," *For Crying Out Loud: Women's Poverty in the United States,* Diane Dujon and Ann Withorn (Eds.), (Boston: South End Press, 1996), pp. 313–316. Reprinted by permission of the publisher.

through the air. To me, that noise and confusion represented what family was *supposed* to be.

I am a product of the system, so to speak. I was a child of five years old in a single-female-headed household with four siblings, and we were on welfare. Memories of everyday living were not too bad. We were used to having no heat until Thanksgiving, and we never had hot water in the summertime. We lived in our own home and envied the families living across the street from us in the projects. They *always* seemed to have heat and hot water all year round. Their electricity *never* got shut off. They received repairs if anything broke down and had their apartments painted every other year automatically. It seemed to me that living in the projects was luxury!

My mother was (and is) a proud woman and a very hard worker. As an adopted, only child of a doting, elderly, immigrant couple, she was ill-equipped to cope with five children in poverty and an ex-husband who never paid her any child support. But she did the best she could.

Mother did not like her social worker, Mrs. Brown, who always made her feel like a loser. She would come to our house unannounced and ask to look in closets and cabinets as if my Mother was hiding something or someone. To this day, I can see the tension and feel the anxiety this worker provoked in my mother's life.

We did not have a bad life; we did not really know we were poor. We did not own a car; we had no phone. But Mother managed, somehow, to get us all into parochial school. She always told us education was the key to success, although she had had very little education herself. My mother's influence lasted only until the eighth grade. After all, I was a teenager and my mother was the *last* person I listened to!

At 16 years old (after another night with my mother) I eloped, thinking it was the way to a better life. (Wasn't the point to "at least get him to *marry* you"?) A son was born of this union, the only good part about it. Although I was madly in love, after my first child was born, reality set in and I knew my marriage wouldn't last. Two years later, we parted and my world fell apart. I was only 18 years old!

I loved my baby son, but alone with no income, I did not think I would be able to keep us together. So I went to Mom's house for help.

I divorced at 20, worked for several years at factory work and waitressing jobs, went to night school for a while, then married again. This marriage lasted six years. I had two more children and, when the fighting got real bad, this husband just disappeared, and we have not seen him since. At 28, I was divorced again!

I had just about given up on the love-and-marriage bit; I went back to night school and was set to stay a single parent, when husband #3 showed up on the scene. He was kind, affectionate, and took an interest in me and my children. I fell passionately in love and thought this was meant to be!

I had married this last time out of my culture, into one I could not understand. Things that seemed odd and uncommon to me, I chalked up as different ways, traditions, customs, and language. We were different! I went along with it: different dress, different conversations, recreations and working conditions. I just wanted to be a good wife and mother, to take care of the home, go to the PTA meetings, bake, shop, keep myself attractive, and be there for my man. But through day-to-day experiences, I eventually realized what was happening, and this was not the reality I had expected for my family!

What had happened to love? This was not what I thought it would be. Yes, he professed to love me and the children and showed compassion and kindness. Yes, he vowed to love and care for us forever. Yes, he could be sweet and gentle, but look out! *Emotionally, Freddy Kruger lived here.* I couldn't close my eyes for too long; if I slept, anything could happen in the dark.

I knew I would have to hide from him because he was not about to let us go. I was running, escaping for my life and my sanity! With my children (the baby in my arms and the three others in tow), I fled from an abyss of cruelty, deceit, and oppression that I had never known existed. I had been a romantic fool, brain-washed to believe in love.

I stayed in a battered women's shelter for a month. I finally managed to get him out and get our home back. When I looked toward the future, it seemed desperately bleak and uncertain. My self-esteem was nil and I had no money. My children and I had been physically, mentally, and emotionally battered for a long time and needed many years of therapy and counseling to be able to deal with it; and after two decades, we are still haunted by the abuse. When my youngest child went to school, I knew I needed to do something to better myself economically. We had been subsisting on welfare benefits that could not decently support a family, so I thought I should go back to school and earn a degree that would enable me to earn a breadwinner's wage. I had never gone to high school and was told I needed a GED to get admitted to college at U-Mass/Boston, College of Public and Community Service (CPCS). When I was eventually admitted to CPCS, the first thing I did was buy four pairs of knee-socks and I was ready for a new start in my life!

In September 1979, I was finally on my way—to where or what, I had no idea, but I felt it would be O.K. I was getting educated! This college was not what I expected; it was comprised of adult working people and many single mothers on welfare trying to do the same thing as I. I had found my niche and I thrived!

In my second semester, I entered a class called "Basic Organizing." This class was made up of 13 welfare-recipient mothers and a few human service professionals. Ann Withorn was our instructor, and she made me feel as if I had come to the right place. Was I in for a surprise when I found out my life experience was really a valuable asset in her class! I had just ended my third marriage; and I was a former abused and battered wife of a substance abuser.

Some of the other student mothers were so smart, I thought I could not keep up, but we learned to become a self-help group and helped each other in many ways to earn credits by working together in groups. And what a dynamic group we were! We actually became a sisterhood—sort of a sorority of poor women—sharing our most intimate secrets, experiences, hopes, dreams, and disappointments. We developed a collective knowledge, which we were able to use to help each other fend off the Welfare Department. We adopted a principle to never go to the Welfare Department alone—we became each other's advocates at fair hearings. We exchanged clothing, shared childcare responsibilities when our childcare arrangements fell through, compiled lists of wealthy suburban communities' trash pick-up days, and organized furniture shopping sprees for the nights before trash collections. Individually, we were weak, but together we were formidable!

The "Basic Organizing" class began organizing on campus and developed into a Recognized Student Organization, which allowed us to obtain office space, a telephone, and a small budget with which to work. We voted on a name and were now called "Advocacy for Resources for Modern Survival" (ARMS). We voted to become a chapter of The Coalition for Basic Human Needs (CBHN), which was the state-wide welfare rights organization. Our priority was to advocate for welfare recipients' access to higher education. We began to serve on many advisory committees and on boards of directors of antipoverty agencies that affected our lives, such as daycare centers, health care providers, fuel assistance agencies, tenants' rights organizations, clothing and food distribution centers, etc.

Many of us felt intimidated and unable to even know what was being said at the meetings, but we took notes, came back to ARMS, and discussed all that we had heard and educated each other. This was a wonderful time getting closer to the other women and their children and beginning to trust each other. Working together, we were able to keep ourselves informed on several fronts at once. We were able to monitor proposed changes in the service delivery of a variety of agencies, assess their often conflicting policies, make holistic appraisals of their effects on our lives, develop recommendations, and, most importantly, significantly impact the final decisions. *We were making a difference!*

In this "Basic Organizing" class, the group decided to organize around welfare issues. The Aid to Families with Dependent Children program was very important to all of us because we derived our income and health benefits from it, but it was an inadequate, punitive system that harassed and demeaned us. We all decided to fight back using techniques that would enable us to earn our sheepskins. We started to research poverty issues going all the way back to the Elizabethan Poor Laws, and we found out that poor people always had it bad! There were the manors and the serfs, the Pharaohs and the slaves, the Old South and the Blacks, and now we had billionaire politicians and Workfare participants!

Learning the theories, history, and practice of organizing saved my life; actually, it brought me to life! I finally had something worthwhile to live for.

Josefina Flores: A Veteran
of the War in the Fields

DAVID BACON

Josefina Flores is a field organizer for the migrant workers' union, United Farm Workers. At the time of this interview; she was engaged in a campaign to organize the strawberry industry in the face of sometimes violent opposition by the companies involved. Think about the role of unions in the lives of poor, minority laborers. What are the pros and cons of labor unions? What particular problems exist in trying to collectively organize farm laborers?

Josefina Flores, a woman in her sixties, looks a little weather-beaten, from a life spent in the sun. "I was born in Calexico, in the Imperial Valley," she remembers. "I worked in the fields from the time I was 7 years old, in the lettuce, in the beets, the carrots, and finally, the grapes. My family worked the *corrido*—we traveled with the crops, making the same circuit every year."

"In those years, no one ever demanded that the children of farm workers go to school. I just went a few days in one place and a few days in another. I wanted to go to school. I could see the other children playing and learning things. But I couldn't, because of the economic situation of my family. I was the oldest child—I had to help, so I went to work. This was in 1937 and 1938, and the wages were 30¢ an hour. At first if just worked helping my parents. Adding what I did to their work, we all just made a little more."

Flores was born in the United States, and so is a U.S. citizen. "But even so, we were just seen as poor people, as Mexicans," she recalls. "Being poor and being Mexican was just about the same thing."

She got married at 21, and had nine children. Only three are still living, and her husband died when the oldest was 10. "Afterwards, I just went on working," she, says. "I brought my kids to the fields, the way my parents brought me. We had

SOURCE: David Bacon, "Josefina Flores: A Veteran of the War in the Fields," *Dollars and Sense*, Number 231 (September/October 2000), pp. 38–39. Used by permission of the author.

a little *corrido*—just from Arvin to Selma and back [two small towns in California's Central Valley]."

Today, Flores is an organizer for the United Farm Workers, a veteran of the labor wars that have swept California fields since the 1960s. Driving through the Pájaro Valley around Watsonville, she stops from time to time to speak with workers at the edge of the strawberry fields. There they work, doubled over, for ten hours and more every day. Most are very young—eighteen or twenty years old.

Flores calls them to come talk with her. She takes down, in a thick, spiral-bound notebook, careful notes about what they say. Every name is written down—what each person says about their wages, the problems of their job, the name of their foreman. She keeps this record partly to help the union organize. But who else is going to write down what happens to these young men and women of the strawberry fields? The spiral-bound notebook is the record that each person was here, that each thought a certain way about their situation. Josefina Flores has become an archivist for the voiceless.

"I never learned to read and write when I was a child—not until much later," she says. "I learned in the union. Organizers would teach me a little here, and a little there, long after I was already grown up."

Flores became a member of the United Farm Workers when the union first began. "In 1965 we began to hear that César Chávez was organizing a union for farm workers. I didn't know what a union was," she explains. "I was working on a ranch near Selma, and there was a strike. I saw that the union was trying to do something good, just trying to get the wages up a little, and get bathrooms in the fields. So I joined."

In 1968, the union struck the grape harvest, as it did every year from 1965 to 1970. That year, Flores went with her daughter to collect food donations at a local restaurant. "While I was inside, a foreman came in and shot me. He shot seven bullets into my body." It took Flores two years to recover. Afterwards, she became a UFW organizer and a leader of the huge 1973 grape strike, when growers tore up their union contracts and brought in the Teamsters. That epic battle was called off after two other workers were shot and killed on the picket line.

When Flores looks at the young immigrants who make up the workforce in the strawberry fields today, she sees workers who have little idea of the sacrifice she and the other union veterans made over the years to build a union. "People come here from far away in Mexico," she explains. "They know very little about their rights as workers. We have to explain the whole history of the farm workers' movement to people who not only weren't here when it happened—many of them hadn't even been born. To them, César Chávez is a boxer." (She refers to Julio César Chávez—the Mexican boxing champion.)

"If they don't come here [to the United States], they don't eat," she adds. "They tell me—'we're not here because we want to, but because we have to.' In the little towns they come from, there's no clinic, and sometimes no school. They can't read and write. And of course the labor contractors threaten them. A lot of workers have no papers, so it's not hard to scare them. That's the biggest problem—for us and for them. They know so little."

Flores looks at the young workers and sees herself as she was when she was young. "They're tired of being poor and ground down," she concludes, "just like I was. And while some are afraid, these young people are still not as accepting of things as farm workers were when I was their age. Their expectations are higher than ours were. That's why I think our movement can help them."

"They want something better. I hope they're willing to fight to get it."

How Predatory Lending Victims Fought Back and Won

DAVID SWANSON

Author David Swanson is the former Communications Coordinator for ACORN, the Association of Community Organizations for Reform Now. ACORN is the largest community organization fighting for the rights of low- and moderate-income families, representing approximately 350,000 families and 850 neighborhood chapters in over 100 cities in the United States. In this piece, Swanson demonstrates the power of collective action and what can be accomplished when people work together towards a common goal. As you read this selection, think about this model of collective action. What made their efforts so successful?

If someone told you that a bunch of low-income people, most of them African-American or Latino, most of them women, most of them elderly, had been victimized by a predatory mortgage lender that stripped them of much of their equity or of their entire homes, you might not be surprised. But if I told you that these women and men had gotten together and after three years of work brought the nation's largest high-cost lender to its knees, forced it to sell out to a foreign company, and won back a half a billion dollars of what had been taken from them—one of the largest consumer settlements ever—you'd probably ask me what country this had happened in. Surely it couldn't have been in the United States of the Second Gilded Age, the land of unbridled corporate power and radical government activism on behalf of the rich and the greedy.

And yet it was. These victims of predatory lending identified the problem and named it "predatory lending" in the late 1990s, and their campaign to reform Household International (also known as Household Finance and as Beneficial) played out from 2001 to 2003, concluding with a settlement that includes a ban on badmouthing the company. That's part of why more people haven't heard about

SOURCE: This article is a chapter in *The Wealth Inequality Reader by Dollars and Sense and United For a Fair Economy* (2004). www.dollarsandsense.org/bookstore/wealthinequality.html. Reprinted by permission of *Dollars & Sense,* a progressive economics magazine (www.dollarsandsense.org).

this. The families who fought back and defeated Household are barred from bragging about it or teaching the lessons they learned, because that would require recounting the damage that Household did to homes and neighborhoods. These families are members of ACORN, the Association of Community Organizations for Reform Now. I was ACORN's communications coordinator during much of the Household campaign but left before it ended. No one has asked me not to tell this story.

In low-income minority neighborhoods in the United States, what little wealth there is, is in home equity. Home equity makes up 74.9 percent of the net wealth for Hispanics in the bottom two income quintiles (0–40 percent), and 78.7 percent of the net wealth for African-Americans in the second income quintile (20–40 percent). There have been gains in minority home ownership over the past few decades, in part as a result of the work by community groups like ACORN and National People's Action to force banks to make loans in these communities. But the home ownership is fragile and not protected by additional savings. Lenders in the past decade have focused on stripping away equity, and community groups have been forced to focus on keeping out loans that are worse than no loans at all.

Most high-cost loans are refinance loans. Too often they are marketed aggressively and deceptively, including through live-checks in the mail that result in very high-cost loans that the lender will be only too happy to refinance into a new mortgage. Often these loans are made with excessive, sometimes variable, interest rates, outrageously high fees, and fees financed into the loans so that the borrower pays interest on them and often is not told about them. They are made with bogus products built in, on which the borrower also pays interest. Hidden balloon payments force repeated refinancings for additional fees each time. Mandatory arbitration clauses attempt to prevent borrowers from taking lenders to court. The practice of loaning more than the value of a home traps borrowers in loans they cannot refinance with a responsible lender. Consolidation of additional debts further decreases equity, placing the home at greater risk. Quiet omission of taxes and insurance from a mortgage that previously included those charges results in a crisis when the yearly bills arrive.

Predatory lenders turn the usual logic of lending upside down. They make their money by intentionally making loans that the borrowers will be unable to repay. They charge fees for each refinancing until finally seizing the house. Fannie Mae has estimated that as many as half of all borrowers in subprime (high-cost) loans could have qualified for a lower cost mortgage. High-cost loans are not just made to people with poor credit. They're often made, rather, to people who have poor banking services in their neighborhoods. After HSBC bought Household, it announced that 46 percent of Household's real estate-backed loans had been made to borrowers with 'A' credit. Household made no 'A' loans.

ACORN members don't take abuse of their neighborhoods lying down, and Household was a leading cause of the rows of vacant houses appearing in ACORN neighborhoods in the 1990s. ACORN launched a campaign to reform Household that included numerous strategies. One, an old ACORN stand-by, was direct action. Repeatedly, ACORN members in numerous cities around the country simultaneously protested in Household offices to demand reform. At the same time, ACORN was working to pass anti-predatory lending legislation in local and state governments and Congress. ACORN members made sure that in each case the victims testifying were victims of Household and that Household's abuses were highlighted. When ACORN released major reports on predatory lending, the examples included were always from Household.

ACORN also worked with the Coalition for Responsible Wealth to advance a shareholder resolution that would have tied Household's executives' compensation to ending its predatory lending. In 2001 Household held its shareholders meeting in an out-of-the-way suburb of Tampa, Florida. A crowd of ACORN members was there with shark suits and shark balloons to protest. The resolution won 5 percent. Over the next year, ACORN pressured state pension funds and other shareholders. Household held its 2002 meeting an hour and a half from the nearest airport in rural Kentucky. ACORN members made the trip by car from all over the country. The protest may have been the biggest thing the town of London, Ken., had seen in years. The resolution won 30 percent.

As a result of ACORN agitation, various local and state governments threatened to divest from Household. ACORN also put pressure on stores like Best Buy that used Household credit cards. At the same time, ACORN Housing Corporation was assisting many Household victims in either refinancing out of their Household loans or at least canceling some of the rip-off services built into their loans, such as credit insurance. And ACORN was getting the word out through local ethnic media to stay away from Household.

ACORN wrote up numerous accounts of Household predatory loans and took them to the attorney generals in state after state urging investigations. ACORN similarly pressured federal regulators to act. And ACORN assisted borrowers in filing a number of class-action suits against Household targeting those of its practices that were clearly illegal even under existing law. ACORN let Wall Street analysts know what Household stood to lose from these law suits, as well as from various reforms that Household periodically announced in its attempt to hold off the pressure from ACORN.

But ACORN members never let up. They protested again and again at Household offices and held press conferences in front of homes about to be lost to Household. They protested the secondary market that was putting up capital for these predatory loans. And they held a major protest at the trade group that lobbied in Washington for Household and its fellow sharks. Then, in the summer of 2002, ACORN members took the step that Household executives would bring up again and again in later negotiations. On a beautiful summer day in the unbelievably wealthy suburbs north of Chicago, victims of Household from around the country simultaneously poured out of busses by the hundreds and thousands onto the lawns of the board members and CEO of Household. They knocked on the doors and spoke to those who had hurt them from a distance. When the police made them leave, ACORN members plastered "Wanted" posters all over the neighborhood telling the board members' neighbors what crimes the Household executives were guilty of.

Through all of this, we worked the media. I kept a database of victims' stories and contact info and put them in touch with reporters whenever the reporters were willing to tell not just the victimization story but also the story of fighting back. We generated several hundred print articles and several hundred TV and radio stories about Household's predatory lending practices. We worked the small neighborhood papers, flyers in churches, posters on walls. We produced lengthy articles in the New York Times, Washington Post, Wall Street Journal, Los Angeles Times, and Forbes Magazine. We kept up an endless barrage in the trade press: the American Banker, National Mortgage News, etc. We maintained an enormous website about Household that no longer exists.

A handful of ACORN staff people with great expertise and unrelenting effort organized thousands of members to drive this campaign until Household agreed to pay victims $489 million through the 50 states attorneys general, and later agreed to pay millions more through ACORN, as well as to reform its practices.

This campaign was an example of what can be done if enough different angles are pursued at once and the company ripping you off is put on the defensive and constantly hit with the unexpected. And this campaign was a success by the one and only measure ACORN judges campaigns by: it increased the size and power of ACORN to effect future progressive change. This is good news for low-income neighborhoods, but bad news for Wells Fargo, the predatory lender who is next on ACORN's list.

Reflection Questions

FOR PART VI

After finishing the section on agency, reflect on the following questions from Part VI:

1. Think of the terms *agency, empowerment,* and *collective action.* How does each of the readings demonstrate these terms?
2. Which do you think is more empowering—individual or collective action? Why?
3. Compare/contrast the readings in this section with one another. Which methods are more effective in bringing about change? Why?
4. Think about this final section in relation to previous ones. What lessons can you take from this section regarding housing, welfare, parenting, schooling, and work?
5. Select one particular essay and analyze it, first *without* using a sociological imagination and then analyze it again *with* a sociological imagination.

Afterword

We end this book of voices of the poor with a sermon by a Unitarian Universalist minister who grew up in poverty. Reverend Bumbaugh, with a keen sociological imagination, reflects back on his childhood and then looks at the condition of the poor in contemporary society. He is scandalized and wants all of us to be scandalized by an affluent society that is structured in ways that allow its poor and especially its poor children to suffer. Along with sharing his insights about poverty, he implores us to be morally outraged by a society that turns its collective back on its poor children.

The Forgotten Children of Affluent America

DAVID E. BUMBAUGH

As I prepared for this sermon, I frequently heard a voice in my inner ear speaking with great authority. "It's no disgrace to be poor," said my Aunt Martha, talking like an adult to two small boys who desperately wanted something she could not give them. "Why," we had asked, "do we have to be poor?" "It's no disgrace to be poor," she repeated, more to herself than to us, "it's just damned inconvenient!" It was the kind of comment I would hear her make many times as we were growing up. As she sat at her old treadle-powered sewing machine, manufacturing shirts for us and blouses and dresses for herself out of old flour sacks, she would mutter with a sigh, "It's no disgrace to be poor. We should be grateful for what we have." As we stood together in the kitchen, working over a pile of spotty green beans or tomatoes well past their prime or corn left to grow tough on the cob, culling the usable from the useless and preparing it for canning so there would be food for the winter, she would murmur, more to herself than to me, "It's no disgrace to be poor, but does it have to be so tough?"

As she conducted her frequent war against the vermin which inhabited the walls of the old apartment building in which we lived, sprinkling a deadly green powder on the floors and sweeping it into cracks and crevices, pouring the same powder under the paper which lined the silverware drawer and the shelves of the kitchen cabinet, or as she pulled apart the beds and poured an equally deadly liquid along the edges of the mattresses to discourage bedbugs, she reminded herself that being poor was no excuse not to be clean and free of bugs. And as we listened to the frequent sounds

SOURCE: David E. Bumbaugh, "The Forgotten Children of Affluent America," www.uc.summit.nj.uua.org/Sermons/DEB/98049.html. Published by permission of the author.

of ambulances and police cars screaming through the neighborhood in response to drunken brawls and family violence, she admonished us that just because we were poor was no reason not to be proud of ourselves and careful of our behavior.

She and my uncle worked hard to create an island of calm and peace and tranquility in the midst of a world which was chaotic and unpredictable and sometimes dangerous. And like many poor parents, they invested their lives and their hopes in their children, in a future which would be qualitatively better than the lives they had known. They used to joke with us about that far-off day when one of us would be living in the White House, and how proud they would feel when we invited them to visit. We all knew that it would never happen, but we also heard in that standing joke the expectation that our lives would be better than theirs had been.

Like most poor parents, they had learned that life was never going to be much better for them and so they had invested their hopes for the future in their children. And like most poor parents, they simply did not know how to make that hope come true. They did what they could to protect us from the environing hazards of our world. They could be fierce when they perceived an unjust attack upon us. At the same time, they felt cowed and impotent in the face of authority and they did not know how to use the system to transform dreams into reality. They were often reduced to futile rage against a society which treated them as ciphers, which failed to honor their dreams, which saw their children not as promise or opportunity but as burden and expense.

We boys made our way through a public school system which regularly telegraphed to us the message that not very much was expected of us and then out into a world in which neither of us felt welcome, or at home. And of the two of us, one escaped that world of our childhood and one did not. And society tried to convince us—and itself—that the difference was the result of merit. Both of us knew, and still understand, that it was more a matter of luck which of us would escape and which would become part of that forgotten America. I tell you this so you understand my prejudice, and where I come from; for I have never forgotten whence I have come or my responsibility to speak for the forgotten children of America.

I was born in the midst of the Great Depression. But the world I experienced was not shaped by that economic catastrophe; the nations' financial collapse only served to make forgotten America more visible. Nor did that world end with the Depression. Rosemary L. Bray, who was born more than 20 years later, describes very much the same world in her memoir, *Unafraid of the Dark*. Rosemary's world was the urban ghetto of Chicago and her poverty was complicated by racism and sexism. But the family she describes, its relation to the larger world as it struggled to survive on the fringes of the mainstream economy, is very similar to the milieu in which I grew up. Not much changed in those 20 years.

Rosemary's family, however, benefited from a welfare system which, while never generous, never intended to do more than keep people living on the thin edge of poverty, did provide the center piece for a patchwork of economic support which, when supplemented by the occasional, low-paying, unpredictable job and the sustaining structures of family and church, made it possible to raise a family of children, to give them a minimal level of health care, to keep them in school, and to provide them with a full-time mother who was present to protect them from the dangers, temptations and seductions of the outside world.

Rosemary's family had a greater success rate than mine—all of the children made it out of the culture of poverty in which they grew up. Rosemary Bray, herself an affirmative action baby, went from the Chicago ghetto to Yale and then on to a career in journalism, and is now preparing for the Unitarian Universalist ministry. Her siblings hold responsible jobs and lead solidly middle-class lives. After her children were grown, Rosemary's mother was able to leave the welfare system, as did most recipients of welfare. Reflecting on her own journey, Rosemary says:

> *We thought it would be enough to get an education and a job, to marry and start a family, to pay our taxes and vote, be ordinary and unexceptional citizens. It now appears that we were wrong. In attempting to downplay the circumstances of our early lives we left others—mothers and children such as we once were—at the mercy of ignorant and vicious ideologues who have never regarded the poor with anything but contempt. Changes in the welfare system since the late 1980s have made it nearly impossible for this story to happen today.*

Reflecting on my own experience, and on the engrossing story my friend Rosemary Bray relates, I understand the despair I feel when I think about the plight of the poor in this vastly affluent nation, the even deeper despair when I think about the children who have been abandoned, who have been forgotten, who have fallen through the safety net as we pursue with determination a social policy shaped and driven by free-market values rather than human values.

There is a scandal at the heart of our national life. . . . In this nation. . . . we choose not to remember our fellow citizens who are not riding this wave of economic growth; we choose not to remember that our unprecedented prosperity is occurring in the context of the greatest disparity between rich and poor in the recent history of this nation; we choose not to remember that social policy has been structured so as to deprive the poor of the crumbs which once were their right as entitlements and to encourage the continuing concentration of resources in fewer and fewer hands; we choose not to remember that we have evolved the best political system money can buy—one which deprives the poor of any effective voice. As the Dow zig-zags . . . and we calculate what it will mean for the small part of it we own in retirement funds or investments, we choose not to remember that children under 6 years of age comprise the poorest age group in this nation and that our social policies are designed to beggar them even more.

There is a scandal at the heart of our national life. . . . It has to do with the fact that, finding ourselves in the midst of the hottest housing market in decades, busily buying and selling and building houses as if they were commodities, no longer worried about having to pay capital gains taxes on our profits, we choose not to remember in the midst of this frenzy that there are over 2 million homeless children in the United States. We choose not to remember in the midst of this frenzy that the average age of a homeless person in the United States is 9 years of age—the average age. While we congratulate ourselves on having the most dynamic economy in the world, we choose not to remember that we have failed to house our poorest citizens.

Statistics are telling and not all of them are moving up. In the wake of the program "to end welfare as we know it," we have determined that everyone must have a job and that there must be a life-time limit for any kind of public assistance. But we have failed to insist that in exchange for full-time work, a person should receive a living wage. For a single mother with a preschool child in New Jersey, the cost of housing and day care

are estimated to be $725 a month. If that mother can find a full-time job paying $5.10 an hour, she will take home about $700 a month. She will be in deficit before she begins to consider the cost of food, clothing, health care, and transportation.

And what is true in New Jersey is true in most of the nation as we who have never known welfare congratulate ourselves that we have "ended welfare as we know it." What we have done is to reincarnate the old work houses of Dickens' England. Only now they are low-paying jobs with no future, with no benefits, and no hope of ever moving out of poverty. At the same time, this policy separates children from their mothers' care for much of their young lives. The underlying effect of the ending of welfare, no matter how we dress it up in the moral language of the dignity of work, is to secure a steady source of low-paid workers for the economy. In their book, *The Breaking of the American Social Compact*, Piven and Cloward quote from Lawrence Mead's *Beyond Entitlement* to demonstrate the forces driving the recent assault on the poor. They quote Mead as saying in urging the attack on welfare:

> Low-wage work apparently must be mandated just as the draft has sometimes apparently been necessary to staff the military. Authority achieves compliance more efficiently than benefits. Government need not make the desired behavior worthwhile to people. It simply threatens punishment (in this case, the loss of benefits) if they do not comply.

And, of course, forcing people to accept jobs which fail to pay a living wage does not guarantee that such jobs will always be available for the unskilled and inexperienced. Statistics recently released suggest that across the nation only about 30 percent of those forced off welfare have been successful in finding jobs, and that statistic counts as successful anyone who has earned at least $100 in a three-month period. It is small wonder that food banks all over the country are reporting a 17 percent increase in requests for emergency food aid. And it is telling that almost two-fifths of those receiving emergency food aid are 18 or under, that nearly one-half of the families receiving such aid from food banks have children under 5. And these statistics are from the early part of 1997, before some of the largest cuts in food stamps and other resources for the poor took effect. In the midst of the nation's dynamic and vibrant economy, America's forgotten children are going hungry.

Poor people, by and large, have accepted the reality that they probably will not escape the trap of poverty, but they continue to hope that with a little luck, their children might. Even the most poverty-stricken ghettos are not devoid of dreams for the future. In his book *There Are No Children Here*, Alex Kotlowitz chronicles the lives of two small boys growing up in a Chicago housing project. Over and over again, like a small candle flickering in the overpowering gloom of poverty and despair, one hears in the voices of the boys and of their mother the inchoate hope that the children somehow will escape. Most of them do not. Once more, the fierce disparities between the rich and the poor drain that hope of any reality.

In 1991, Jonathan Kozol explained in his book *Savage Inequalities* part of the reason that the flickering hope for the children of the poor so often dies. He examined the vast gulf between the schooling of the children of the rich and the children of the poor. Poor children are concentrated in systems which spend significantly less per child upon education, and in districts where a significantly larger percentage of the school budget must be spent upon maintaining aging and derelict buildings. Poor children have fewer books and resources, less well-equipped libraries and labs, less experienced teachers, and larger class sizes than their affluent contemporaries. We in New Jersey know about this, as our courts struggle against entrenched political realities to enforce some kind of equality of resources on the state schools. Most of us would be quite willing to have equality in schooling, provided it did not affect the quality of our schools. In defense, we often insist that money is not the key to education, that if those other districts were better run, they would get more return on their investment, all the while fiercely fighting any effort to reduce the money spent by our schools, for fear that it would have a negative impact upon the quality of our children's education. And year after year the inequality grows and the children graduate from their unequal schools, some to promise and some to despair.

There is a scandal at the heart of our national life. . . . The scandal has to do with the fact that . . . two societies have been created—one of affluence and one of poverty, one of hope and one of despair, one fully in command of the national birthright and one condemned to be forever outside the charmed circle of the American dream. The scandal has to do with our determined blindness to the fact that what is at stake in our policies toward the poor, toward affluent America's forgotten children, is nothing less than the soul of the nation. We cannot continue a policy which subordinates human beings to market values without destroying our own humanity. A people is judged by how it treats its poorest, weakest, least advantaged members.

In his book *Waiting for the Barbarians*, Lewis Lapham remarked:

> The barbarian implicit in the restless energies of big-time, global capitalism requires some sort of check or balance, if not by a spiritual doctrine or impulse, then by a lively interest in (or practice of) democratic government. The collapse of communism at the end of the Cold War removed from the world's political stage the last pretense of a principled opposition to the rule of money, and the pages of history suggest that oligarchies unhindered by conscience or common sense seldom take much interest in the cause of civil liberty.

What Lapham remarks about the global condition is equally true of our national condition. Our children—and they are all our children, regardless of the political jurisdiction in which they live or the school districts in which they are educated—lay upon us a moral responsibility. We cannot be a moral people and permit our children to go hungry and homeless while the rich grow richer; we cannot be a moral people and educate some of our children for success while grooming others to provide the forced labor at the bottom of the labor market or starve; we cannot be a moral people if we accept luxury as our right and forget those, especially the children, who are condemned to lives of despair by the very policies which benefit us. We cannot be a moral people if we do not demand social policies which seek to ameliorate the discrepancies between the rich and the poor, policies which seek to provide the kind of support which allowed Rosemary Bray and countless others to emerge from poverty and to make of their talents a gift to the nation and the world.

"It is no disgrace to be poor," said my Aunt Martha. And she was right. But it is a disgrace to be affluent in America and to forget those others, who were children when we were children, who are contemporaries of our children and our grandchildren, who are not so blessed. It is more than a disgrace. It is a sin to turn our backs on the forgotten children of affluent America.

Reflection Questions

FOR THE BOOK

1. Make a list of the major points from the two theoretical perspectives. Overall, do you find more support for one theoretical perspective over another? Find at least one selection from each chapter to justify and support your answer.

2. At this point, you should fully understand the sociological imagination and be able to apply it to all of the readings in the book, as well as to your own life. Take a moment to analyze your own life situation. How have you been affected by social structures and forces?

3. What social policies would the two theoretical perspectives advocate for solving the problem of poverty?

4. Reflect on the essays in Part III. How would you be affected by the loss of an important family member, a devastating illness that inhibited your ability to work, a divorce, a natural disaster that destroyed your home? How close are you to falling through the safety net?

5. Reflect on the essays in Part IV. How do poor people adapt to and cope with their difficult situations? How are their experiences structured by race, class, gender, age, and location?

6. Consider the selections in Part V. How are the life chances of poor people affected by society's institutions?

7. Regarding agency, will positive social change occur if it is left up to those in power? If not, what is the best course for social change?

8. All of the selections in the book are meant to teach us something about poverty from the perspectives of those experiencing poverty. Make a list of lessons from Parts II though VI and state the policy implications of each lesson.

GLOSSARY

agency *See* human agency

alienation The separation of human beings from each other, from themselves, and from the products they create.

ascribed characteristics Personal characteristics inherent in individuals over which they have no control such as age, family of origin, race, and sex.

assimilation The process by which individuals or groups voluntarily or involuntarily adopt the culture of another group, losing their original identity.

caste A stratum in the stratification system that is fixed at birth and is permanent.

culture of poverty The view that the poor are qualitatively different in values and lifestyles from the rest of society and that these cultural differences explain continued poverty.

cultural genocide The deliberate and systematic extermination of a national or racial group.

empowerment The feeling of control over outcomes.

environmental racism/classism The concentration of poor and racial minorities near hazardous and toxic environments.

fatalism The acceptance of all things and events as inevitable.

gentrification The redevelopment of poor and working-class urban neighborhoods into middle- and upper-middle class enclaves; often involves displacement of original residents.

grassroots organizations Collective efforts by common people to produce social change in their interests.

hierarchy The arrangements of people or objects in order of importance.

human agency Individuals are not passive. They actively shape social life by adapting to, negotiating with, and changing social structures.

institutional racism Occurs when the social arrangements and accepted ways of doing things in society disadvantage a racial group.

life chances The chances throughout one's life-cycle to experience the good things in life.

living wage A wage that places the worker above the poverty threshold.

Medicaid The government health program for the poor.

Medicare The government program that provides partial coverage of medical costs for the elderly.

meritocracy A system of stratification in which rank is based purely on achievement.

near-poor People with family incomes at or above their poverty threshold but below 125 percent of their threshold.

poverty A standard of living below the minimum needed for the maintenance of an adequate diet, health, and shelter.

poverty threshold The poverty line established by the government based on the minimal amount of money required for a subsistence level of life. The threshold varies with the size of the family.

progressive tax An income tax where the rates increase with income.

race A group socially defined on the bases of a presumed common genetic heritage resulting in distinguishing physical characteristics.

regressive tax   A tax rate that remains the same for all people rich and poor. The result is that poor people pay a larger proportion of their earned income than do affluent people.

severely poor   People living at or below half of their poverty threshold.

social class   A number of people who occupy the same relative economic rank in the stratification system.

social Darwinism   The belief that the principle of the survival of the fittest applies to human societies, especially systems of stratification.

social determinism   The assumption that human behavior is explained exclusively by social factors.

social mobility   Movement by an individual from one social class to another.

social movement   A collective attempt to promote or resist change.

social stratification   Occurs when people are ranked in a hierarchy that differentiates them as superior or inferior.

socioeconomic status   The measure of social status that takes into account several prestige factors such as income, education, and occupation.

stereotype   An exaggerated generalization about some social category.

stigma   A label of social disgrace.

structural approach to poverty   The understanding of poverty resulting from factors external to individuals.

subculture   A relatively cohesive cultural system that varies in form and substance from the dominant culture.

subprime loan rate   Home loans available at a high interest rate. Those individuals with a poor credit history usually have to pay a subprime rate.

sweatshop   A substandard work environment where workers are paid less than the minimum wage and where other laws are violated.

underclass   The term used by culture of poverty theorists to denote the 10 to 20 percent of the poverty population that is mired in poverty with a strong propensity for crime and other anti-social behaviors, welfare dependency, and out-of-wedlock births.

underemployment   Being employed at a job below one's level of training and expertise.

undocumented immigrants   Immigrants who have entered the United States illegally.

upward social mobility   Movement from a social class to a higher class (e.g., from poverty to working class).

welfare   Receipt of financial aid and/or services from the government.

workfare   The imposition of compulsory work programs and other mandatory requirements on welfare recipients with the goal of maximizing work participation while reducing reliance on welfare.

WEB SITES

POVERTY: GENERAL

Center on Budget and Policy Priorities
www.cbpp.org
Articles and information on economic issues, including poverty and welfare.

Children's Defense Fund
www.childrensdefense.org
A children's advocacy group that provides data and analysis of trends concerning the plight of children.

Economic Policy Institute
www.epinet.org
Brief articles and data on various economic problems.

Inequality.org
www.inequality.org
A clearinghouse for information on social class issues.

Joint Center for Poverty Research
www.jcpr.org
JCPR seeks to advance our understanding of what it means to be poor in America.

U.S. Bureau of the Census.
www.census.gov/hhes/www/poverty.html
Official data on poverty, published annually.

Worldbank.org.
www.worldbank.org/poverty
Worldbank provides resources and support for people and organizations working to understand and alleviate poverty.

TOPIC AREAS

Activism

ACORN
www.acorn.org
The largest community organization of low and moderate income families, working for social justice and stronger communities.

Center for Law and Social Policy
www.clasp.org
CLASP seeks to strengthen policy for low-income families.

Homeless Advocates Newspaper
www.bigissue.com

National Center for Law and Economic Justice
www.welfarelaw.org

National Law Center on Homelessness and Poverty
www.nlchp.org

Southwest Center for Economic Integrity
www.economicintegrity.org/index.htm
The Southwest Center seeks to protect marginalized people from bad business/corporate practices such as payday and mortgage lending.

Health

Kaiser Family Foundation
www.kff.org

National Center for Health Statistics
www.cdc.gov
The government's clearinghouse for health information, including health statistics on the poor.

U.S. Census Bureau: Health Insurance Coverage Statistics
www.census.gov/hhes/www/hlthins/hlthins.html

U.S. Department of Health and Human Services Administration on Aging
www.aoa.dhhs.gov

Housing/Homelessness/Neighborhoods

ACORN
www.acorn.org
The largest community organization of low and moderate income families, working for social justice and stronger communities.

National Coalition for the Homeless
  www.nationalhomeless.org

National Law Center on Homelessness
and Poverty
  www.nlchp.org

U.S. Census Bureau: Housing and
Household Economics Statistics
  www.census.gov/hhes/www/housing/
  ahs/ahs.html

Parenting/Children

Action Alliance for Children
  www.4children.org
  AAC focuses on current trends and policy
  issues affecting children and their families in California.

Administration for Children and Families
  www.acf.dhhs.gov

Center on Fathers, Families, and
Public Policy
  www.cffpp.org

Center for Research on Child Well-Being,
Princeton University
  http://crcw.princeton.edu

Children's Defense Fund
  www.childrensdefense.org

Handsnet
  www.handsnet.org
  Handsnet offers resources for organizations to strengthen their programs and
  policies for children and families.

National Center for Children in Poverty
  http://nccp.org

Racism/Discrimination

Administration for Native Americans
  www.acf.dhhs.gov/programs/ana

Applied Research Center
  www.arc.org
  ARC focuses on the advancement of
  racial justice through research, advocacy,
  and journalism.

Center for Immigration Studies, Publications
and Policy
  www.cis.org

Institute on Race and Poverty,
University of Minnesota
  www.irpumn.org/website

National Association for the Advancement
of Colored People
  www.naacp.org
  The NAACP is a civil rights organization
  for ethnic minorities in the United States.

Schools/Schooling

Institute for Urban and Minority Education
  http://iume.tc.columbia.edu

National Institute for Urban School
Improvement
  www2.edc.org/urban

U.S. Department of Education, National
Institute on the Education of At-Risk
Students
  www.ed.gov/offices/OERI/At-Risk

Survival and Finances

America's Second Harvest
  www.secondharvest.org
  This website provides information on
  hunger in the United States and related
  public policies.

HungerWeb
  http://nutrition.tufts.edu/academic/
  hungerweb
  HungerWeb is for those interested in
  finding solutions to hunger at the global,
  national, community, and household
  level.

U.S. Census Bureau: Income Statistics
  www.census.gov/hhes/www/income/
  income.html

Welfare

American Public Human Services
Association
  www.aphsa.org
  Articles and information on welfare
  reform.

The Finance Project (formerly the Welfare
Information Network)
  www.financeproject.org/irc/win.asp.

Making Wages Work
www.makingwageswork.org
Reports on programs that supplement income and wages in order to help families escape poverty and welfare dependency.

Work

Bureau of Labor Statistics
http://bls.gov

Environmental Justice Resource Center
www.ejrc.cau.edu

Rockefeller Foundation
www.rockfound.org

U.S. Department of Labor: Employment and Training Administration (ETA)
www.doleta.gov

INDEX